Vision and Response
in Modern Fiction

Vision and Response
in Modern Fiction

Arnold L. Weinstein

Cornell University Press

ITHACA AND LONDON

Acknowledgment is made to:

George Braziller, Inc., for material from *The Flanders Road* by Claude Simon, tr. Richard Howard; reprinted by permission of the publisher; copyright © 1961 by Claude Simon.

New Directions Publishing Corporation for material from the following selections from *Labyrinths* by Jorge Luis Borges: "Three Versions of Judas," tr. James E. Irby; "Deutsches Requiem," tr. Julian Palley; "Tlön, Uqbar, Orbis Tertius," tr. James E. Irby; "The Garden of Forking Paths," tr. Donald A. Yates; "Emma Zunz," tr. Donald A. Yates; "The God's Script," tr. L. A. Murillo; "Funes the Memorious," tr. James E. Irby; "A New Refutation of Time," tr. James E. Irby; copyright © 1962, 1964 by New Directions Publishing Corporation; reprinted by permission of New Directions Publishing Corporation.

Simon & Schuster, Inc., for material from *Passing Time* by Michel Butor; copyright © 1960 by Faber and Faber; reprinted by permission of Simon & Schuster, Inc.

First published 1974 by Cornell University Press.
Published in the United Kingdom by Cornell University Press Ltd., 2-4 Brook Street, London W1Y 1AA.

International Standard Book Number 0-8014-0833-4
Library of Congress Catalog Card Number 73-20793

Printed in the United States of America by York Composition Co., Inc.

To A. C. W.

Acknowledgments

The origins of a book are never entirely traceable. I would like to acknowledge, however, the significant influence that Laurence Holland exerted on my undergraduate studies; my thinking about the problems of vision in literature and about the interrelations between feelings and systems owes a great deal to his Princeton lectures on James and Faulkner. My studies of Faulkner, Butor, Simon, and Robbe-Grillet began to take shape in my doctoral dissertation, and I am grateful to Harry Levin and W. M. Frohock for their willingness to let me pursue a recalcitrant subject and attempt the type of informal-formal comparison that characterizes this book as well. In scope and aim, however, this book goes far beyond my original interest in "reconstructive" narration in order to pursue larger questions of mystery and knowledge among a wider spectrum of authors and national literatures.

I am especially grateful to the National Endowment for the Humanities for the generous grant during 1971–1972 which enabled me to devote a full year to thinking through, deepening, and writing down the ideas and analyses that make up this book.

My next debt is a broader one: the undergraduates and graduates at Brown University whom I have taught in my courses on the modern novel have had an immense influence on my thinking and my writing. My conviction that literary criticism is not a matter solely for specialists, that the impact a book has on a reader is part of its meaning, that the most appropriate style (for me) in which to write about literature is the biased, oral style I use every day: this is the result of my teaching experience, and I am grateful for it. My greatest debt, however, is to my wife, Ann, who has lived with this book more years than I care to recall. To her distrust of professionalism I owe some measure of equilibrium; to her fundamental agreement that vision and response make sense in life as well as in literature I owe still more.

Finally, grateful acknowledgment is extended to the following for permission to reprint copyright material:

Grove Press, Inc., for material from *Two Novels* by Alain Robbe-Grillet, tr. Richard Howard; reprinted by permission of Grove Press, Inc.; copyright © 1960 by Grove Press, Inc.

Alfred A. Knopf, Inc., for permission to quote from the following copyrighted works: *The Trial* and *The Castle*, by Franz Kafka, translated by Willa and Edwin Muir; *The Good Soldier*, by Ford Madox Ford; "Notes Toward a Supreme Fiction" from *The Palm at the End of the Mind*, by Wallace Stevens.

W. W. Norton & Company, Inc., for material from the Norton Critical Edition of *The Turn of the Screw* by Henry James; reprinted by permission of the publisher; copyright © 1966 by W. W. Norton & Company, Inc.

Random House, Inc., for permission to quote from the following copyrighted works: *Ulysses*, by James Joyce; and *The Sound and the Fury* and *Absalom, Absalom!*, by William Faulkner; and for permission to reproduce the drawing of the human eye from page 388 of *The Sound and the Fury*.

Schocken Books Inc. for material from *The Penal Colony* by Franz Kafka; reprinted by permission of Schocken Books Inc.; copyright © 1948 by Schocken Books Inc.; and for material from *The Trial* by Franz Kafka; reprinted by permission of Schocken Books Inc.; copyright ©1937, © 1956 by

Alfred A. Knopf, Inc.; copyright renewed, 1964, by Alfred A. Knopf, Inc.

Janice Biala, for permission to reprint material from *The Good Soldier* by Ford Madox Ford.

The Bodley Head for material from *Ulysses* by James Joyce.

Curtis Brown Ltd for material from *The Sound and the Fury* and *Absalom, Absalom!* by William Faulkner.

Calder and Boyars Ltd for material from *In the Labyrinth* by Alain Robbe-Grillet, tr. Richard Howard.

Jonathan Cape Ltd for material from *The Flanders Road* by Claude Simon, tr. Richard Howard.

Faber and Faber Ltd for material from "Notes Toward a Supreme Fiction" from *The Collected Poems of Wallace Stevens* and for material from *Passing Time* by Michel Butor, tr. Richard Howard; reprinted by permission of Faber and Faber Ltd.

Librairie Plon for permission to quote material, in my translation, from *Monsieur Ouine* by Georges Bernanos; copyright © 1946 by Librairie Plon.

Martin Secker & Warburg Ltd for material from *The Trial*, *The Castle*, "Metamorphosis," and "A Country Doctor" by Franz Kafka.

The sections on Georges Bernanos and Michel Butor have appeared in an earlier, modified version as articles in journals. I am grateful to the Syracuse University Press for permission to reprint parts of "Bernanos' *Monsieur Ouine* and the Esthetic of Chaos," *Symposium* (Winter 1971); and to the Purdue Research Foundation for permission to reprint parts of "Order and Excess in Butor's *L'Emploi du temps*," *Modern Fiction Studies*, XVI, Number 1 (Spring 1970), 41–55, copyrighted *Modern Fiction Studies* © 1970, by Purdue Research Foundation, Lafayette, Indiana.

Although all the material in this book appears in English

(either an established translation or my own translation), I read the French and German works in the original language. In some cases these works may be better known by their original titles, and I am therefore listing them for the benefit of those who read French and German:

Balzac, *Le Père Goriot*

Bernanos, *Monsieur Ouine*

Kafka, *Der Prozess, Das Schloss,* "Die Verwandlung," "Ein Landarzt," "In der Strafkolonie," "Ein Hungerkünstler"

Butor, *L'Emploi du temps*

Proust, *A la recherche du temps perdu*

Simon, *La Route des Flandres*

Robbe-Grillet, *Dans le labyrinthe*

ARNOLD L. WEINSTEIN

Providence, Rhode Island

Contents

Vision and Response
in Modern Fiction

In place of a hermeneutics we need an erotics of art.
                             Susan Sontag, *Against Interpretation*

Introduction

"Vision" and "response" denote our perception of the world and our reaction to it. Most novels illustrate that paradigm doubly. First, they *depict* an education: the protagonist or narrator—Rastignac, Pip, Marlow, James's governess, Quentin and Shreve, Joseph K., Proust's Marcel, Butor's Jacques Revel, Robbe-Grillet's soldier—confronts and tries to interpret the world around him. Second, they *constitute* an education: the reader turns the pages in a sequential enterprise of progressive enlightenment, as the substance of the book becomes less opaque and more intelligible, and as its meaning emerges. In this context all novels are mystery stories, and all novels both describe and engender the acquisition of knowledge. The knowledge arrived at, and the itinerary taken, are usually divergent for reader and protagonist, and the joint educational process is variously informed by content, style, structure, and, of course, the reader's expectations. To analyze the ways in which specific novels achieve their meaning and posit their reality is the goal of this study.

This epistemological perspective enables us to see writers in a special light. Balzac and Dickens write out of different traditions, and they have different aims; each writer, however, utilizes the mystery form, builds his work around the effort to penetrate codes, to perceive (and honor) the human bonds obscured by rigid societal norms. Likewise, Faulkner and

Bernanos have little in common *except* the effort to tap the affective potential that the forms of ellipsis, mystery, and disorder afford. Although I make no attempt to unearth an ignored formal tradition, I do enlist the comparative groupings and parallels to illustrate the different uses to which similar narrative strategies can be put, as well as the often striking affinities between writers whom literary historians usually separate. Finally, the groupings I use and the development I try to chart may be, at worst, nothing more than the itinerary of my *idée fixe*, but, at best, evidence that the forms of narrative from Balzac to Robbe-Grillet, if interrogated, bespeak an evolution in credibility and depth, a radically changing sense of what the novel has to teach us, and—by extension—what we can know.

Implicit in my approach, and essential to my thinking, is the contention that literary criticism depends on disciplined scrutiny of the work and disciplined awareness of the self. "Disciplined" has nothing to do with "systematic." I believe that literature is always more than a system and that literary analysis involves personal judgments and subjective biases. Even if impartiality could be achieved in criticism, or a work of art be equated with a mere instance of conventions, traditions, or principles, such a feat would be, in my opinion, an impoverishment rather than an accomplishment. This study stems from the conviction that literature is realized only through the intense, often idiosyncratic response of each reader. It will therefore come as no surprise that I take sides in this book (just as most of the novelists in question take sides), that my inquiry is neither disinterested nor distanced. The very terms "vision" and "response" are double-edged, implicating the reader's perception and beliefs in that act of understanding dramatized by the work. No novel has ever spoken for itself. Reading, even the impartial, objective variety favored by academia, is always an appropriation, a connivance; I would even argue that it is an appetite, an aggression on the written word.

To understand a literary text, we welcome expertise of all kinds: biography of the author, history of the period, structure of the language. But we also need to understand our understanding, to see what we are doing to the book, to grasp how the book becomes—internally for its characters, externally for us—knowledge.

The process of knowing and the reader's stake in fiction are the two central concepts that account for the particular novels I have chosen to analyze and the particular evolution that this book is meant to trace. For the ways of knowing change. From Balzac and Dickens to Borges and Robbe-Grillet the resources of mystery (delayed disclosure, hidden identities, innumerable devices which tease and lure the reader) are exploited, but the nature of the investigation tends to evolve. Balzac ends in a glaring curtain call where true identities and authentic motives are unfailingly revealed; clarity, in Dickens, is already more elusive, and the protagonist's path toward it is more sinuous, requires more revision and doubling back. Above all, we shall see that Dickens posits the primacy of the unseen but felt patterns against the weight of visible evidence. In Conrad, Ford, and James the unseen, the suspected and desired begin to reign: the drama is always just beyond the scope of the narrative, luring on reader and character, convincing both that what is seen is but appearance, foil to reality, and stimulus for the endless speculations that alone are real. In Faulkner and Bernanos the conventions of character description, discursive prose, and linear development are rejected as inadequate to convey the kind of sensuous, affective experience which alone constitutes knowledge; here we see the extreme versions of an art form, two writers who violently dislocate tradition in order to go beyond words, to transcend their medium altogether. In all of these novelists, the text is rich in secrets and meanings; the job of character and reader is that of interrogation and creation, transforming the evidence into humanly valid truth. Rastignac must see the connection between *le beau monde* and *la maison Vauquer*, just as Pip must learn to go beyond appearances to grasp the real nature of Estella and the convict. The task becomes more conjectural, more definitively murky in James and Ford, for there are no solid contours beyond the perceptions and inventions of the characters. Bernanos and Faulkner hallow the felt rather than the seen, and in their work the text, the givens, are but a springboard to the realm of passions and affections which inform human conduct but mock semantics and syntax. In all of these writers, the act of reading is equivalent to a kind of moral grammar, a conferring of depth and resonance to the surface text. The characters and situations harbor truths: Vautrin exposes them in *Père Goriot;* Pip suffers them in *Great Expectations;* Dowell is destroyed by them in *The Good Soldier;* Quentin and Shreve create them in *Absalom, Absalom!* This manipulation of the text is the desired aim of the author's technique. In each case there is penetration. The characters and the reader must plumb the givens, discover the depth and volume that are concealed or suggested by the words. Vision and response effectively characterize the nature of that operation.

In the novels I discuss in Chapter 4, entitled "Eclipse," the struggle to achieve order and knowledge becomes integrated into a larger network of forces. In the work of Kafka and Joyce, human configurations of meaning are superseded. Kafka dwarfs his characters by placing them in situations grotesquely beyond their control, and Joyce tends, crudely speaking, to transform his into multifaceted, aesthetic pawns. Michel Butor illustrates a synthesis of these strains, and *Passing Time* depicts the impasse of individual order, the vital resistance between the world and our need to harness it. My last chapter deals with the alienation between the vision and the perceiving agent. In Proust, Borges, Claude Simon, and Robbe-Grillet, we witness the growing autonomy of perception. To impose depth and meaning on a series of events is a form of self-assertion; mysteries with human explanations (even tragic ones like that of Oedipus) testify to a world that is humanly measurable and humanly interrogated. The works studied in the final chapter are, with varying emphases, articulated by principles of composition and harmony that have no human dimensions. The world of the perception, the world of the text, are liberated from the referential constraints of plot, character, and depth psychology. Penetration becomes a useless metaphor and mystery a misnomer in the circular texts of Borges, the transformations of Simon, and the analogies of Robbe-Grillet. Yet, amid these surface designs, there are dangling characters, pirouetting and responding (although with little vision) to the impulses they receive.

Thus, Chapters 4 and 5 call into question much that is advanced in the first half of the study. To be sure, Balzac, Dickens, James, and Faulkner do not make up a single family of writers, but they evince a belief in a certain kind of reading, a certain kind of knowledge through literature which can no longer be sustained in the authors considered in the last two chapters. My contention is that such choices of belief and disbelief go beyond literary confines and authorial whims: they point to the uses of language and fictions in dealing with reality; they reveal the adequacy and inadequacy of literature as a tool for knowledge, orientation, or assertion. Finally, because all art is order, all literary criticism is, in some sense, a search for governing principles and authority; from Balzac to Robbe-Grillet, the novel reveals how man makes sense of things, and the cogency and structure of art lead us obliquely but inevitably to the priorities and assumptions of the age.

I would like to say a word about the strategy and rationale of my book. The methods of analysis used are eclectic because, in my opinion, anything is good that works. Discussions of syntax in Faulkner are followed by a study of metaphor in Simon and an inquiry about the whereabouts of the narrator in Robbe-Grillet. Although my format may be misconstrued as a series of self-contained book reports or as the result of a reluctance to generalize, I would like to argue for the virtues of arriving at literary history via intense analyses of single works. Much has been advanced in recent years about the conflicting claims of generic studies and single "readings," about the distinction between the specificity of the work and its constants, the sameness which relates it to the larger generic network. Unquestionably, the interests of clarity and arrangement are served by the larger formal or generic approach; specific readings, arguing the wholeness of a single work rather than its place in the literary continuum, are often viewed as perceptive, but necessarily insufficient. Implicit in much of the best critical discussion of our time—specifically the work of structuralist critics such as Barthes and Todorov, but generally the work of all those with either formalist or structuralist leanings—is the nostalgia for a science of literature, a yearning for that perfect system which could both order all the individual works of literature and elevate the study of such works into the grand scheme of a Great Classification. A certain stereotype of the eighteenth century comes to mind, with its clock and clockmaker images of intricate, interlocking structures, its array of anatomists and Encyclopedists. The question is not so much whether the schemes and charts, emphasizing how works correspond to and deviate from the norms, tell us anything about literature, but, rather, how such information can be of value. Why do we need the charts? What are we trying to learn?

Admittedly, no book exists in a vacuum, and readers as well as authors are conditioned by the contextual existence of other forces (aesthetic or nonliterary altogether). But individuals read specific books that individuals have written, and all our awareness of the tradition, the impersonal, collective forces behind our specificity, will not alter the intimacy of that one-to-one confrontation. I am not trying to resurrect Ptolemy or the nineteenth-century self or biographical criticism or even New Criticism; our awareness of deep structures, of determinism (socioeconomic, genetic, sexual, what-have-you), of history itself, has effectively destroyed any lingering myth of free agents or wholly original works of art. Yet, single selves—both those who write and those who read—and single books do exist; moreover, they alone exist. We may choose to regard the text as primarily an instance of "literariness" and even the reader as the particularized product of impersonal forces. The modern intellectual climate favors such a view. Much of the fiction studied in this book reflects the diminishing authority of character and the growing appeal of systems; much of our literary criticism tends to view the work of art as either an expression of other forces or a repository of techniques. However, our disinclination for the particular and our interest in the general may cause us to overlook, rather than give us an overview. We may be rich in schemes and patterns, but blind to the visible, tangible world we inhabit.

Again it is a question of what we are looking for. Do I *understand* a man better when I study an X ray of his bone structure, when I know how he anatomically relates to the species? A single book, a single poem, has much more to tell us than how it is incorporated in the writer's *oeuvre*, the period's productions, the country's heritage, the genre's laws, the language's structures. Beyond all those claims, it is also a thing in itself; and it has, because it is, integrity. Insistence on the singleness of the work of art need not be myopic, nor need it slight the aesthetic dimension; rather, I am suggesting that we redefine the *context* of art (especially fiction) so as to include our response, that is, our response to a particular form. Because the design of each novel shapes our understanding, the conventions and strategies of fiction are too important and too controlling to be dealt with in abstract and generic terms; form is an affective and intimate matter. Our rage for abstraction sometimes makes us confuse charts with knowledge, knowledge with love. Love may well be the proper mode for our intercourse with art. I mean love as an opening rather than a finalizing mode of response, love as a widening perception of art's fullness and our need. In this light, knowledge means response; it means perceiving and hallowing the uniqueness of the work rather than abstracting it into pattern. Susan Sontag has argued forcefully that ours is an age replete with interpretation and short on immediacy:

> Like the fumes of the automobile and of heavy industry which befoul the urban atmosphere, the effusion of interpretations of art today poisons our sensibilities. In a culture whose already classical dilemma is the hypertrophy of the intellect at the expense of energy and sensual capability, interpretation is the revenge of the intellect upon art.
>
> Even more. It is the revenge of the intellect upon the world. To interpret is to impoverish, to deplete the world—in order to set up a shadow world of "meanings." It is to turn *the* world into *this* world. ("This world"! As if there were any other.)
>
> The world, our world, is depleted, impoverished enough. Away with all duplicates of it, until we again experience more immediately what we have.[1]

To generalize may well be the most insidious, evasive form of interpretation; as Borges has classically shown in the story of Funes, to generalize is to forget, to close one's eyes to the uniqueness of the world. We live in a universe of discrete people and discrete objects; classifications are mental constructs and have, as yet, never been seen, touched, or smelled. People and books are more than, and more real than, the schematic reductive meanings we foist on them. People have a way of fighting back, undoing and unhinging our best-laid plans; but books cannot react, even though their power and endurance dwarfs what we customarily have to say about them. Thus, I intend to be something of an ombudsman in this enterprise, to speak at great length about single works, to

[1] Susan Sontag, *Against Interpretation* (New York: Laurel, 1970), p. 17.

prize them as formal achievements but to interrogate those forms and strategies, to eschew reflections on the genre in favor of sustained confrontation with the fullness of each piece. There is a volume, a resonance, an inexhaustibility in great art that we cannot begin to perceive until we live with it, reread and respond anew, open ourselves sensuously and morally as well as aesthetically and rationally to its statement and its mode of discourse. If novels are to be more than casual pastimes on the one hand or the ingredients of a Great Classification on the other, then we must take them seriously and attend to them as single works. Only then do they, like the people and things that we love, begin to open up, to disclose their riches and, thereby, our own. Faulkner's *Absalom, Absalom!* is a model for us in this respect, because it poses the question of the kind of knowledge, the kind of interpretation, even the kind of criticism that is worth having; only after disciplined scrutiny, after affective identification, only then does the story fully open up, revealing the tragic circularity of its themes, the fearful order of its materials, the rewards and costs of its "overpass," the reality of its conventions, the truth of its history. Art requires a commitment commensurate with that which Quentin and Shreve give to the story of Thomas Sutpen. It is a large order, requiring a personal rather than a professional engagement, and there are no guaranteed methods to ensure success. But it may be that the most precious things in literature can only be discovered through such single-minded courtship. Ultimately, I am contending that a sequence of full-blown studies will, despite its selectiveness and incompleteness, better render the evolution of a form, the history, and the use of a genre, than will the more comprehensive, theoretical overview.

To be sure, I do not always follow my principles, and there is more than a little literary history, abstraction, and polemicism in this book. Some of my discussions (on Conrad, Kafka, and Borges) clearly emphasize the *oeuvre* rather than the single work, but the bulk of my argument does rest with individual novels, and it is for the reader to judge whether the narrow view gains in depth what it sacrifices in scope.

I do not justify my choices, for they are manifestly the result of my taste as well as my thesis. Other novelists could have been included, and some of those discussed may seem less comfortable than others in my alignment. My aim, however, is not to pin down the practitioners of a new genre, but to illuminate a certain evolution in a number of novelists from the mid-nineteenth century to the present. Perhaps one cannot speak of development in the sequence of chapters, but rather of changing modalities of vision. But the tandem of vision and response is closely related to the way we order our lives as well as our art. The mystery beyond us incites illumination in Balzac, ambiguity in James, sentience in Faulkner, and charts in Butor. Reliable depth in Dickens becomes impenetrable marshland in Ford and surface embroidery in Robbe-Grillet. These changes signify. I hope that the following chapters will both shed a new light on the particular novelists and reveal something about the larger issue: the ethics of perception and the relevance of form.

1 | Solvable Mysteries: Balzac and Dickens

Père Goriot and *Great Expectations* are so unalike—language, cultural and literary tradition, intent of the author—that any comparative study should state its rationale and its expectations at the outset. Both novels make extensive use of mysteries, suspense, and withheld information. Each work is shaped out of the tension between human, often familial bonds and the inhuman behavioral codes required for social success. In each book the search for answers to the questions—the missing identities and backgrounds in *Great Expectations*, the full story of Goriot's relations to his daughters in Balzac's novel—constitutes the educational process for the youthful protagonist. What is at stake is the integrity of feeling within a mechanized society. Solving mysteries is akin to discovering relationships and ties that were not visible at the beginning. The discovery (and sanctity) of relationships is both a formal and a substantive matter: the new patterns that emerge are the result of more than a completed puzzle. It is true, of course, that identities must be revealed, ellipses filled in, and so on, but more crucially there must be a change in vision if the newly constituted (and dearly purchased) reality is to be perceived.

The mystery form is always used to express a world of hidden depths. Surfaces are filled with signs, and in the course of the novel the *otherness* of appearances, the content to which they refer, is made explicit. In the development of fiction since the nineteenth century, however, the notion of depth has become problematic. The strategy of suspense and mystery continues to be used, as the work of James, Conrad, Ford, Faulkner, Bernanos, Robbe-Grillet, and Butor amply demonstrates. But it undergoes some fascinating changes, as the concomitant belief in depth, in something to be revealed, evolves and then wanes. Traditionally, the literature of otherness has taken the form of allegory or symbolism. The words used were, in some sense, merely an entry, a key to larger realms of meaning which could be brought to expression only by indirect means. Surely, fiction such as *Lord Jim* and *Absalom, Absalom!* springs from the allegiance to depth, to the almost ineffable content of life (or one man's life) which must be conveyed through the autonomous structures of language and syntax. The entire enterprise is brutally thrown into question by Robbe-Grillet: "Literature, in any case, would always, and systematically, consist in talking about *something else.* There would be a world that was present, and a real world; the first would be the only visible one, the second the only important one. The novelist would be supposed to act as a mediator: by his fake description of visible—but completely unreal—things, he would evoke the 'real' which was hiding behind them."[1]

Balzac and Dickens are especially interesting in the light of this development, for they are apparently two of the greatest exponents of depth and revelation. However, we shall see that the ratio of mystery to clarity is quite different in each writer; between the lucid, didactic stance of Balzac and the strangely reticent, Gothic vision of Dickens the novel takes a stride in the direction of ambiguity, of unexpressed but reliable depth. Finally, mystery and suspense must be considered in the way they shape vision, Rastignac's and Pip's as they

[1] Alain Robbe-Grillet, *Towards a New Novel,* tr. Barbara Wright (London: Calder and Boyars, 1965), p. 179.

learn to penetrate and re-evaluate the world they live in, but also our vision as we apprehend their stories and confront their obstacles. By comparing the uses of mystery and the corresponding modes of vision in *Père Goriot* and *Great Expectations*, we can see the shift from an aesthetic of total illumination to one of double vision.

Balzac, perhaps more than any other writer, uses the mystery form to express a world filled with content, depth, keys, hidden stories, monstrous secrets. There are no false leads in his work; the reader's curiosity is constantly assaulted, but never frustrated. Paris is brimming over with signs for the initiated observer. Balzac's famous description of the city as a "veritable ocean" is more than romantic myth-making; the language of depth is ubiquitous: "Sound it: you will never touch bottom. Survey it, report on it! However scrupulous your surveys and reports, however numerous and persistent the explorers of this sea may be, there will always remain virgin places, undiscovered caverns, flowers, pearls, monsters— there will always be something extraordinary, missed by the literary diver."[2]

More striking than the nature of the unknown is its reliability. Balzac's material has infinite potential; he will focus on the Maison Vauquer, and in particular on Rastignac, Vautrin, and Goriot. But he could have easily spotlighted other lives: Madame Vauquer, Bianchon, even Poiret and Michonneau have pasts and futures that are bristling with stories, rounded events. Thus, Rastignac's particular interest in Goriot, his "desire to unravel the mystery of a frightful situation that had been concealed with great care by its creators and its victim alike" (p. 14), is merely an instance (the material for this work) of a larger truth: "there was in all of them a suggestion of drama, either already over or still being enacted"

[2] H. de Balzac, *Père Goriot*, tr. Henry Reed (New York: New American Library, 1962), p. 17. Subsequent quotations are from this edition.

(p. 15). Balzac's way of presenting these mysteries is well known. His exposition usually describes preceding events and facts necessary to make intelligible what follows. Some have even claimed that the stories themselves are redundant, tautological. The rhythm of many of his novels is therefore quite jerky: the dramatic action is consistently halted while the narrator piles on still more information. Moreover, things and faces reveal their inner secrets easily to the clairvoyant narrator. The Maison Vauquer is the material expression of Madame Vauquer, just as the individual faces suggest possible histories and pasts. Balzac's version of *correspondances* and the pseudoscience of Lavater dignify this expressivity of surfaces, but of interest to us is the ease with which appearances yield their meaning. *Père Goriot* is an exercise in sleuthing. On the one hand, the *pensionnaires* harbor stories that are ripe for the picking. Along with this figurative detective work there is also, however, the real thing. Rastignac, on several key occasions, eavesdrops on Goriot and discovers crucial information; Vautrin is quite literally tracked by the police, and even the sellout between Michonneau and the police agent is overheard by Bianchon. Balzac neglects no means of getting information, and *Père Goriot* is an ongoing series of discoveries, all real. There is no waiting, no mistakes, no delusions. To be sure, Balzac—like Stendhal and Flaubert—describes in his novels the gap between the naive expectations of his protagonist and the cynical operation of society. As a theme, "lost illusions" could apply to a great many nineteenth-century novels. But the modern theme of boredom, of the discrepancy between our desires and life's offerings, a theme central to Baudelaire and Flaubert, is only marginally or tentatively present in Balzac: the blasé character in his stories is ever on the threshold of stupendous adventures. The frustration experienced by Emma Bovary of a world that falls drastically short of her expectations, or even the ironic, wry "n'est-ce que ça?" that typifies the Stendhalian hero, are inconceivable in Balzac. Such a balance between desire and compensation seems to reveal an unperturbed confidence in depth, in the ultimate cogency and harmony (known, of course, only by Balzac) of these mysteries. The reader is little more than a spectator, and his itinerary is one of constant revelation and, more profoundly, gratification. The most horrible secrets of the *beau monde* or the Maison Vauquer are still full and concrete. The stories, all rounded out and replete with details, emerge from the shadows, the closed doors of squalid boarding houses and elegant salons. Little will be left for the imagination. There is none of the empty, amorphous disorder that might in fact be found if we lifted the roof off a *pension* and observed the lives below.[3]

However, there is a price for the clarity that finally reigns in *Père Goriot*, and it is, metaphorically at least, a double one. On the one hand, as the mysteries are solved and the secrets are exposed, the characters seem to diminish in interest and in depth; on the other hand, this process of diminution is not merely a narrative penalty (perhaps the inevitable result of explicit storytelling), but it also constitutes the fundamental theme of *Père Goriot*—Rastignac's transition from fullness to shallowness.

This transition is not entirely the result of the student's own personality; it stems, in large part, from the lessons learned by the example of Vautrin, Goriot, and Mme de Beauséant. Rastignac, like Pip in *Great Expectations*, will have to pierce the façade of romance if he is to perceive the true configurations of reality. The following exchange at the Maison Vauquer perfectly illustrates Vautrin's role in sharpening the student's vision. Eugène is recounting his impressions of Anastasie at the ball and then near the boarding house:

[3] We can observe a comparable emphasis on the spectacular in Zola's roof-lifting novel *Pot-Bouille,* but some half a century later Michel Butor characteristically rejects such rounded fictions and plumbs the spatial unities for themselves in *Passage de Milan.*

"Anyway," said Eugène, cutting him short, "I danced with one of the most beautiful women at the ball, a ravishing countess, the most enchanting woman I've ever seen. She had peach blossoms in her hair, and some other flowers at her waist—real ones, they scented the air—but oh, well, anyway, you'd have had to see her to know what I mean. It's impossible to describe how *alive* a woman looks when she's dancing. Well, this morning I actually *saw* this divine creature, about nine o'clock, on foot, near *here*, in the Rue des Grès! I can't tell you how my heart thumped, I imagined . . ."

"That she was coming here," said Vautrin with a searching look at Eugène. "She was quite certainly going to see Papa Gobseck, the money lender. Go deep enough into any woman's heart in Paris and you'll always find the moneylender's even more important than the lover. Your countess's name is Anastasie de Restaud. She lives in the Rue du Helder." [p. 48]

The language of depth characterizes Vautrin's attitude: "searching look (*regard profond*)," "go deep enough (*fouillez*)," "you'll always find." Such realistic deflation, however, closes the discussion, for there is little to add to the data introduced by Vautrin. The impulse toward lyricism, or even fabulation, is effectively throttled by the criminal's statement. Thus, not only is knowledge gained, but such flights of emotion are ridiculed and become far less likely to occur in the future. Rastignac's education seems the precise opposite of Pip's: the French student will learn to hide, and finally, to destroy true feelings, while Pip must learn to perceive and acknowledge real ties after being blinded by false codes.

Vautrin, one of Rastignac's chief mentors, is a penetrator of all enigmas and himself impenetrable. Somewhat like Jaggers in *Great Expectations*, the criminal knows what is hidden to others; however, Vautrin goes on to pull the strings of the plot itself, to be the *force motrice* behind the scenes: "I myself will take on the part of Providence; I'll make up God's mind for Him" (p. 113). He becomes destiny for the Taillefer family and very nearly does so for Rastignac as well. Clair-voyant concerning the motives of others, Vautrin consistently exposes Rastignac's ambitions and *mauvaise foi*. Above all, however, he charts the wilderness, applies to the inchoate material of Parisian life not only names and labels, but an entire behavioral system. His sketch, almost computerlike in its fullness and immediacy, of Rastignac's legal and social prospects, testifies to a vision that is unclouded, not to say omniscient. Vautrin thus illuminates the scene, edifies us by explaining away the mysteries. All of the above characteristics assert Vautrin's role as a surrogate of the author himself, and his advice to the student is not surprising: "You must either cut through this mass of men like a cannon ball, or creep into it like a plague" (p. 109). Balzac's cult of energy is well known,[4] but it would seem that Rastignac chooses to follow the second precept of Vautrin: "creep into it like a plague." Artifice and strategy are more congenial to the student than explosions of will power. Vautrin's message is, as Rastignac realizes, a cruder version of Mme de Beauséant's words:

"The more coldly you calculate, the further you'll go. Strike without pity; and you'll be feared. Look on men and women simply as post-horses, and leave them behind as soon as they are exhausted. In that way you'll reach your goal. . . . And if you have any real feeling, hide it like treasure. Never let anyone suspect it, or you'll be lost. . . . If you ever fall in love, don't show it!" [p. 82]

Now, the emphasis on secrecy, with regard to love, is hardly a new concept; one need merely think of Racine or Mme de La Fayette. What is at stake in Balzac, however, is integrity of the secret itself, the authentic vital core of character which must be shielded from exposure or treachery. Phaedra's pas-

---

[4] See Leo Bersani's discussion of the strategies of containment in *Balzac to Beckett: Center and Circumference in French Fiction* (New York: Oxford University Press, 1970), pp. 24–90.

sion remains fatal and intact; Rastignac will learn to be a man without depth, an actor who can ape feelings and exploit others while remaining detached. There is a movement toward exposure, or surface, in Balzac. The crannies are illuminated, the secrets are exposed, the stories are told, the characters are emptied. The process is gradual, and the result is a kind of attrition or entropy—moral, psychic, physical—symbolized elsewhere in terms of desire by *la peau de chagrin*, realized here in the tension between depth (integrity, secrecy) and façade (illumination) in *Père Goriot*. Balzac himself characterized this notion in the following way: "Perhaps a work . . . painting the devious ways by which an ambitious man of the world gets the better of his conscience as he tries to skirt around evil, so as to achieve his aim while preserving appearances, might be . . . both fine and . . . dramatic" (pp. 129–130). The statement is literally true, for the "appearances" alone are "preserved" at the end of the novel.

However, *Père Goriot* is not about Rastignac the finished, emptied product; it focuses instead on the dynamics of selling out, the transition from depth to surface. In such a world there is still room for the equivocal, and, although the reader has a privileged vantage point, Rastignac must learn to orient himself. What is façade and what is authentic expression? The *beau monde* that flocks to Mme de Beauséant's party is described wholly in terms of glittery surfaces:

The drawing rooms were lit up with the dresses and smiles of the most beautiful women in Paris. The most distinguished from court, ambassadors, ministers, illustrious men from every walk in life, bedecked with crosses, stars, and multi-colored ribbons, were crowding around the viscountess. The orchestra boomed out its music under the gilded ceilings of a palace that was now a desert to its queen. Mme de Beauséant stood at the door of the first drawing room to receive her so-called friends. She was dressed in white, and her simply braided hair was without ornament; she appeared calm, and showed [*affichait*] no sign of sorrow or pride or artificial gaiety. No one could read her thoughts [*lire dans son âme*]. [p. 245]

The last statement is extraordinary, coming from Balzac. Mme de Beauséant cannot survive, but she does resist the inexorable movement toward surface and signboard. What are the implications of such a movement? First, it is important to note the *undoing, dissolving* effect of such constant revelations. Ever since Baudelaire, critics have recognized the visionary—as opposed to the "realistic"—dimension of Balzac's work. The carefully structured exposition, with its endless accumulation of detail, frequently goes up in smoke. No amount of factual, causal information can adequately serve as a ballast for the passions of Goriot, Grandet, Balthazar Claës, Hulot. In *Père Goriot*, the Maison Vauquer has been evoked with exquisite care: everything about it is drenched with human meaning and cogency. It seems to rule over the story and permeate the characters with its squalid, well-defined, serene identity. Yet the deterministic (and, ultimately, reassuring) order it posits is a very fragile one; there is little in Balzac that matches the exodus from that seemingly stable, despotic center of action. The *pension* becomes little more than a house of cards, as each character changes his mask and assumes a new role: Vautrin, Trompe-la-Mort; Rastignac, a bachelor in his stylish apartment; Victorine, the rich heiress; Michonneau, the traitor. Harry Levin has remarked that Balzac's universe, like Shakespeare's, is filled with cataclysmic upheavals;[5] it could then be argued that the notion of *correspondances*—implying a metaphoric, dualistic, depth sense of reality—is not permanently viable. The Maison Vauquer, described, narrated, and (literally) emptied, is no longer a cogent, signifying thing at the end of the novel. It is as flat as the empty coaches that are sent to Goriot's funeral procession. Perhaps the best example of the diminishing referential system

[5] Harry Levin, *The Gates of Horn* (New York: Oxford University Press, 1966), p. 156.

in *Père Goriot* is the little glove box that Mme de Beauséant gives Rastignac as a souvenir:

"I would like to give you a token of my friendship. I shall often think of you. You seem to me good and noble, young and frank, in a world where such qualities are very rare. I hope you will sometimes think of me too. . . . Ah, yes," she said, glancing around the room, "here is the box I used to keep my gloves in. Every time I took them out, before going to a ball or a theater, I felt I was beautiful, because I was happy, and I never touched it without leaving some pleasant thought with it. There's a great deal of me in it, a whole Mme de Beauséant who no longer exists." [p. 246]

This little speech is both pathetic and crucial. Things can possess or retain human significance only through the consent, and even complicity, of the human beings who live among them. Such complicity grows out of a reverence for spirit, for depth, for some kind of transcendence. But the system breaks down in *Père Goriot*. At the close of the novel, it is evident that the glove box is empty, little more than a coffin like the one Goriot is buried in.

One of the great ironies of *Père Goriot* is that the mentors, the teachers of exploitation and artifice, are among the only characters who retain opaqueness and integrity of feeling. Despite the lucid strategies for survival that Rastignac learns from Vautrin and Mme de Beauséant, the criminal and the *grande dame* escape the clarifying (and emptying) gaze of the narrator. Vautrin's accusation of his fellow *pensionnaires*, "flabby limbs of a gangrened society" (p. 196), is reinforced by the real content of his boast: " 'Have any of the rest of you ten thousand brothers ready to do anything on earth for you?' he demanded proudly. 'There's goodness here,' he said, striking his breast. 'I've never betrayed anybody!' " (p. 197). Those ten thousand brothers are enshrouded with mystery, just as Vautrin's affection for Rastignac is enigmatic. The older man's feelings for the boy resist classification perhaps, but a depth of tenderness in that relationship makes a mockery of Eugène's behavior with Delphine or Victorine. And the reductive vocabulary of a gangrened society (ours or theirs), labeling such feelings "homosexual," will not do. Balzac relentlessly emphasizes the indifference and egotism of the inhabitants of the Maison Vauquer, and *Père Goriot* dramatizes the breakdown of older codes of order and selfless commitment. In this light, Goriot's passion for his daughters—revealing a world of endless depth and suffering—is also a kind of mystery, transcending cause and effect, never fully explicated. If Vautrin and Mme de Beauséant explain the rules, it is Goriot who provides the example for Rastignac, who illustrates the cost of authentic (even if fanatic) feeling. The mystery form elicits a search for relations, and Goriot is the savagely torn link between the Maison Vauquer and the *beau monde*. Later, in Dickens, or more clearly still in Faulkner, the strategy of withheld information and ellipses will generate a new vision, one which can perceive the deeper patterns and laws of reality. Goriot is a negative puzzle, the example of broken, trampled laws. All the melodramatic paraphernalia Balzac decks him with, such as the "Christ of Paternity," emphasizes still more grotesquely the malfunctioning of his role. He stands on the ruins of a world of depth: "I have justice on my side, everything on my side, nature, the law! *I protest!* The country will perish if fathers are trodden underfoot. Of course it will. Society, the whole world, turns on fatherhood. Everything will collapse if children don't love their fathers" (p. 259).

The world does not collapse, but Rastignac's commitment to feeling does. The process of counterfeiting, of replacing real values and ideals with imitations or abstractions (money), is, as Lukács observed,[6] central in Balzac. What we are left

[6] Georg Lukács, *Studies in European Realism* (New York: Grosset & Dunlap, 1964), pp. 47–65.

with, in *Père Goriot,* is a world of pure appearances. The three full characters, Goriot, Mme de Beauséant, and Vautrin, receive the supreme epithet "sublime" from Balzac; their affections dwarf the sensibilities of the student, and they possess a kind of depth and generosity which will disappear from the fully lit scene. At the close of the novel, their mysterious passion has been narrated. They are gone. There are no secrets left to tell. Rastignac alone is there, scheming his plans for survival and masquerade.

To go from the omniscient narrator of *Père Goriot* to Pip's first-person narrative in *Great Expectations* is to enter the realm of limited vision. Irony and discrepancy inevitably result from the contrast between Pip's narrow view and the reader's broad view: we are able to detect his snobbishness and foresee the ruin of his great expectations. It would seem that the reader's own sensibilities and acumen are enlisted and tested in Dickens' novel. Finally the novel is built on a series of mysteries: the identity of the benefactor, the outcome of Pip's love for Estella, the attempt to escape with Magwitch. Yet, the fact of the matter is that Dickens is not terribly interested in exploiting the ironic potential of point-of-view narrative. To be sure, there are the "plump" mysteries which Pip ignores, but an essential ingredient of Pip's storytelling is the prodigious amount of explanation that accompanies and clarifies the story at every moment. Here we are very far from the controlled, dramatic irony of *Bleak House* where Esther's limited vision is contrasted and complemented with the omniscient narrator's; instead we have two Pips, the child whose life is recounted and the middle-aged man who is telling it. This combination makes for very little darkness because the inchoate, unlabeled child's vision rarely achieves authority. Characters are usually accompanied with clarifying details, rather than perceived with immediacy. Consider, for example, the first introduction to Mrs. Joe:

My sister, Mrs. Joe Gargery, was more than twenty years older than I, and had established a great reputation with herself and the neighbors because she had brought me up "by hand." Having at that time to find out for myself what the expression meant, and knowing her to have a hard and heavy hand, and to be much in the habit of laying it upon her husband as well as upon me, I supposed that Joe Gargery and I were both brought up by hand. She was not a good-looking woman, my sister, and I had a general impression that she must have made Joe Gargery marry her by hand. . . .

My sister, Mrs. Joe, with black hair and eyes, had such a prevailing redness of skin that I sometimes used to wonder whether it was possible she washed herself with a nutmeg-grater instead of soap. She was tall and bony, and almost always wore a coarse apron, fastened over her figure behind with two loops, and having a square impregnable bib in front that was stuck full of pins and needles.[7]

Other characters, including Pumblechook, Trabb's boy, and Wopsle, are introduced in similar, detailed fashion, and indeed Dickens is renowned for precisely those colorful character portraits. Of course, there are unheralded, unlabeled characters in this book, such as the first appearance of the convict, Jaggers, and Herbert. But more on that later. At the moment it is important to ascertain the generally clear, fully drawn nature of the things and people Pip perceives. As soon as Joe mentions Tickler, Pip hastens to explain (to us): "Tickler was a wax-ended piece of cane, worn smooth by collision with my tickled frame" (p. 15). When Mrs. Joe announces that she is going to "dose" Pip, the boy is quick to elaborate on the meaning of such a ritual. In general, Pip provides a kind of running commentary concerning his style and the events that befall him. Tickler and "dosing" as such have no tremendous import, but other, more crucial issues are also

[7] Charles Dickens, *Great Expectations* (New York: New American Library 1963), p. 14. Subsequent quotations are from this edition.

illuminated in this fashion, so that the reader is very rarely in the dark. After Pip's encounter with Miss Havisham and Estella, he conscientiously informs the reader of his reaction: "I had never thought about being ashamed of my hands before; but I began to consider them a very indifferent pair. Her contempt for me was so strong that it became infectious, and I caught it" (p. 70). So careful is Dickens to avoid unwanted ambiguity that he never lets a potentially misleading statement stand alone. Thus, Pip is acutely aware of his growing snobbishness, and he tries to ensure our certainty on that score as well; regarding Joe's education, we have the following confession: "Whatever I acquired, I tried to impart to Joe. This statement sounds so well that I cannot in my conscience let it pass unexplained. I wanted to make Joe less ignorant and common, that he might be worthier of my society and less open to Estella's reproach" (pp. 123–124). In the same vein, Pip's decision to take the London coach by himself has the characteristic follow-up: "I am afraid—sore afraid—that this purpose originated in my sense of the contrast there would be between me and Joe, if we went to the coach together" (p. 175). In short, Pip keeps us thoroughly informed about his real motivation; his "mistakes" are highlighted as he makes them, and the reader has little need to interpret or decipher on his own. Many critics have noticed the "anti-fairytale" nature of *Great Expectations,* but it should be emphasized that the romance is exposed and punctured early in the story. At the beginning of Chapter 29, Pip is musing over his future, and we have the following passage in which the mature narrator clearly exercises his double vision:

She had adopted Estella, she had as good as adopted me, and it could not fail to be her intention to bring us together. She reserved it for me to restore the desolate house, admit the sunshine into the dark rooms, set the clocks a-going and the cold hearths a-blazing, tear down the cobwebs, destroy the vermin—in short, do all the shining deeds of the young knight of romance, and marry the princess. [p. 252]

This passage well illustrates the rich ironic potential that Dickens has chosen to ignore, for without the all-shattering conclusion about romance, Pip would be a finely deceived protagonist with good reason to be so. Notice the progressive sense of excitement and lyricism in the passage, the sure logic of Pip's deduction. Finally, it is striking to note the soundness of Pip's illusion. He is not grasping for straws or daydreaming; rather he is incorporating all the assorted Gothic details into a convincing whole. Yet Dickens unhesitatingly pulls the rug out from under his feet, deflates the bubble at once rather than exploiting the blindness and lyricism. We have only to consider what Faulkner has done to the Sutpen story to see that Dickens is not significantly interested in developing false leads or sustaining a distorted perspective. Instead, Dickens is striving for on-the-spot elucidation, and the reader is constantly edified at the protagonist's expense. The confused, murky texture of experience, of making mistakes and being deluded, of *being* a snob (rather than merely announcing it) is never really transmitted to the reader. The clarifying stance of Pip the narrator effectively shunts off the immediacy of the child's view, and the reader's ethical landscape is considerably more charted than the child's. Therefore it may seem that there are no abysses in this novel, no hidden depths that might escape the rectifying double vision of the narrator; Dickens, like Balzac, appears to explain and illuminate as he goes. A final reassurance of moral order and stability is furnished by the scattered bits of philosophical wisdom which dot the narrator's reminiscences. Statements such as "Heaven knows we need never be ashamed of our tears, for they are rain upon the blinding dust of earth, overlying our hard hearts. I was better after I had cried than before—more sorry, more aware of my own ingratitude, more gentle. If I had cried before, I should have had Joe with me then" (p. 177), or "so throughout life our worst weaknesses and meannesses are usually committed for the sake of the people whom we most despise" (p. 238) bespeak a kind of future certainty that smugly undermines the tentativeness of the ongoing narrative. (To be sure, the first-person narrative has a built-in protective device, and the very story we are reading gives evidence of the narrator's survival.)

This assessment of Dickens' use of suspense is not meant to be a criticism of the author for not having written a Jamesian novel of delayed revelations. My focus is on the way the reader and narrator come to knowledge; my purpose is to indicate the actual role of mystery and its relation to vision in *Great Expectations*. It is important to acknowledge the clarifying and redressing impulse of the novel, Dickens' strategy of setting things straight as they unfurl, because there are—on a more subterranean level that we are now going to explore —enigmas that remain.

One must first concede that Dickens holds back many of the important answers in the novel, disclosing them at the proper dramatic moment. Pip manages to persevere for some time in the delusion that Miss Havisham is his benefactor and that Estella is destined for him. Most readers have doubtless dismissed Miss Havisham long before the boy does, and we are more attentive to Estella's warnings than he is. Yet, that bizarre old lady is surely a more plausible and palatable candidate for benefactor than the convict is. It may be a law of art that everything signifies (and therefore, the convict, once introduced into the novel, must have a role to play), but few of us attach such importance to the random events of our real lives. Dickens has contrived to keep the convict before our eyes, but it is perfectly natural that Pip should not imagine his identity. Just before his final departure from the village, the boy gives a brief thought to that meeting on the marshes; the passage illuminates the defects of our knowledge, the cleavage between the puny, myopic logic we apply to events and the harsh patterns of necessity and meaning which we finally, unwittingly, enact:

> If I had often thought before, with something allied to shame, of my companionship with the fugitive whom I had once seen limping among those graves, what were my thoughts on this Sunday, when the place recalled the wretch, ragged and shivering, with his felon iron and badge! My comfort was that it had happened a long time ago, and that he had doubtless been transported a long way off, and that he was dead to me, and might be veritably dead in the bargain. [p. 164]

The shame Pip feels toward the convict is different from the embarrassment caused by his humble origins; it is more akin to fear, a reluctance to acknowledge the dark side of life, and, ultimately, of oneself. The romance consists in believing that one can live sheltered from such forces. In *Bleak House*, Lady Dedlock's secret, Jo's blighted existence, the pestilence of Chancery and Tom-All-Alone's testify to a kind of evil that must be exposed, acknowledged, and lived with; acquiring such knowledge has its price, and Esther's maturity will cost her her beauty. Pip too must come to terms with evil, must acknowledge not only Magwitch, but Compeyson and Drummle as well. Only then will Estella and Miss Havisham cease to be picturesque surfaces and yield their terrible human secrets; more importantly, the village world will no longer be a mere bucolic, humble façade, but will achieve—when it is too late—its lacking third dimension of depth, feeling, and reality. The authentic mystery of *Great Expectations* does not emanate from mistaken identities; it lies in the discovery that our discrete labels and ordered lives are but a thin crust overlaying long reaches of blackness. That nether world dictates the plots in Dickens' novels, and the paths of knowledge lead inexorably toward it. The mysteries can be "solved" once Pip's vision has been broadened beyond the confines of the fairy tale. Pip's education will consist of linking together the seemingly distinct halves of his experience:

I consumed the whole time in thinking how strange it was that I should be encompassed by all this taint of prison and crime; that, in my childhood out on our lonely marshes on a winter evening, I should have first encountered it; that it should have reappeared on two occasions, starting out like a stain that was faded but not gone; that it should in this new way pervade my fortune and advancement. While my mind was thus engaged, I thought of the beautiful young Estella, proud and refined, coming towards me, and I thought with absolute abhorrence of the contrast between the jail and her. [p. 285]

Contrary to Pip's expectations, there is nothing strange about being tainted with prison and crime; that an event "happened a long time ago" is no comfort that we are free of its consequences; quite the contrary. The threads of life commit us to patterns we ignore: "Pause you who read this, and think for a moment of the long chain of iron or gold, or thorns or flowers, that would never have bound you, but for the formation of the first link on one memorable day" (p. 83). To solve the mystery is to find and interpret those links. Recognition of ties and bonds may be seen as either imprisonment[8] or relatedness; the distance between those two kinds of vision is the journey Pip must make.

In this light the opening of the novel yields its true richness. A child is alone in a graveyard seeking to imagine his parents, trying to grasp the "identity of things" (p. 9). Suddenly a figure emanates from the marshes and graves threatening to cut the child's throat:

a fearful man, all in coarse grey, with a great iron on his leg. A

[8] For a discussion of the prison motif in Dickens, see Lionel Trilling's essay on *Little Dorrit* in *Charles Dickens: A Collection of Critical Essays* (Englewood Cliffs, N.J.: Prentice-Hall, 1967), pp. 147–158.

man with no hat, and with broken shoes, and with an old rag tied round his head. A man who had been soaked in water, and smothered in mud, and lamed by stones, and cut by flints, and stung by nettles, and torn by briars; who limped, and shivered, and glared, and growled; and whose teeth chattered in his head, as he seized me by the chin. [p. 10]

This is the identity of things. Although it will be many pages later before Magwitch says to Pip, "Look'ee here, Pip. I'm your second father" (p. 345), the evidence is on the opening pages if one can accede to it. Dickensian mystery is not a matter of playing games with the reader, of hastily tying the strands of plot together and removing the masks at the novel's close; it is, in the words of Martin Price, "a world of heightened significance, a world of unrelieved and often frightening relevances, a world where crime and disease are not discrete experiences but dimensions of a larger and more oppressive dehumanization. It is a world of doubles and counterparts, of actions that reticulate into a vast mesh of consequences."[9] We can now redefine the nature of vision in *Great Expectations*. The very considerable amount of clarity, details, and explanations offered by the two Pips illuminates a narrow path and permits us, in a naturalistic fashion, to follow Pip in his journey; the full scope of the boy's experience and the meaning of his education are revealed only after we have learned to interpret the whole picture, to perceive the tangential, underlying, often symbolic reality with which any event in Dickens is fraught. Dorothy Van Ghent has commented on the distinction between the reality principle in Dickens and the reductive, pedestrian naturalism generally applied to experience:

Coincidence is the violent connection of the unconnected. Life is full of violent connections of this sort, but one of the most rigorous conventions of fictional and dramatic art is that events

[9] Martin Price in *Charles Dickens: A Collection of Critical Essays*, pp. 7–8.

should have a logically sequential pattern; for art is the discovery of order. Critics have frequently deplored Dickens' use of coincidence in his plots. But in a universe that is nervous throughout, a universe in which nervous ganglia stretch through both people and their external environment, so that a change in the human can infect the currents of air and the sea, events and confrontations that seem to abrogate the laws of physical mechanics can logically be brought about.[10]

Beneath the surface phenomenon of a young blacksmith who turns into a snob is a tableau of less visible, but more elemental passions. For example, the rather contained, explanatory narrative Pip provides is counterbalanced by disturbing outbursts of his subconsciousness in the form of nightmares or visions during sickness. The boy also has hallucinations of seeing Miss Havisham hanging by the neck, and this repressed desire will very nearly boomerang when Orlick traps him with a noose at the limekiln. Pip identifies all too readily with the story of George Barnwell at the time of the attack on his sister, just as he has visions of himself in prison. Not only dreams and visions are used to give vent to the desires and fears of the protagonist, but events and characters are also at the command of these "nervous ganglia." This sense of a disturbed inner life rarely surfaces in the controlled narrative actually articulated by the two Pips, just as Dickens cannot explicitly *say* what is happening under the surface of his fairy tale. But the events and rhythm of the novel, if interrogated, tell the darker story. For instance, critics have pointed out[11] that Orlick is not so much the villain as Pip's alter ego. As soon as it becomes clear that Orlick is doing to Mrs. Joe what Pip would like to do, we begin to see what is hidden in Dic-

[10] Dorothy Van Ghent, *The English Novel* (New York: Harper and Row, 1967), p. 163.

[11] See *ibid.*, and especially Julian Moynahan, "The Hero's Guilt: The Case of *Great Expectations*," *Essays in Criticism*, X (1960), 60–79.

kensian mystery. Likewise, the scene in which Pip tries to save Miss Havisham has distinct overtones of rape and murder: "we were on the ground struggling like desperate enemies, and . . . the closer I covered her, the more wildly she shrieked and tried to free herself" (p. 431). It is the full resonance of Pip's narrative that must be grasped, that larger, dimly lit area untouched by the narrator's commentary, if we are to fully penetrate his story.

Whereas Balzacian mystery sheds light on the breakdown of interrelations, Dickens requires the reader to see the interrelatedness of ordinarily discrete elements, to see, for example, the connection between an early reference to the cold distant stars and Estella (p. 59), or the irony of Magwitch's remark about Compeyson after their fight in the marshes: "He's a gentleman, if you please, this villain. Now, the hulks has got its gentleman again, through me" (p. 44). If we can see Orlick as Pip's alter ego, then not only the attack on Mrs. Joe, but also the murderous assault on Pip himself reveals its true significance. Pip must come to terms with Orlick, as the embodiment not only of evil, but also of his own repressed fears and desires. The final confrontation, with its setting on the marshes, its mud and ooze and ghostly vapor of the kiln, unmistakably suggests a kind of initiation, a descent into hell, a climax to the arduous journey of self-knowledge. Orlick, like Magwitch, is the identity of things, the dark underside which must be perceived. Orlick's breathless "explanation" of the mysteries—resolving many of the puzzles—is like death itself, and Pip dizzily sees both his past and future life rush by. It is a moment of truth, briefly dispelling the mists and vapors; yet it is a glimpse of the real enigmas of life, the irrationality of evil, the abyss of envy. The story opens in the marshes, and they, along with the mists, the taint of crime, and the shadow of Newgate, constitute the real medium in which Dickens' novel unfolds. Clarity is ever momentary, and the marsh imagery breaks into the fragile constructs of order whenever a deep chord or true passion is touched. When asked by Herbert to drop Estella, Pip is savagely struck: "I turned my head aside, for, with a rush and a sweep, like the old marsh winds coming up from the sea, a feeling like that which had subdued me on the morning when I left the forge, when the mists were solemnly rising, and when I laid my hand upon the village finger-post, smote upon my heart again" (p. 271). We are of the marshes, Dickens is saying, and there is an indelible stain on the makeshift, orderly edifices we try to erect. The scene is always haunted by ghosts like Compeyson. Disorder and fear and guilt are primordial here. In *Little Dorrit*, Arthur Clennam *knows* (proof will always be found later) that there is something dark beneath his family's fortune; Chancery and Tom-All-Alone's and the fog pollute the moral atmosphere of *Bleak House;* the dust of *Our Mutual Friend* permeates the novel with its aura of crime and decay. If one tends to forget the hidden guilt in *Great Expectations*, Jaggers is there to remind us of the potential crimes we are harboring. The hidden feelings that Jaggers awakens are not fanciful; they must be brought to light and acknowledged.

In a book filled with suspense and errors, Jaggers best illustrates the phenomenon of vision without response. The formidable lawyer is a power behind the scenes; he knows everybody's secrets and regards Pip and his friends as "very obvious and poor riddles that he had found out long ago" (p. 264). Jaggers, very much like Bucket in *Bleak House*, knows the answers to most of the enigmas that abound in the novel. He knows the secret of Pip's benefactor, knows about Estella and Molly; yet Pip and Esther, not Jaggers and Bucket, undergo a veritable initiation into these mysteries. Jaggers shuns personal commitment; he honors only facts and evidence. He is therefore ignorant of the only things in Dickens' world that are ultimately worth knowing: Wemmick's touching attachment to "the aged one," Joe's love for Pip, Pip's feeling for Estella. The magnificent scene in which the unillusioned, chastened boy confronts Jaggers and Wemmick together, batters down their protective wall of "evidence" and "portable property," and forces them into humanity is a key to the whole novel:

I made a passionate, almost an indignant appeal to him to be more frank and manly with me. I reminded him of the false hopes into which I had lapsed, the length of time they had lasted, and the discovery I had made. . . . I wanted assurance of the truth from him. And if he asked me why I wanted it and why I thought I had any right to it, I would tell him, little as he cared for such poor dreams, that I had loved Estella dearly and long, and that, although I had lost her and must live a bereaved life, whatever concerned her was still nearer and dearer to me than anything else in the world. [pp. 442–443]

Then, in a brief moment of vulnerability and humanity, Jaggers acknowledges the integrity of such poor dreams and reveals the whole truth about Estella's origins. The pieces have all fallen into place, but the resultant pattern is more than a completed puzzle; like the web the spider creates out of his own body, the picture of order has been achieved through pain and effort. Pip can forgive Miss Havisham because he knows her story and has suffered. Finally the completed pattern enables Pip to make one ultimate act of redemption. Although he has lost Estella and his own poor dreams, Pip can bequeath to the dying Magwitch his own great expectations:

"Dear Magwitch, I must tell you, now at last. You understand what I say?"
A gentle pressure on my hand.
"You had a child once, whom you loved and lost."
A stronger pressure on my hand.
"She lived and found powerful friends. She is living now. She is a lady and very beautiful. And I love her!" [p. 494]

It is the supreme fairy tale, the higher world of truth which does not depend on evidence; at once it redeems both Pip and the detective-story form Dickens has used to tell his story. The pieces have not merely fallen together, yielding an unbroken surface, but rather the boy, in finding and suffering the answers, has created depth which was not there. Pip has embraced his father and asserted his bond with humanity. Although "not related to the outlaw, or connected with him by any recognizable tie" (p. 481), Pip obtains permission to hold the convict's outstretched hand during the trial. At the close of the trial, Pip's vision has been so transformed, the visible world of evidence and societal codes has so receded into the background, that only Magwitch and his poor humanity are real while the gallery looks like a "large theatrical audience."

Critics have long pondered the relative merits of the two endings Dickens gave to *Great Expectations;* yet neither is truly happy, and both reflect the cost of vision. Whether Pip is reunited to Estella or not, the unquestioning love and happiness of his childhood (Joe and Biddy) are forever gone. When Joe nurses the sick Pip back to health and becomes progressively distant as the boy returns to his old self, we have merely a confirmation of the boy's nightmarish reactions to Wemmick's note: "Don't go home." Home and all it represents—security, innocence, grace—must, in some sense, be sacrificed before it can be seen, sounded, and appreciated. Esther Summerson and Eugene Wrayburn are disfigured, and Arthur Clennam is half-broken and far into middle age, before they achieve a measure of happiness. Regardless of the ending, Pip's knowledge and maturity have been purchased at a comparable price.

In conclusion, the relative clarity and solidity of the protagonist's stance is seen to be a foil. Pip is able to tell us that he is becoming a snob, and he accurately describes the bullying of his sister and the appearance of the convict; he cannot tell us that Orlick's attack on Mrs. Joe suits him or that Magwitch is his father and ties stronger than leg irons will bind them together. The mysteries encountered by the child will be understood only when the naturalistic setting has been subsumed by a larger moral framework. As in Balzac, the world of evidence is not finally reliable; but whereas it tends to become illuminated façade in the French writer, Dickens makes it subordinate to the demands of spirit, and the strange designs it conceals must be perceived by the spirit. In such a fictional universe the reader must learn to go beyond the concrete details, enlarge his frame of reference, return to the scene, and effect a final synthesis. In contrast to the emptied mysteries of Balzac, Dickens does not leave the stage suffused with light; instead, the mists are still there, filled with depth and suggestiveness, and the physical and moral contours have grown dim and depend on the eyes of the viewer.

2 | Enclosed Vision:
Conrad, Ford, and James

From the illuminated façade of the Beauséant reception to Pip's struggle at the limekiln, we can discern one of the movements of modern fiction. Each scene lays bare the mysteries that confront the young hero, but whereas Balzac converts all into light (and hustles his opaque characters from the stage), Dickens entrusts his meaning to the texture and resonance of the event itself. Unstated, perhaps unstateable, Dickens' theme, not circumscribed by the finiteness of any text, acquires its fullness and depth only through the cooperation of the reader. The writers to be discussed in this chapter have gone far beyond Dickens in the pursuit of mystery and the consequent interest attached to the suggested and unseen. Conrad, Ford, and James dramatize the act of imagination itself and tend to make it the subject of their fiction.

The scope of the mystery is drastically altered. Through his sleuthing and his mentors, Rastignac uncovers no less than the operative laws of Parisian life; Pip's discoveries, less generic and more private, are already enlisted in the task of self-knowledge. *Lord Jim*, "Heart of Darkness," *The Good Soldier*, and virtually all of James's fiction can be seen as an unending scrutiny of motive. There are no more Vautrins who hold the keys to the riddles. Already Jaggers' effectiveness in *Great Expectations* is undermined, as knowledge is more and more equated with insight rather than fact. Omniscient author-narrators yield to unreliable author-narrators; vision is increasingly restricted as the fictional enterprise itself becomes more open-ended. Balzac hoists his answers and keys and laws from within the precincts of the work; the original *donnée* is replete with its future possibilities. Dickens, as we have seen, uses mysteries for which factual answers are inadequate. That act of going beyond the evidence, of seeing more and more deeply than logic warrants, extends the bounds of the fictional world. In Conrad, Ford, and James that realm beyond the confines of the novel, beyond the purview of the narrator, entices forth the book we read. The source of the work, the reality principle it is intended to reveal, is always beyond and beckoning. As Wayne Booth has abundantly and critically illustrated,[1] what counts in such suggestive, conjectural art is not so much moral judgments as sensitivity, the quality of the vision rather than the value of the action. Such a shift in narrative modes can never merely be a question of aesthetics; the omniscient author dies because one can no longer share his certainties, because his statement is too complete to command our belief or engage our vision. Ford's "saddest story" seems, at first, a virtuoso display of ferocious irony and blindness, leaving little doubt as to its scheme of reference; but there is a fundamental openness in *Lord Jim* and *The Good Soldier*, an implicit belief that appearances are all we have to go on and that the only viable humanism consists in seeing as finely and richly as we can, projecting on or inferring from the array of surfaces some pattern of depth that will redeem them and us.

Unquestionably, the work of Conrad does not countenance fully relative value schemes. His view of ethics is not blurred, and his major work deals with the precise conflict between the image of the self and the patterns of conduct which fate

[1] See Wayne Booth, *The Rhetoric of Fiction* (Chicago: University of Chicago Press, 1961), *passim*.

causes us to enact. This clash usually takes the shape of a betrayal of trust, and the only reconciliation in Conrad, not unlike the acceptance Pip must arrive at, is to acknowledge both parts of the self: the inviolate image and the equally representative acts, even when they are dark. Such an assessment of Conrad's moral drama may be overly schematic, but it indicates the real codes and boundaries that shape the world of the novels. Where, then, are the uncertainties? First, they reside in the question posed by Stein: "how to be?" The code is clear, but the problem of living with it is not. How does one apprehend that seam in life where principles and people interact? Jim's reaction to the determining event of his life resembles that of Razumov in *Under Western Eyes:* shock. The inscrutable, unalterable nature of their act and the rigorously logical network of consequences give rise to a strange monologue in Conrad, wherein the protagonist queries in disbelief how such a damning pattern can, in fact, be his life. The problems of self-knowledge are matched by a corresponding epistemological impasse: how does one learn of others? The public dimension looms large in Conrad; one's image, as Sartre and the existentialists were to show much later, is the function of others, and *Lord Jim* focuses more on Jim's impact on others than on his self-opinion. From this point, no single authority can suffice. The variety of responses to Jim (Brierly, Chester, Brown, Marlow, the reader) asserts both the tentative, arbitrary nature of judgment and Conrad's interest in perception as theme.

Of course, the elaborate Conradian presentation may be viewed as the author's failure to distinguish between matter and manner. Thus we have Wayne Booth's query: "Is 'Heart of Darkness' the story of Kurtz or the story of Marlow's experience of Kurtz? Was Marlow invented as a rhetorical device for heightening the meaning of Kurtz's moral collapse, or was Kurtz invented to provide Marlow with the core of his experience of the Congo?"[2] Posing the question in terms of either-or, however, suggests a kind of critical dissection that is alien to the work. Similarly, we might ask what Marlow's function in *Lord Jim* is and why the story of Razumov in *Under Western Eyes* should be presented by the old English professor? Why does Conrad always insist on the conjectural framework, the structures of scrutiny? If we ponder this, we will see that Booth's question does not, in fact, go far enough; rather than view Marlow as the *device* for getting at Kurtz (although he is surely that as well), let us consider him the indispensable alien lens through which the self takes on its existence, that is, Marlow is enlisted even more for ontological than aesthetic reasons. This is particularly obvious in *Lord Jim*, where Marlow is joined by a host of other witnesses. Jim himself offers very little self-portraiture, not merely because he is rather simple and incurious, but because he is perhaps least suited to discover and define his self. Conradian characters are strangely inaccessible to themselves; they brood incessantly on their images, but the creation and apprehension of that image is the work of others. Nostromo's itinerary consists in moving beyond the legendary, fixed, and false image that he has unquestioningly and complacently accepted; but he arrives at bitterness and betrayal, not self. Decoud, seemingly independent and iconoclastic, fatally discovers that he cannot exist without recognition by others. Razumov, in order to be effective politically, must be acknowledged, must be seen and responded to, even though the man he becomes is abhorrent to him. In short, the search for the self, instigated from the inside or the outside, constitutes the visible impulse of Conrad's work, but the desired object is at best elusive, at worst nonexistent.

All we really see is the apparatus of observation. The po-

<hr />

[2] *Ibid.*, p. 346.

litical or ideological or even moral conflicts seem to matter less than the problems of scrutiny, interpretation, surveillance, and surmise. Conrad is drawn to secret agents, double agents, speculating professors, and philosophical men of the sea because the mechanics of inquiry strike him as more real, possibly even more ethical, than the fatal gestures themselves. Much has been written about the premise that character is fate in Conrad, that the novelist's mastery, in Dorothy Van Ghent's words, "is his ability to make the circumstance of 'plot' the inevitable point of discharge of the potentiality of 'character.' "[3] But Conrad is more modern than Greek in that his characters refuse to abide by such revelation; thus, they steadfastly view themselves as victims of circumstances, whereas we are invited, as Van Ghent says, to see them as "character exposed by circumstances."[4]

It is a question of taking the narrative structures seriously, as edifices important in themselves and not just for what they supposedly do. The endless debate over the authenticity or inauthenticity of particular acts in Conrad (such as whether Jim is ultimately traitor or hero in his pact with Brown, whether Razumov's final gesture is redemptive or not) may obscure the other, truly starker elements of his fiction: namely, the reader and Marlow never get beyond name-calling, affixing labels, testing hypotheses, preparing judgments, conjuring up phantoms, striving for some kind of "real" Jim who would "really" either be or not be "one of us." The chase is endless because there is no real self, nothing but speculation. In this light we better understand Jim's and Razumov's refusal to recognize themselves as betrayer; "betrayer" is as fabricated as "hero." What emerges from Conrad is not that our uncontrollable acts expose us, but rather that life erratically and brutally foists roles upon us, and we are stuck with

[3] Van Ghent, *English Novel*, pp. 283–284.
[4] *Ibid.*, p. 284.

them. For the truth is a void, and, rather than accept that, we live out the procedural drama of fighting against masks. The most authentic note in Conrad is that the masks do not fit. But they are all we have. That is why codes are so precious to Conrad, especially the seaman's code. The allure of roles, of fixity, is irresistible, and it helps to explain why Jim cannot naysay Brown (who, a white man, is for Jim "one of us") or Heyst, Jones or Marlow, Kurtz. Beyond that, however, it accounts for the formalism of the work, the dualities and hidden affinities, the massive interest in the machinery of perception, the awesome verbosity of the style itself; all testifies to a desperate belief in form, in the categories of value. In Conrad form is called on to generate essence, to replace or even engender the substance it usually orders. The life of Oedipus is illuminated in the fatal act of his past: character is fate, and plot is revelation. With Jim we are left wondering if codes alone remain, if Jim contains anything to be illuminated. His act and his reaction make fine drama, but the correspondence scheme has broken down, and all the effort, theatrics, and posturing will not put it back together.

The suspicion that the self is extinct explains much of Conrad's art. For our need remains. The search for the self, the need for the strictest codes, are more imperious than ever in a world without center. Conrad is modern because he has to make what was given to Sophocles. He needs that machinery. He cannot show his cards because he does not possess them. That is why there seems to be almost a bluff, a calculated risk, in his fiction. His dazzling solution is to overwhelm us with the reality of the quest in the hope that we will also accept the illusion of the vision. Thus we have the famous preface to *The Nigger of the "Narcissus"* where Conrad, after articulating his intention "that the light of magic suggestiveness may be brought to play for an evanescent instant over the commonplace surface of words: of the old, old words, worn thin, defaced by ages of careless usage," defines his single objective:

"my task which I am trying to achieve is, by the power of the written word to make you hear, to make you feel—it is, before all, to make you *see*."[5] Rather than interpreting this Maupassant-derived statement in a naturalistic vein (in which case it clearly does *not* describe Conrad's work), let us take account of the emphasis placed on the reader himself. The mystery form generates a need for clarity and penetration. Kurtz's experience (and Marlow's) in "Heart of Darkness" is ineffable partially because "the old, old words, worn thin" will not convey its intensity, but also, one suspects, because it may be unavailable, verbally or otherwise, to the author. But, if the strategy works, the reader is obliged—because the narrator is obliged—to project his own vision. And that vision may be more real, the more it is strained. Hence, there is insistence, in *Under Western Eyes*, on the opaqueness of the Russian soul, its infuriating sublimity which resists the grids of logic and language. The core of *The Secret Agent* is Mrs. Verloc's tragic suspicion that "life doesn't stand much looking into," and Conrad's story bears her out, as her discoveries lead to death. Conrad's fiction depends on belief in these dark, ineffable realms, for they generate the compulsion of his work. Despite the verbosity and the analytical passages, the novels never clarify or lay bare the sources of energy. They cannot. There is a wager in such an aesthetic, almost a plea that the expressed appearances do, in fact, hint at, or stem from, something too fine or too prodigious for language. Should we decide that Jim is small beer and Marlow has been wasting his time, or that Kurtz is merely deranged, or that the Russian soul is gibberish, there is little "evidence" to convince us of the contrary. In this light Conrad is vulnerable to the criticism leveled at him by E. M. Forster, that "he is misty in the middle as well as at the edges, . . . the secret casket of his genius

[5] Joseph Conrad, *The Nigger of the "Narcissus," Typhoon* and *The Shadow Line* (London: Everyman's Library, 1945), p. 5.

contains a vapour rather than a jewel."[6] Yet his particular stoicism stems directly from his suspected emptiness.

Because of its emphasis on vision and its sense of the void, the Conradian novel can emerge only when fact, or the straightforward narration of a story, no longer carries the credibility or the "magic suggestiveness" that its author needs for his faith and defines as the condition of his art. Conrad's codes and forms are more truly generative than prescriptive because the sought-after self can be brought to life only through the complicity of character, narrator, and reader. Pip's put-down of Jaggers and Wemmick, the authority of the subjective as opposed to the weight of evidence, has, in Conrad, been transformed into narrative credo.

The Good Soldier reminds one, in many ways, of Conrad. The collaboration between the two writers is, of course, well known, but there is also considerable internal evidence of a shared aesthetic: the break with linear chronology, the "impressionistic" rendition of character, the interest in point-of-view narrative. But, within the perspective of this study, Ford's novel poses far more radically the problem of vision in an opaque world. Ford records the cost of blindness as well as the arduousness and vagaries of perception. Conrad's characters (Jim, Razumov, Nostromo, Heyst) are frequently paralyzed by a defective but rigid image of themselves that is challenged or belied by their actions; the anguish rarely permeates the narrative process. The conjectural, probing nature of Marlow's reconstructive narrative underscores the elusiveness of character, but it never places in doubt the validity, however tentative, of the emerging portrait. In *The Good Soldier* false appearances, inflexible conventions, and deficient self-knowledge are no longer contained or redressed by the

[6] E. M. Forster, *Abinger Harvest* (New York: A Harvest Book, 1964), p. 138. In fact, Forster's strictures refer to Conrad's essays, but we may easily apply them to the novels as well.

ironic wisdom of a Marlow. The old dichotomies between appearance and reality, ignorance and knowledge no longer function in the restorative, corrective manner to which we are accustomed.

Such a verdict of confusion may seem excessive. For it seems obvious that the narrator of *The Good Soldier* is, somewhat like Jason in *The Sound and the Fury*, so wrongheaded and clearly deceived as to be reliable. Thus his disorder would be our order; his blindness, our vision. Literature frequently edifies us by such exemplary reversals, and Dowell is an easy target. Dowell is a catastrophically limited character, a full-scale Prufrock incapable of action and feeling. He is lonely, rootless, bewildered, idiosyncratic, in turn exploited or babied, and monstrously gullible. Florence does not long mystify the reader (who early realizes what her family is trying to intimate to Dowell), and the nature of their *ménage à trois* in Paris could only escape a moron: "You see, that fellow impressed upon me that what Florence needed most of all were sleep and privacy. I must never enter her room without knocking, or her poor little heart might flutter away to its doom."[7] Such statements strengthen the reader's position, flatter his sense of clairvoyance. In a maze of appearances and subterfuges, Dowell's kind of knowledge is hopelessly wrong; his surefooted sense of orientation at Nauheim is a triumph of absurdity:

Yes, I could find my way blindfolded. I know the exact distances. From the Hotel Regina you took one hundred and eighty-seven paces, then turning sharp, lefthanded, four hundred and twenty took you straight down to the fountain. From the Englischer Hof, starting on the sidewalk, it was ninety-seven paces and the same four hundred and twenty, but turning righthanded this time. [p. 22]

[7] Ford Madox Ford, *The Good Soldier* (New York: Vintage Books, 1951), p. 88. Subsequent quotations are from this edition.

For the more careful reader, however, Dowell's narrative is still more subtly and insidiously colored than might be suggested by the ridiculous deficiencies just mentioned. His willingness to accept a nonconsummated union, the thinly disguised fear at Florence's elopement ("I must have received her advances with a certain amount of absence of mind. I was out of that room and down the ladder in under half a minute" [p. 83]), his general priggishness and fastidiousness, all militate against the outlandish, perhaps most telling statement of all: "I don't know that analysis of my own psychology matters at all to this story" (p. 103). The remarks of a Dowell we can cheerfully and precisely discount; the mistakes and losses he records are to be expected. Such irony is, finally, not disturbing.

Ford has very carefully structured his novel in such a way that Florence's story—a farcical, grotesque, ironic comedy of errors—precedes the serious treatment of Leonora and Edward and Nancy. Yet, even during the farce, we would do well to reconsider Dowell's predicament. He is, as all critics recognize, the dupe of conventions. For ten years he regards Edward and Leonora solely as "good country people," and he never questions the weak heart of his wife. Is it so evident that we would have had better vision? In discovering the treachery of his wife and friend, Dowell uncovers the manifold uncertainty of all appearances. Our life is built on the tacit assumption that the coins we deal in are not counterfeit, for who of us could tell:

Upon my word, I couldn't tell you offhand whether the lady who sold the so expensive violets at the bottom of the road that leads to the station was cheating me or no; I can't say whether the porter who carried our traps across the station at Leghorn was a thief or no when he said that the regular tariff was a lira a parcel. The instances of honesty that one comes across in this world are just as amazing as the instances of dishonesty. After forty-five years of mixing with one's kind, one ought to have acquired the habit of being able to know something about one's fellow beings. But one doesn't. [p. 36]

The Good Soldier relentlessly reminds us how little we know. After remarking that he doesn't know whether Leonora was proud of a particular deed, Dowell will characteristically question what anyone has to be proud of. Or when mentioning that Edward didn't look like the sort of person with whom one shouldn't leave one's wife alone, Dowell then adds, "that is, if you can trust anybody alone with anybody" (p. 11). The skepticism quickly becomes infectious and generic. It is a story of rampant disillusion and dissolution. The part of the book dealing with Florence is so grotesque that we feel sheltered from the weaknesses of the narrator. However, as we read further and the characters assume more flesh, the stereotypes and the firm judgments waver. But Dowell's lament is unchanging. At the outset he exclaims: "I know nothing—nothing in the world—of the hearts of men" (p. 7). The point will be driven home when he describes his dealings with young Carter in America: "I have said just now that, in my present frame of mind, nothing would ever make me make inquiries as to the character of any man I liked at first sight. . . . For who in this world can give anyone a character? Who in this world knows anything of any other heart—or of his own?" (p. 155). Dowell cannot judge or condemn, not because he is too weak, but because the categories of judgment have eroded. The description of Edward's love for Nancy is a case in point: "And in speaking to her on that night, he wasn't, I am convinced, committing a baseness. It was as if his passion for her hadn't existed; as if the very words that he spoke, without knowing that he spoke them, created the passion as they went along. Before he spoke, there was nothing; afterwards, it was the integral fact of his life" (p. 116). What kind of code can withstand or cope with that?

As Mark Schorer has pointed out,[8] Ford's novel abolishes the reassuring dichotomy between appearances and reality; Dowell has discovered that nothing is unreal or untrue:

And yet I swear by the sacred name of my creator that it was true. It was true sunshine; the true music; the true splash of the fountains from the mouth of stone dolphins. For, if for me we were four people with the same tastes, with the same desires, acting—or, no, not acting—sitting here and there unanimously, isn't that the truth? If for nine years I have possessed a goodly apple that is rotten at the core and discover its rottenness only in nine years and six months less four days, isn't it true to say that for nine years I possessed a goodly apple? [p. 7]

The statement throws an interesting light on the notion of "truth" in literature (and, possibly, in life as well). Honest Iago and Tartuffe, *le pauvre homme*, are true enough if we happen to be Othello or Orgon. Or, to go a step further, one could argue that those beleaguered old men of literature, forced at last to accept their just deserts—Lear, Creon, Oedipus—have lived rather well. At what point do we step in and gauge their lives? While they are enjoying power and happiness, or after they have been co-opted into a fatal pattern that, while they were living, had little or no bearing on their consciousness? Such speculation is heresy, of course, with regard to the reasonably clear world view of Sophocles and Shakespeare, but the gentlemen in question are in question because they ignore or do not accept that world view. Punishment (if it comes late) and death (whenever it comes) add immeasurably to the pattern of life we are enacting; they dot the "i's" and cross the "t's," provide sober, definitive, harmonious contours to the enigmatic, open-ended quality of every man's life as he lives it; but these ponderous bringers of order can hardly be said to be retroactive, even if they are retrospective. What living life has the unity and cogency of a biography? *The*

[8] See Mark Schorer, "An Interpretation," in *ibid.*

Good Soldier makes a pitiful plea for the integrity of the limited view, and it is, as Dowell repeatedly laments, a sad story.

It is sad because sanity and civilization rest on the viability of conventions:

Upon my word, yes, our intimacy was like a minuet, simply because on every possible occasion and in every possible circumstance we knew where to go, where to sit, which table we unanimously should choose; and we could rise and go, all four together, without a signal from any of us, always to the music of the Kur orchestra, always in the temperate sunshine, or, if it rained, in discreet shelters. No, indeed, it can't be gone. You can't kill a minuet de la cour. You may shut up the music-book, close the harpsichord; in the cupboard and presses the rats may destroy the white satin favors. The mob may sack Versailles; the Trianon may fall, but surely the minuet—the minuet itself is dancing itself away into the farthest stars, even as our minuet of the Hessian bathing places must be stepping itself still. Isn't there any heaven where old beautiful dances, old beautiful intimacies prolong themselves? Isn't there any Nirvana pervaded by the faint thrilling of instruments that have fallen into the dust of wormwood but that yet had frail, tremulous, and everlasting souls?

No, by God, it is false! It wasn't a minuet that we stepped; it was a prison—a prison full of screaming hysterics, tied down so that they might not outsound the rolling of our carriage wheels as we went along the shaded avenues of the Taunus Wald. [pp. 6–7]

Refinement and elegance have always been marked by convention, and they are dealt a heavy blow in *The Good Soldier*. Peire Vidal's pathetic showing with *la Louve*, who ferociously refuses to play the game, sets the tone for the novel. The reversal of the chivalric code by bestiality can be seen in capsule form in Florence's invitation to the Ashburnhams: " 'Why shouldn't we all eat out of the same trough—that's a nasty New York saying. But I'm sure we're all nice quiet people and there can be four seats at our table. It's round' " (p. 31). Lest the resonance of the last detail be unnoticed, Ford repeats two pages later: "And then Florence said: 'And so the whole round table is begun.' " *The Good Soldier*, like Kafka's "Hunger Artist," prefigures, in terms of savagery destroying and replacing refinement, the social and moral overthrow of a culture that erupted with the Great War. The heavy irony and ludicrous blindness of the first half of the novel, focusing on Florence and thereby keeping Edward, Leonora, and Nancy relatively undefined, obscures rather than serves this theme. After the garish revelations have been recorded, culminating in the melodramatic death of Florence, the tone of the novel shifts perceptibly, and Dowell concentrates on the murky human motivation that could have made possible such behavior. The emerging picture of Edward, Leonora, and Nancy, with its emphasis on their past and the complex forces that shaped the three of them, gives depth and poignancy to the silhouettes of the early part of the book. For a gullible fool, Dowell has some acute insights into the personalities he depicts. If one had to deduce the cause of such waste and destruction, it is blindness, the unavoidable blindness of being oneself and not others: Edward's inability to sense the inadequacy and anachronism of his sentimental "feudalism," Leonora's Catholic conditioning and her failure with Edward, Nancy's adolescent cruelty and inexperience. How could they be otherwise?[9]

The only clairvoyant character in the novel is Florence. The American girl knows what she wants and how to get it. In a drama of misleading appearances, Florence conceives of her role as a bringer of light. She provides about as much enlightenment as her orange-distributing uncle. Florence's de-

---

[9] In contrast to the modern critical emphasis on unreliable or neurotic narrators, Theodore Dreiser felt that Ford's novel was "tragic in the best sense that the Greeks knew tragedy, that tragedy for which there is no solution."

ception is comparable to the minuet; manners and conventions have always clothed less aesthetic, more instinctive needs. The whole matter is one of protection: form as shield, form as foil. Dowell has spent his life trying to shield Florence, while Leonora has just as earnestly shielded him from the reality of their situation for the last nine years. In each case, the aim is to spare the heart, to keep it unexposed. *The Good Soldier* is about the failure of both those protective ventures. All of the "things" which Dowell keeps from Florence, the "things" most clothed in convention, "love, poverty, crime, religion, and the rest of it" (p. 16), are precisely what emerge as central in Ford's novel. And they emerge with a shattering force, strewing debris about the book: Edward's life, Nancy's sanity, Dowell's happiness.

Ford's triumph is to have rendered that tragic lesson. He has chosen the hard way, by beginning the novel with Dowell's enlightenment rather than showing the before and the after. Ford's well-known insistence that the right way to start a novel is with a strong opening impression has been subjected to a great deal of criticism.[10] Yet no criticism could be

---

[10] Ford's point is made as follows (*Joseph Conrad: A Personal Remembrance* [Boston: Little, Brown and Co., 1924], pp. 136–137):

> "It became very early evident to us that what was the matter with the Novel, and the British novel in particular, was that it went straight forward, whereas in your gradual making acquaintanceship with your fellows you never do go straight forward. You meet an English gentleman at your golf club. He is beefy, full of health, the moral of the boy from an English Public School of the finest type. You discover gradually that he is hopelessly neurasthenic, dishonest in matters of small change, but unexpectedly self-sacrificing, a dreadful liar, but a most painfully careful student of lepidoptera and, finally, from the public prints, a bigamist who was once, under another name, hammered on the Stock Exchange. . . . Still, there he is, full-fed fellow, moral of an English Public School product. To get such a man in fiction you could not begin at his beginning and work his life chrono-

stronger than what is dramatized in *The Good Soldier*. The reader meets a destroyed narrator. Dowell has depended wholly on first impressions, has, as the "good people" do, taken things for granted. The novel measures the enormity of his error. And the technique is decidedly more than impressionistic. It is, rather, a process of vision and revision, impression and query, probing and guessing. As the harsh but clear contours of Florence's story yield to the muted, entangled character relationships between Edward, Leonora, and Nancy, our picture of the whole is altered. The irony, cynicism, and melodrama become credible and moving through our reconstruction. Edward's sentimentality; Leonora's Catholic conscience; flat, grotesque scenes culminating in bizarre statements such as Leonora's " 'Don't you know that I'm an Irish Catholic' " or Leonora striking Maisie Maidan; all these "excesses" become resonant, even necessary after we have acquired background information. Surely it is a technique designed to shape the reader's response. The tone of the book is increasingly imploring. Scenes, once casually or melodramatically mentioned, must be rethought, and Dowell only initiates the process: "Consider her [Leonora's] position when she burst out over the Luther-Protest. . . . Consider her agonies" (p. 185), or

"you have to imagine my beautiful Nancy appearing suddenly to Edward, rising up at the foot of his bed, with her long hair falling, like a split cone of shadow, in the glimmer of a night-light that burned beside him. You have to imagine her, a silent, a no doubt agonized figure, like a spectre, suddenly offering herself to him—to save his reason! And you have to imagine his frantic refusal—and talk. And talk! My God!" [p. 201]

---

logically to the end. You must first get him with a strong impression, and then work backwards and forwards over his past."

For a critique of this kind of realism (as the sole desirable realism), see Booth, *Rhetoric of Fiction*, pp. 40–41.

As the book progresses, we must call into question our notion of irony, of melodrama. We are forced to re-evaluate those earlier scenes, reconsider our judgment of Dowell. Our task, in fact, mirrors the education and reversals that Dowell himself has undergone.

To alter an opinion, to be forced to see things and oneself differently, is always hazardous. *The Good Soldier* both describes and elicits such an enterprise. The starkest example of this education can be seen in Nancy's change from innocence to consciousness and guilt. The entire section III of Part IV is devoted to this transformation, and some may find it overdone, altogether too literary for their taste. It begins with Nancy reading about a divorce suit. Here is how Ford conveys Nancy's gradual understanding of the term "adultery":

She knew that one was commanded not to commit adultery—but why, she thought, should one? It was probably something like catching salmon out of season—a thing one did not do. She gathered it had something to do with kissing, or holding someone in your arms. . . .

And yet the whole effect of that reading upon Nancy was mysterious, terrifying, and evil. She felt a sickness—a sickness that grew as she read. Her heart beat painfully; she began to cry. She asked God how He could permit such things to be. And she was more certain that Edward did not love Leonora and that Leonora hated Edward. Perhaps, then Edward loved someone else. It was unthinkable.

If he could love someone else than Leonora, her fierce unknown heart suddenly spoke in her side, why could it not be herself? [p. 219]

During her three weeks of introspection Nancy ponders over the nature of love:

she remembered to have heard that love was a flame, a thirst, a withering up of the vitals—though she did not know what the vitals were. She had a vague recollection that love was said to render a hopeless lover's eyes hopeless; she remembered a character in a book who was said to have taken to drink through love; she remembered that lovers' existences were said to be punctuated with heavy sighs. . . .

She remembered that Edward's eyes were hopeless, she was certain that he was drinking too much; at times he sighed deeply. He appeared as a man who was burning with inward flame; drying up in the soul with thirst; withering up in the vitals. . . .

And, after that thought, her eyes grew hopeless; she sighed as the old St. Bernard beside her did. At meals she would feel an intolerable desire to drink a glass of wine, and then another and then a third. Then she would find herself grow gay. . . . But in half an hour the gaiety went; she felt like a person who is burning up with inward flame; desiccating at the soul with thirst; withering up in the vitals. [pp. 223–225]

The progression is exemplary: from abstract, exaggerated convention to awareness of others to awareness of self. Each discovery is more corrosive than the last, leading to a world and a self of random, terrifying disorder. Nancy's universe quite simply discards its protective cover: "the burning logs were just logs that were burning and not the comfortable symbols of an indestructible mode of life" (p. 220). Mad, the child's face will become for Dowell "a picture without a meaning." Dowell himself never goes insane, but he can make little more sense of his experience than the girl can. The ordered picture (and there can be orderly pain and punishment too) has been beset by meaningless discord: "Or are all men's lives like the lives of us good people—like the lives of the Ashburnhams, of the Dowells, of the Ruffords—broken, tumultuous, agonized, and unromantic lives, periods punctuated by screams, by imbecilities, by deaths, by agonies? Who the devil knows?" (p. 238).

We are far from Balzac and Dickens. Education in *Père Goriot* and *Great Expectations* consists basically in insight, penetration of the societal codes in favor of human bonds. Ford too dramatizes insight, but it is a devastating insight, one that erodes and paralyzes more the more one sees. Dowell stated at the outset, in only seemingly exaggerated terms, that "it is not unusual in human beings who have witnessed the sack of a city or the falling to pieces of a people to desire to set down what they have witnessed for the benefit of unknown heirs or of generations infinitely remote" (p. 5). It is for the reader to make more of it than Dowell does.

The Good Soldier illustrates a theme that haunts much twentieth-century fiction: how to orient oneself in a world of collapsing conventions. As children of Eliot and Joyce and Pound, it is somehow difficult to respond fully to such a theme because we are too accustomed to dealing with it purely aesthetically, to encountering it as means of artistic economy. Or else, we are often inclined to scoff at conventions, to brand all conventional behavior as blind or vulnerable, to expect (almost gleefully) comeuppance, intrusion of reality into the sheltered confines of decorum and tradition. The savage, brutal truth, we say, will out. Truth is, indeed, savage enough, but conventions are not (for better or for worse) made of papier maché. Perhaps it is hard, from the vantage point of the latter twentieth century, to see *The Good Soldier* as other than ironic; the pieties of Dowell and Edward and Leonora risk seeming so prehistoric as to be preposterous. But Ford may have thought otherwise; although his book is a scathing critique of conventions, it is also a poignant recognition of the fact that conventions are real: Edward *is* his sentimentalism; Dowell *is* his gullibility; Leonora *is* her Catholic upbringing. The pathos of *The Good Soldier* lies in the fact that our blindness and our conventions are part of our flesh.

Yet if we are never to have more of life than our own limited vision affords, *The Good Soldier* is suspiciously larded with corrective, quasi-authorial wisdom. Dowell is almost embarrassingly forced into those awkward postures of earlier omniscient fiction: peeping at keyholes, having long, clarifying conversations with the characters, and the like. In short, the vision is controlled. Background, history, and fact are brought in to ballast the wavering impressionistic narrative, and although the result makes for little order, one nevertheless feels that the whole Ashburnham tragedy has been told. Dowell places the burden of interpretation on the reader, but Ford has arranged the presentation with a sure hand. The "guideless" novel of pure surfaces, where vision is problematic from beginning to end and the reader's own experience constitutes the sole authority, may not be possible; but it begins to loom over the horizon in the scenic art of Henry James.

If any writer is preoccupied with the themes of vision and awareness, it is Henry James. Perhaps one should say the *forms* of vision and awareness, for James, through example and especially theory, inaugurates the literature of perception and creates the narrative strategies to embody it.[11] Those strategies—center of consciousness, use of the *ficelle*, innuendo, and conjecture rather than explicit statement—form one of the cornerstones of modern fiction, and it is no small irony that the uncontrolled, often savage ventures of contemporary literature are the progeny of such a fastidious, authority-conscious craftsman. Critics have argued that James's theories outdistanced (and overschematized) his work, making him a favored target for critical debate and exegesis. His richest, fullest works, like *The Ambassadors,* do not have the insolence and challenge of such formal experiments as *The Sound and the Fury* or Beckett's trilogy or *Pale Fire* or much of the *nouveau roman.* Yet, if the modern treatment of perception seems more radical than it is in James, one may question whether any other author has comparably delved into the moral ramifications of vision. Faulkner's idiot and Beckett's Molloy tell

---

[11] Although, chronologically, James obviously precedes Conrad and Ford, I have placed him last because his work deals with the moral dimension of all perception more fully—and more disturbingly—than that of any other author in my study.

stories far more despotically and hermetically controlled by "center of consciousness" than is Strether's account of his trip to Paris. Even when the Jamesian narrator is suspect—as in *The Aspern Papers* or *The Turn of the Screw*—the signs and syntax of sanity remain. James is ever lucid, and his characters are endlessly interpreting and refining their observations, rather than entrusting the entire burden to the reader. But it is arguable that *The Ambassadors* makes a deeper statement about the moral posture of the observer than do the novels of Faulkner and Beckett. Most of us are neither idiots nor living in urns, but we are all observers, and we tend to value subtle reasoning as a virtue. It is a particularly academic virtue, and in a world of crumbling values, it may stand alone for a time as a guide to sanity. But my study of James will show that speculation and scrutiny may violate as well as refine.

The international theme of *The Ambassadors* is perfectly suited to an ethic of vision: place a foreigner in an alien culture and let him gradually discern the patterns and forms that are operative. The dramatic method limits us to Strether's awareness, his prodigiously growing awareness, and the novel thus educates us as well as him. Among the many ambiguities of the novel is the particularly unsettling one that involves the tension between perception and action, seeing and doing. Strether urges Little Bilham to live, for a man has only his experience. Likewise, Strether is able to go beyond his Woollett preconceptions and acknowledge the "necessity" of the sexual relation between Chad and Mme de Vionnet. Yet it is a novel of abdication,[12] for Strether willingly chooses only to apprehend such knowledge, not to embody it. There are doubtless many reasons: the fearful sense of the price of sexual passion, symbolized in the theory of the "sacred fount"

---

[12] For a penetrating analysis of this paradox, see Philip M. Weinstein's chapter on *The Ambassadors* in his volume, *Henry James and the Requirements of the Imagination* (Cambridge, Mass.: Harvard University Press, 1971).

and fully realized in the suffering of Marie de Vionnet and the flourishing of Chad; the fundamental inability of the celibate writer to accede to passion by any means other than imaginary, vicarious. However, the contrast between Strether's growing knowledge and Strether's inaction may be only apparent, because the testimony of the whole novel is overwhelmingly in favor of refined insight. To be sure, Chad has become what he is through his love affair with Mme de Vionnet, but it is Strether who earns the unstinting admiration of Maria Gostrey, Mme de Vionnet, Little Bilham, and Chad himself by virtue of his refined vision. In a sense, the book consists of little more than Strether's bouts with strange, opaque circumstances, and the real issue of each contest, beyond the particular information to be imparted, is the exhibition—almost always to an admiring, if not awed, public—of the quality of Strether's thought. There is a real enough moral drama in *The Ambassadors*, but it tends to be wholly internalized at the expense of the tangible, visible world of appearances. The dialogues are competitive, characterized by the faintly obscene, teasing quality of disrobing one's mind, exposing its suppleness and the subtleties of which it is capable. Strether's manner of perception does not so much highlight as replace the substantive discoveries he makes; one might in fact say that the plot of *The Ambassadors* can be seen as a backdrop for the protagonist's thinking processes. To be sure, the novel is more than a display of Strether's thinking. There is concrete and sensuous detail, and Strether's education consists, in part, in opening himself to the beauties and delights of the physical world: Paris itself, Gloriani's garden and the fine appearances there, dining with Maria Gostrey, Mme de Vionnet, the Cheval Blanc, the textures of clothes, the beauty of women.[13] But the very narrative structure, built around the

---

[13] Consider, for example, the exquisite rendering of simple sensuous things in Strether's lunch with Mme de Vionnet:

"How could he wish it to be lucid for others, for anyone, that

device of the *ficelle*, requires constant assessment of these solid events. The Woollett mentality and, it must be said, the Jamesian aesthetic place more emphasis on meanings than surfaces. As a result, one can have the feeling that the physical world is just so much grist for the refining powers of the mind; by virtue of sheer bulk alone, the reflective, interpretive, abstract dimension of *The Ambassadors* outweighs—and portentously outweighs—the moments of sensuous depiction of people and things.

The emphasis on manner at the expense of matter accounts for the strange mixture of minute precision and large confusion in the later works. The endless, dialectical discussions (in which the actual subject matter may easily be forgotten) refine and internalize the givens of the story; essentially dramatic, these exchanges build a kind of ladder of Jamesian logic that is soundly constructed but leads in no visible direction. Yet the dialogues do in fact carry out the work for which they are intended: that progressive display of suppleness and agility—ballet as well as strip tease—that constitutes a fine mind in action. The abdication that crowns Strether's activities is an honest acknowledgment that his real business is neither that of Woollett nor of Paris, but that of the discriminating, only vicariously committed imagination. Strether's goodness and integrity cannot conceal the autonomous nature of his excel-

---

he, for the hour, saw reasons enough in the mere way the bright, clean, ordered water-side life came in at the open window?—the mere way Mme de Vionnet, opposite him over their intensely white table-linen, their *omelette aux tomates*, their bottle of straw-colored Chablis, thanked him for everything almost with the smile of a child, while her gray eyes moved in and out of their talk back to the quarter of the warm spring air, in which early summer had already begun to throb, and then back again to his face and their human question" (New York: New American Library, n.d., p. 185).

The temptation for such mere things to be enough genuinely bothers James; *The Spoils of Poynton* dramatizes this tension.

lence; the authority of his refinement—for it is the abiding
authority of James's work—is gauged by its internal cogency,
by the force and beauty of its performance, not by success or
failure. A blunt truth may not be worth a fine error. Better to
make rather too much of things than to fall short. Despite the
loquaciousness of Jamesian characters, the interminably decorous instances of social intercourse, this world is threatened by
blind, egomaniacal behavior, affording virtually no communication, bordering on solipsis.

Whereas Lambert Strether is making more than conjectural
stabs at the nature of reality, his activity and his prowess nonetheless consist in incessant scrutiny. This is the same posture
assumed by some of the more disturbing members of James's
gallery to whom we now turn: the narrator of *The Aspern
Papers*, the narrator of *The Sacred Fount*, John Marcher in
"The Beast in the Jungle," the governess in *The Turn of the
Screw*. *The Aspern Papers* is possibly James's most caustic
critique of the "truth-seeker." This theme is treated even more
luridly in Ibsen's *Wild Duck*, but James's "publishing scoun-
drel" obviously does double duty as artist-figure as well. His
very real hunger to know the whole Aspern story is not in
itself problematic, but James characteristically puts a human
price tag on all such knowledge. The influence of Hawthorne
may be detected here, for characters such as Chillingworth
and Ethan Brand illustrate the ravages of prying lucidity. The
element of exploitation—the violence implicit in *knowing*—is
less obviously but still more profoundly present in *The Sacred
Fount*. In this exasperating story, the narrator has chosen to
shield the victim of the love relationship that he is simultane-
ously deciphering and depicting. The narrator seeks to get to
the truth, but to veil it, whereas Mrs. Brissenden wants, above
all, to expose and dominate. It is a chilling tale, for the ramifications of the "fount" theory of replenishment and loss extend
to the narrative focus as well, and at the close, the narrator
has indeed shielded May Server, but he is, like Guy Bris-

senden, a depleted, older man. If there is a tendency, already in *The Ambassadors*, to value the quality of the imagination beyond any of its achievements, one has the spectacle of the imagination functioning nearly *in vacuo* in *The Sacred Fount*. Tony Tanner has compared James's baroque use of foils and screen and ambiguities to that of *Last Year at Marienbad*,[14] and I shall analyze in a later chapter the wholly autonomous imagination in Robbe-Grillet. *The Sacred Fount* is entirely hypothetical, and each hypothesis is at least at one remove from us, since in a world of screens one must constantly surmise, conjecture, refine, reverse, even sublimate the infinitely malleable givens. And James gives little indeed in this story: elliptic bits of conversation, views of people with their backs to us, enigmatic facial expressions. At the end, Mrs. Brissenden refuses to cooperate with the narrator, dismisses him as crazy, and scatters his imaginative scaffolding to the winds. It is a strained narrative, James's purest example of fiction as conjecture, and it stands among his works as a reminder that the endlessly refining imagination may completely lose touch with the outer world by obeying its inner compulsion.

Unlike *The Sacred Fount*, "The Beast in the Jungle" does present the evidence against which the imaginative thrust can be measured—in terms of efficacy and not merely fineness. We no longer receive mere innuendoes, but rather we watch the full, drawn-out spectacle of John Marcher watching his life. We witness the growing intimacy with May Bartram and the deepening of their pact. There is no surmise, no hypothesis; we truly see what Marcher cannot: that the event of his life, the real substance—far from being some marvelous happening for which he has been singled out—is the business of living, the commitment to experience and growth that he grotesquely abstracts into *attente*. The waste dramatized by "The Beast in the Jungle" comes from a very particular kind of blindness:

[14] See the Introduction to *Henry James: Three Novels*, ed. Tony Tanner (New York: Harper & Row, 1968).

the assumption that the shape of a life corresponds with one's conscious grasp of it. Those of our actions or words which seem trivial to us, or even escape our attention altogether, may well be our defining characteristics in the eyes of others. Every moment, as Dickens has shown, we are unwittingly forging the chains that will bind us. James is content to dramatize consciousness, even to confer authority to it, but he takes pains to show just enough behavior and action to keep the reader on his guard. The trick to "The Beast in the Jungle" is to see that the real pattern of Marcher's life makes a horrible mockery of the conscious pattern that obsesses him. In reading James, one is obliged to see the whole picture, to mark postures and gestures as well as thoughts. Living is relentless, for it tallies up everything: dull and empty experiences as well as momentous ones, hours lost in sleep as well as spent in action. Waiting for life is a form of living, and watching for something to happen is a form of activity. We are frequently blind to these realities because of the fallacy of content and the despotism of consciousness. In "The Beast in the Jungle," James exposes the liabilities of such beliefs: Marcher's life perversely transcends and undermines his grasp of it. The reader who has looked only to Marcher for the meaning of his story may well be caught too.

All of these odd strains of vision are interwoven in James's most haunting tale of observation and imagination: *The Turn of the Screw*. The critical debate between the Freudian and the "straight" interpretation has tended to make the story a *cause célèbre*, an entity in itself, and most critics, caught in the melee, have neglected the parallels between *The Turn of the Screw* and James's other works. There is no need to review all the arguments, and, as Robert Kimbrough has amply shown, more recent criticism of the tale strikes out in new directions.[15]

[15] See the Norton Critical Edition of *The Turn of the Screw* (New York, 1966), esp. pp. 235–274. All quotations are from this edition.

Nonetheless the two critical positions can be briefly summarized in the following manner. The "straight" reading takes James's word for it (in the Preface and Notebooks) that he has "ruled out subjective complications" for the governess; hence the ghosts are real, and she makes a valiant, if partially unsuccessful, effort to save the children. The Freudian interpretation suspects the governess's narrative, brings in those "subjective complications," and judges the ghosts to be hallucinations of a diseased mind. The governess's background, her feeling for the uncle and for Miles—in short, her own personality—account for her visions, and everything she says is to be filtered in that light. The two readings comprise a critical impasse, for they raise the question of the integrity and authority of the literary statement. Is everything open to interpretation and juggling? As Wayne Booth has insistently pointed out, it does make a difference which reading we accept, but at the same time James manifestly made it hard for us to choose. Let us then consider whether, in the light of our previous remarks about James's treatment of vision, such an impasse is legitimate.

One must focus on the total scene, leaving aside both James's notebooks and the background of the governess. We note from the beginning, regardless of James's later disclaimers, the characteristic fusion of imagination and vision. At the outset we are told that Douglas, interrupted by one of the women, "took no notice of her; he looked at me, but as if, *instead of me, he saw what he spoke of*" [my italics] (p. 2). Likewise, Douglas acknowledges that the governess's love for the uncle is intricately related to the story: "Yes, she was in love. That is, she *had* been. That came out—she couldn't tell her story without its coming out" (p. 3). A last instance, in the story proper this time, of the interrelatedness of the governess's feelings and her vision of the ghosts occurs on the very first discovery of Quint:

It was plump, one afternoon, in the middle of my very hour: the children were tucked away and I had come out for my stroll. One of the thoughts that, as I don't in the least shrink now from noting, used to be with me in these wanderings was that it would be as charming as a charming story suddenly to meet some one. Some one would appear there at the turn of the path and would stand before me and smile and approve. . . . That was exactly present to me—by which I mean the face was—when, on the first of these occasions, at the end of a long June day, I stopped short on emerging from one of the plantations and coming into view of the house. What arrested me on the spot—and with a shock much greater than any vision had allowed for—was the sense that my imagination had, in a flash, turned real. He did stand there! [pp. 15–16]

The "confusion" between Quint and the uncle has, of course, been duly assessed by the Freudians; our interest is less in the source of such a confusion (which the story does not deal with) than in the "prepared" nature of the vision, the inevitable sense that such a specter has not merely—coincidentally —materialized but is, even if enigmatically, in connivance with the governess's own thoughts.

At this point, it might be instructive to consider James's interest in the ghost story as a genre. In the New York Preface, James mentions his affection for the "good, the really effective and heart-shaking ghost-stories" and his distaste for "the new type . . . , the mere modern 'psychical' case, washed clean of all queerness as by exposure to a flowing laboratory tap."[16] However, it does not follow that "subjective complications" would reduce the tale to a "mere psychical case," and we shall see that an unleashed imagination can be quite compatible with the old terrors that James sought to evoke. The question is whether the terror resides in the ghosts

[16] Henry James, *The Art of the Novel* (New York: Scribner's, 1934), p. 169.

or the fate of the children. Assuming that James himself, like the modern reader, did not believe in ghosts, it follows, as he stated in the Preface to *The Altar of the Dead and Other Tales*, that the author is above all interested in the response to such apparitions, the horror and fear whose reality hardly depend on that of the ghosts. For a writer interested in the scrutiny of opaque situations, the ghost story must possess a very special appeal. It is the extreme promontory in the realm of vision, the point at which what we see becomes a mirror, a reflection of our own mind. James frequently deals with this notion in less radical forms, and we have already noted the tendency toward autonomous vision, the absence of (or disdain for) evidence, in *The Ambassadors*, the wholly conjectural nature of *The Sacred Fount*. Like "The Beast in the Jungle," however, *The Turn of the Screw* presents its evidence as well, gives us the means to gauge the governess's vision.

To be sure, we are treated neither to an authoritative view of the ghosts (!), nor to an unbiased view of the children. But, as the governess relates her experience, we can witness the diminishing authority of the visible and the increasing sway, not to say tyranny, of the speculative, the unseen. Mrs. Grose's first admonition to the governess: "See him, Miss, first. *Then* believe it!" is quite adequate to dispel the governess's original fears about Miles's character. Confidence in the visible deteriorates, however. As the ghosts extend their reign, the visible world is drained of its integrity, tends to become, in the eyes of the governess, a foil, a façade for invisible but evil proceedings. In the encounters with the ghosts we do not expect, from James, much description; but it is more than odd that the governess, as at the first meeting with Jessell, doesn't even look. There are frequent remarks such as "I began to take in with certitude and yet without direct vision the presence, a good way off, of a third person" (p. 29), or "there was no ambiguity in anything; none whatever at least in the convic-

tion I from one moment to another found myself forming as
to what I should see straight before me and across the lake as
a consequence of raising my eyes" (p. 29). Ordinarily, characters in literature are entitled to intuition, and we know the
importance of dreams, omens, and forebodings as paths to
truth (although we sharply distinguish between life and literature in this area). But James insists on the intuitive nature of
her certainty (James could easily have had her *see* without
being obliged to describe to the reader the object of her
vision), and he does so in a story where, as a result of that certainty, one child will die and another will be scarred. The accumulation of inner certainties in *The Turn of the Screw* is
staggering: "on the spot there came to me the added shock of
a certitude that it was not for me he had come" (p. 20); "there
were shrubberies and big trees, but I remember the clear assurance that none of them concealed him. He was there or
was not there: not there if I didn't see him" (p. 21); "I had
an absolute certainty that I should see again what I had already seen, but something within me said that by offering myself bravely as the sole object of such experience, by accept-
ing, by inviting, by surmounting it all, I should serve as an
expiatory victim and guard the tranquillity of the rest of the
household" (p. 26). These inner directives, eschewing any
need for proof, make the silences eloquent, rife with evil:

"I don't change—I simply make it out. The four, depend on it,
perpetually meet. If on either of these last nights you had been
with either child you'd clearly have understood. The more I've
watched and waited the more I've felt that if there were nothing
else to make it sure it would be made so by the systematic silence
of each. *Never*, by a slip of the tongue, have they so much as
alluded to either of their old friends, any more than Miles has
alluded to his expulsion. Oh yes, we may sit here and look at
them, and they may show off to us there to their full; but even
while they pretend to be lost in their fairy-tale they're steeped
in their vision of the dead restored to them. He's not reading to

her," I declared; "they're talking of *them*—they're talking horrors! I go on, I know, as if I were crazy; and it's a wonder I'm not. What I've seen would have made *you* so; but it has only made me more lucid, made me get hold of still other things." [p. 48]

As the unseen takes over the field, we have more and more of the characteristic Jamesian language of scrutiny: "I do mean, on the other hand, that the element of the unnamed and un-touched became, between us, greater than any other" (p. 50). Even within the shadowy décor of *The Sacred Fount*, the sur-mising narrator feels the need to protect the objects of his interrogation; in *The Turn of the Screw* the desire to shield is the strange concomitant of the ghostly vision:

"No, no—there are depths, depths! The more I go over it the more I see in it, and the more I see in it the more I fear. I don't know what I *don't* see, what I *don't* fear!"

Mrs. Grose tried to keep up with me. "You mean you're afraid of seeing her again?"

"Oh no; that's nothing—now." Then I explained. "It's of *not* seeing her." [p. 31]

The premise behind the shield surely seems heroic and sacri-ficial: "I was a screen—I was to stand before them. The more I saw the less they would" (p. 28). At the climax of the story, the same idea is restated: "It came to me in the very horror of the immediate presence that the act would be, seeing and fac-ing what I saw and faced, to keep the boy himself unaware" (p. 85). This impulse is fine, quite Jamesian, but there are two drawbacks. First, the governess's desire to see all the evil leaves one a bit uneasy, and it sounds at times like an invitation for the ghosts to appear. Secondly, and tragically, the governess can protect the children from the ghosts only by pressing upon them at all times her own presence. Screen she may be, but the screen itself is overwhelmingly visible. Once we see the full configuration of the screen she provides, and not merely her intention, a number of things become perceptible.

First, like the narrator of *The Aspern Papers*, she has a propensity to pry, to ferret out information, to force her way into the intimacy of others. She herself acknowledges as much: "Why did they never resent my inexorable, my perpetual society? Something or other had brought nearer home to me that I had all but pinned the boy to my shawl, and that in the way our companions were marshalled before me I might have appeared to provide against some danger of rebellion. I was like a gaoler with an eye to possible surprises and escapes" (p. 54). Each conversation with Mrs. Grose or the children verges on extortion. Imagine, for example, an innocent Flora and her possible thoughts under the weight of the following onslaught: "At the moment, in the state of my nerves, I absolutely believed she lied; and if I once more closed my eyes it was before the dazzle of the three or four possible ways in which I might take this up. One of these for a moment tempted me with such singular force that, to resist it, I must have gripped my little girl with a spasm that, wonderfully, she submitted to without a cry or a sign of fright" (p. 42).

The treatment of Miles is, of course, the most stamped by the smothering protectiveness of the governess. There is little in James more equivocal than the relationship between Miles and the woman who is shielding him from evil. It requires a curious kind of blindness to see the following passage as unambiguous: "I remember in fact that as we pushed into his little chamber, where the bed had not been slept in at all and the window, uncovered to the moonlight, made the place so clear that there was no need of striking a match—I remember how I suddenly dropped, sank upon the edge of the bed from the force of the idea that he must know how he really, as they say, 'had' me" (p. 46).

There are no simple labels for the governess's feelings (just as, in a lesser key, Vautrin's affection for Rastignac cannot be labeled), but the boy recognizes that he is in danger. The scene where he begs, ever so gently, to be let alone should warn us that he is being molested by her voracious need to penetrate him: "It made me, the sound of the words, in which it seemed to me I caught for the very first time a small quaver of consenting consciousness—it made me drop on my knees beside the bed and seize once more the chance of possessing him" (p. 65). Although it hardly makes matters more innocent to describe Miles "as accessible as an older person" (p. 63), or to regard their dinner together in terms of "some young couple who, on their wedding-journey, at the inn, feel shy in the presence of the waiter" (p. 81), my interest is not in transforming Miles into a replacement for his uncle, or any other suitable candidate for the governess; the relationship need not be fitted with a name as long as we see that the governess's hunger for the truth encroaches dreadfully on the privacy and the sex of the child. The last few pages should be quoted in their entirety, for the mixture of truth seeking, desire for possession, and ghost perceiving permeates the whole section. Miles becomes more and more feverish, as the vampirish needs of the governess approach satisfaction:

> It was like fighting with a demon for a human soul, and when I had fairly so appraised it I saw how the human soul—held out, in the tremor of my hands, at arms' length—had a perfect dew of sweat on a lovely childish forehead. The face that was close to mine was as white as the face against the glass, and out of it presently came a sound, not low, or weak, but as if from much further away, that I drank like a waft of fragrance.
> "Yes—I took it."
> At this, with a moan of joy, I enfolded, I drew him close; and while I held him to my breast, where I could feel in the sudden fever of his little body the tremendous pulse of his little heart, I kept my eyes on the thing at the window and saw it move and shift its posture. [p. 85]

Only the most obstinate respect for prefaces or the most arduous belief in the supernatural can prevent us from *seeing* that if there is a ghost, and if there is evil, it is not at the window pane but rather it is the governess herself. Embracing the child, virtually devouring and raping him, she is the sexual evil that she has tried to shield him from.

From the outset James has insisted on a disturbing confusion between the governess herself and the ghosts she sees. Consider, for a first example, the disquieting, hypnotic imitation rite that we are treated to at the second visitation:

> It was confusedly present to me that I ought to place myself where he had stood. I did so; I applied my face to the pane and looked, as he had looked, into the room. As if, at this moment, to show me exactly what his range had been, Mrs. Grose, as I had done for himself just before, came in from the hall. With this I had the full image of a repetition of what had already occurred. She saw me as I had seen my own visitant; she pulled up short as I had done; I gave her something of the shock that I had received. [p. 21]

The passage ends with the excellent, never-to-be-answered question: "I wondered why *she* should be scared." The gover ness describes her own evolution in terms that are ambivalent: "I was queer company enough—quite as queer as the company I received" (p. 25); mentioning Jessel's awful eyes, the gover ness remarks that Mrs. Grose "stared at mine as if they might really have resembled them" (p. 32). Even when James's par ticular style is taken into account, the governess disturbs when she says she "had to smother a kind of howl" (p. 27). More over, all her gestures are so heralded by her intentions that we are likely not to see what she is doing. Much of her time at Bly is spent wandering from room to room, rushing in on Miles or Flora, checking out the grounds: [17] "you may imagine

---

[17] My contention that we must *see* everything that is going on at Bly (and not just the thoughts of the governess) can be better grasped if we compare the effects of the book with that of the cinematic ver sion, "The Innocents." The differences in the two media produce strikingly different results and emphases. The film cannot leave open the question of whether the governess actually sees something; it may

the general complexion, from that moment, of my nights. I repeatedly sat up till I didn't know when; I selected moments when my room-mate unmistakably slept, and, stealing out, took noiseless turns in the passage" (p. 43). This is the stuff ghosts are made of.

If the governess assumed, as we saw, the exact position of Quint, she is served in like manner by Jessel, who sits at her own table and appears "to say that her right to sit at my table was as good as mine to sit at hers" (p. 59), and gives the governess "the extraordinary chill of a feeling that it was I who was the intruder" (p. 59).

The strongest evidence that the governess is herself the evil principle from which she is trying to protect the children is presented in the two final scenes with each of the children. There is no longer any question of ambiguity or interpretation; each child, according to the governess herself, regards her not only as intrusive but downright evil and frightening. After joyously pointing out to Flora the presence of Jessel, the governess is shocked by the child's response: "To see her, without a convulsion of her small pink face, not even feign to glance in the direction of the prodigy I announced, but only, instead of that, turn at *me* an expression of hard still gravity, an expression absolutely new and unprecedented and that appeared to read and accuse and judge me—this was a stroke that somehow converted the little girl herself into a figure portentous" (p. 71). The damage done to Flora is paltry in com-

---

try to beg the question by showing muddled, hazy forms, but it must either show something or nothing when the governess confronts the ghosts; in words, however, James can wisely leave the matter entirely open. On the other hand, it requires no sleuthing on our part to *see* that the governess herself is acting strangely, and strangely like a ghost (we are treated to the whole assortment of flowing white robes, creaking stairs, doors and windows blown open by the wind). In short, the film drastically reduces the vital areas of uncertainty in the novel because it is compelled to render visible, whereas the book makes us do the visualizing.

parison to what is reserved for her brother. Steadily and brutally forcing her way into his intimacy, wringing forth his
pitiful secrets, the governess is frantic that the boy should con-
fess his intercourse with the evil ones. The child, pressed hard
and "knowing" only "what we had done to Flora," gropes
for answers, but can come up with nothing better than "Miss
Jessel, Miss Jessel!" It is not enough for his teacher, so she
shows him that "it was better still than that," and tells him to
look in the window at the coward horror:

At this, after a second in which his head made the movement
of a baffled dog's on a scent and then gave a frantic little shake
for air and light, he was at me in a white rage, bewildered, glaring vainly over the place and missing wholly, though it now, to
my sense, filled the room like the taste of poison, the wide, overwhelming presence. "It's *he*?"
  I was so determined to have all my proof that I flashed into
ice to challenge him. "Whom do you mean by 'he'?"
  "Peter Quint—you devil!" His face gave again, round the room,
its convulsed supplication. "*Where?*"
  They are in my ears still, his supreme surrender of the name
and his tribute to my devotion. "What does he matter now, my
own?—what will he *ever* matter? *I* have you," I launched at the
beast, "but he has lost you for ever!" Then for the demonstration
of my work, "There, *there!*" I said to Miles. [p. 88]

There is only "the quiet day" to be seen, no Peter Quint but
only the devil who, as a tribute to her devotion, has caused
the child's heart to stop beating. We will never know whether
the ghosts were real, but we do know that the child is dead.
Freudian or "straight," the governess has destroyed Miles.[18] It
matters little which way we "read" her, if only we see the
enormity of what she has done.

[18] Asylums are full—and, it would seem, properly so—of people
who see ghosts. Regardless of their intentions, of the exquisite morality which may inform their vision(s), they are removed from society,
because they can do harm—real, measurable, visible—to others.

With all literature, the older, obviously rhetorical, and the newer, seemingly uncontrolled, the final authority must come from the reader-critic, not solely from the work. Wayne Booth has lamented the open-ended post-Jamesian fiction because it leaves ambiguous areas of moral judgment for which clarity is essential. Interpretation of such literature is often fanciful, extravagant, disturbingly closer to the critic than to the work. But literature cannot be purged of its ambiguities and choices; no critical principles can wholly control or eradicate the open-endedness of every human statement. Let us keep our house in order, but let us not convert it into a house of cards. Literature and (even!) literary criticism are not sciences, and the purity of an approach must be subordinated to the quality of what it yields; the method must be evaluated in light of its results. Does a "straight" (or rather, pious) reading of *The Turn of the Screw* really mean a return to order, a respect for the integrity of the literary statement? Should we believe only the interpretation of the governess herself, we are in the drastic position of somehow leaving unchallenged her implied assertion: "I had to destroy the children to save them." Critical irresponsibility may consist of gullibility and blindness as well as overinterpretation. The "straight" reading is a half reading, and it is off center; it must overlook, to use James's own terms, the scenic dimension, the total configuration of the events at Bly. Within this larger picture fall the elements which would make us modify, or even reverse, our opinion of the governess's behavior: (1) what we *see* of her interaction with others and (2) what we must perceive as the diseased nature of her own enterprise and her own vision. There are no laws—in life or in art—for such corrective vision, but our reading must be principled. The final interpretation of a work cannot be based on morally neutral, entirely aesthetic criteria. If we must operate with a bias, let it be a broadly human one rather than a limited parochial one. It is within the framework of human meanings that we must pronounce the governess's vision diseased, for it despotically—even if unwittingly—causes pain and death to two children. We never see the children guilty (we have only their protectress's word for it), but we do see them hounded and hurt. There is a point where ambiguity ceases because we are compelled to choose. Can we leave in question whether the following passage is either shrewd analysis or deranged fancy:

I couldn't abjure [my judgment] for merely wanting to, but I could repeat to Mrs. Grose—as I did there, over and over, in the small hours—that with our small friends' voices in the air, their pressure on one's heart and their fragrant faces against one's cheek, everything fell to the ground but their incapacity and their beauty. It was a pity that, somehow, to settle this once for all, I had equally to re-enumerate the signs of subtlety that, in the afternoon, by the lake, had made a miracle of my show of self-possession. It was a pity to be obliged to re-investigate the certitude of the moment itself and repeat how it had come to me as a revelation that the inconceivable communion I then surprised must have been for both parties a matter of habit. It was a pity I should have had to quaver out again the reasons for my not having, in my delusions, so much as questioned that the little girl saw our visitant even as I actually saw Mrs. Grose herself, that she wanted, by just so much as she did thus see, to make me suppose she didn't, and at the same time, without showing anything, arrive at a guess as to whether I myself did! It was a pity I needed to recapitulate the portentous little activities by which she sought to divert my attention—the perceptible increase of movement, the greater intensity of play, the singing, the gabbling of nonsense and the invitation to romp. [pp. 34–35]

The *Schadenfreude*, the malicious pleasure felt by the governess in pointing out to Mrs. Grose the deviousness of the children, is strange in itself. But does the accusation hold? What are the "signs of subtlety"? What provoked the "certitude," the "revelation" of the governess? What proof of such subtle hypocrisy in the children? The recurring ironical phrase "it was a pity," might well remind us of Othello's "the pity of it, Iago." Shakespeare knew that madness is a question of diseased vision and that innocent children can be destroyed by it. How can we agree that the perceptible increase of movement, the greater intensity of play, the singing, the gabbling of nonsense, and the invitation to romp are a façade? We need not consider the children as Edenic to regard such activities as innocent until proven guilty. It is strange how "appearances" are always suspect in literature. We are accustomed to viewing the visible as a series of masks, of *trompe-l'oeil*, waiting to be exposed and removed so that the true may then be seen. Life provides us with no such comfortable masquerades, and the world we live in may be either all reality or all appearance, but it is surely not a "remove-the-veil" combination. Hence, in life we respect appearances, for they are all we know. The mind's ability to make short shrift of appearances, to deal in meanings rather than surfaces, to imagine a world quite different from, possibly the opposite of, what we see, is a transcendent gift, but it can cause great harm as well as give great delight. We have seen in *Great Expectations* (and we shall see again in *Absalom, Absalom!*) that education consists in transcending the realm of evidence and asserting the primacy of the inner vision. This study is written in the belief that insight and depth alone redeem the inhuman world we inhabit. But *The Turn of the Screw* must stand as a sobering reminder of the destructive and maniacal potential inherent in such a commitment to the unseen.

James's fiction—despite its verbosity—can be so myopic as to border on the autistic. Dialogue is usually a creative chain of hypotheses, each finer and more autonomous than the last. It is indeed a tribute to the authority of the imagination. Yet the "huge spider-web of the finest silken threads suspended in the chamber of consciousness"[19] may claim victims along the

[19] "The Art of Fiction," in *Selected Literary Criticism: Henry James*, ed. Morris Shapiro (New York: McGraw-Hill, 1965), p. 56.

way. Finally, the exquisite conjectural reality that gradually replaces the visible scene may be subtly and insidiously poisoned by the character of the conjecturor. James may have disclaimed "subjective complications" for his governess, but he quite understood the creative power of the imagination; in the New York Preface to *The Turn of the Screw* he clearly described, in terms of reader response, the behavior of his governess: "Only make the reader's general vision of evil intense enough, I said to myself—and that already is a charming job—and his own experience, his own imagination, his own sympathy (with the children) and horror (of their false friends) will supply him quite sufficiently with all the particulars. Make him think the evil, make him think it for himself, and you are released from weak specifications."[20] As a narrative strategy, the statement is seductive. As psychology, however, the notion goes to the very core of *The Turn of the Screw*. In using her own imagination and her own vision, in dispensing with particulars, the governess not only thinks the evil for herself, "better still," the evil becomes precisely her effort to ward off the horror from her charges. If we are to read humanly as well as critically, we must see in her very undertaking those elements of possession and violation that culminate in Miles's death. It may never be known what she saw at Bly, but the real evil that occurred is tangible, visible, and on record.

Balzac clarified his mysteries by banishing his opaque characters and transforming the others into emptied vessels and shiny façades. In Dickens, and still more distinctly in Conrad and Ford, the emphasis tends to be on insight rather than sight, apprehension of moral patterns through the clutter and debris of conventions, appearances, and impressions. James's interest in the unstateable and the unseen is double-edged: on the one hand he considers only the drama of consciousness to be aesthetically effective, and, conversely, he fully recognizes the

[20] James, *Art of the Novel*, p. 176.

biases and dangers that may beset an unswerving commitment to imagination at the expense of visible surfaces. We are accustomed to gracing the inner vision, to hallowing (especially in literature) the felt and intuitive as opposed to the evident. *The Turn of the Screw* is a disturbing test case for such an ethic-aesthetic because it puts the reader on the line and makes his response to fiction a moral one, his adherence to the narrator's authority an abdication of his own. The upshot is something that takes the reader off balance because, whereas the impetus of the work obliges him to focus on the beyond, the real activity may well be going on, unnoticed and uncommented, before his very eyes.

James's experiments with point of view were fecund, and much twentieth-century fiction has never left the subjective labyrinths to which he pointed the way. The following chapters deal with the experiments of post-Jamesian fiction to both honor the private vision and transcend its ambiguities and limitations.

3 | Vision as Feeling: Bernanos and Faulkner

James and Conrad and Ford create what loosely may be called a literature of impressionism. Each writer is interested in the cleft between the private and public dimensions of experience, and blindness—toward others and toward oneself—is one of their major themes. The impressionism of these writers is primarily cerebral, for it presents the personal vision as a structured, even if arbitrary, configuration. We must detect the bias of Dowell's vision, of the governess's story, of Jim's fate, but their experience has form, is a recognizable story. What it all means is quite open to question, but the contours—even when partial as in *Lord Jim*—are perceptible.

In this chapter we will study another kind of impressionism which, unlike the conjectural realism of Conrad, Ford, and James, tends to be visceral and affective in its nature. It renders the impressions of the senses rather than the hypotheses of the mind, and the burdens placed on the reader are of quite a different order. In the two writers discussed, Georges Bernanos and William Faulkner, comprehension at the very basic level has become problematic. To make sense of the narratives of Marlow, Dowell, and the governess is a challenge to our moral judgment, but the texture and configuration of *Monsieur Ouine*, *The Sound and the Fury*, and *Absalom, Absalom!* seem, at first reading, so chaotic and obscure as to be not merely enigmatic, but illegible. The premise behind each novel is that authentic perception, the real drama of consciousness, is a matter of impulses, sensations, fragments of thought and feeling; it is a sensuous, emotive continuum that resists the artificial clarity and cohesiveness of any "story." Of course, these novels are more than random sensory impressions; each has its pattern of selectivity and its cogency. Although Bernanos' novel is relatively unknown, the American novels are such "classics" now, that it may seem naive to speak of their complexity; yet, to any reader opening them for the first time, each book presents the unlabeled, seemingly amorphous flow of consciousness. The emphasis on the nonintellective dimension of experience is double-edged: it creates a narrative strategy of ellipsis, shock, and mystery for the reader, but also prefigures an eventual resolution or "understanding" on an affective level. The appeal to the senses and emotions is an attempt to transcend the subjective prison so well delineated by James, Ford, and Conrad. We shall see how *Monsieur Ouine* and *The Sound and the Fury* adumbrate a vision of spirituality and community, as opposed to the oppressive limitations of individual consciousness. Finally, *Absalom, Absalom!*, with its full array of conjecture, false leads, and subjective complications, will be studied as the most complete embodiment of vision as feeling.

To the general student of literature, the name of Georges Bernanos may be unfamiliar. Even among the specialists of French fiction he is well tucked away in the category of Catholic novelist. Moreover, in those narrower precincts, he is known essentially as the author of *Diary of a Country Priest*. It may, therefore, seem odd to propose *Monsieur Ouine* for comparison with Faulkner. For a number of reasons, however, *Monsieur Ouine* is the only novel of Bernanos that could fit within the framework of a study of vision. It is an immensely, exasperatingly obscure work, seeming at times to be a *Bildungsroman*, at others a mystery story, at others a religious drama. At all times, however, it is chaotic. Among the perplexing factors it presents are (1) a murder that is neither witnessed by the reader nor resolved within the story; (2) a series of mysteries and ambiguities that range from uncertain sexual relations between characters to bewildering use of double and triple names per character, equivocal personal pronouns, and unidentified direct speech; and (3) discontinuity and ellipsis in specific dialogues and entire chapters. In view of such an obstacle course, it might seem fitting to offer at least a plot summary of the novel. However, aside from the real difficulty of putting together such a summary, if this chapter is to illustrate affective power, the novel should be confronted without foreknowledge. Here are the first words:

> She has grasped his small face in her hands—her long hands, her long soft hands—and looks into Steeny's eyes with calm insolence. How pale her eyes are! They seem gradually to withdraw, disappear. . . Here they are, still paler, bluish gray, hardly alive, with a dancing gleam. "No! no!" Steeny cries. "No!" And he jerks back, teeth clenched, his sweet face wrenched with anguish, as if he was going to throw up. My God![1]

This is *in medias res* with a vengeance; the confrontation is hypnotic and compelling, and the reader, assaulted with the "unlabeled" emotive intensity of the relationship, is disoriented. Such undefined violence establishes the tone of the novel. Unexplained, the threat is somehow more compelling; it colors and permeates subsequent events precisely because it is uncontained by specific reference. As we continue with the opening pages, three proper names—Steeny, Miss, and Maman—are bandied about, and we vaguely understand that Steeny's mother is cautioning him about the heat: " 'I thought I heard you yell,' said the tired voice. 'If you go out, be careful

---

[1] Georges Bernanos, *Oeuvres romanesques* (Paris: Bibliothèque de la Pléiade, 1961), p. 1349. Subsequent quotations are from this edition. All translations are my own.

of the heat, dear. It's so hot!' " (p. 1349). Bernanos then treats us to another visceral picture:

It is indeed hot! The air vibrates between the wooden shutters. His face against the blinds, Steeny breathes it in, swallows it, feels it go to the pit of his lungs, to the magic place where reverberate all the terrors and joys of the world. More, still more! It reeks of white lead and putty, a stronger smell than alcohol, one that seems a weird mixture of the moist breath of the big linden trees on the walk. Suddenly sleep has overcome him treacherously, with a blow on the neck, like an assassin, before he's even closed his eyes. The narrow window tilts slowly, sways, then lengthens out of all proportion, as if drawn by suction from above. The whole room follows, the four walls fill up with the breeze, flap suddenly like sails. [p. 1349]

The passage is dizzying, for we must endorse the sensations of a collapsing character. The cinematic technique reminds us of the stability we take for granted in narrative focus. There is something disquieting about the mobility, autonomy—one might say, the demonic nature—of things and people in *Monsieur Ouine*. Notice the violence of the action: "With a blow on the neck, like an assassin"; any murder in this novel, even if only metaphoric, is worthy of interest. There are numerous scenes of violence, fatigue, or drunkenness where Bernanos can "legitimately" render the responses of stunned, off-balance perception: "Hitting the table with his fist, he is amazed to find the bare wood. Before him burns a candle in a modest copper candlestick. At some distance Monsieur Ouine's body, greatly magnified, extends in all directions, with superhuman agility" (p. 1373). This is the "result" of too much wine. Shock and fatigue produce the following:

The road began to move softly, softly under him, like a gilded animal. He sees it between his knees, wild, fleeing, furtive, and as soon as he tries to lift his head, to keep his eyes open, it swells and jumps from one horizon to the next, up to the heavens. So he closes his eyes. But now he feels it under his knees, under his palms—damned road—feels it lift slowly, surely, like soft flanks. A moment earlier fear had thrown him on all fours, and, my God, all he can manage is to keep his balance, to balance that empty head on his shoulders. . . . On his knees? Come on! Up! Up! He tries to lift one hand from the ground, then the other, violently contracts his loins, throws himself backwards. No use! Now it's the whole scene that is sucked in the current, goes under. And the plain, sporadically present then, green and gray now, swells up under the immense blue dome, puffs faster and faster like a toad's throat.

"Philippe! Up! Up. Philippe!" [p. 1414]

At this point the careful reader may well wonder whether this is merely a heightened form of sensory realism, or, indeed, if something else is going on in these passages. The violence of the sun's rays, the gigantic shadow of Monsieur Ouine, the moving road in the sky bristle with meanings that the character's physical state prepares but does not exhaust. Important themes are being sounded in this mode, and Bernanos is attempting, by grounding it in a realistic framework, to extend the limits of perception. Finally, in the last piece, the particular pulsating movement of the road, compared to soft flanks, and increasing in tempo and sway over the boy, has very strong sexual connotations that are strengthened by the woman's voice ("Philippe! Up! Up. Philippe!") and the specific mention of a "first outrage to desire" in the following paragraph. This encounter between Steeny (Philippe) and Jambe-de-Laine (one of the four names she goes by) will never be clarified, nor will its exact measure of sexuality be established —not because Bernanos is either squeamish or teasing us, but because neither of the participating characters perceived it in an unambiguous, defined manner. Thus, the mobility of the narrative focus is emphasized: it disorients us physically, but it also undermines our epistemological footing, forces us to consider whether other, "normative" human exchanges fit into the grids of classical psychology or descriptive behavior that we apply.

Other character relationships are presented in the same baffling, ill-defined, experiential mode. Shortly after Bernanos has shed some light on the Miss-Maman-Steeny entanglement, the next "chapter" opens with direct speech:

"Well, Steeny, all alone?"

It's the *châtelaine* of Wambescourt, Madame de Néréis, who tries to smile but succeeds only in grimacing, as her pitiful deranged head wanders in all directions, seeking some invisible support.

"Mother is here," Steeny answers insolently. "She's taking a nap, I think; Won't you . . ."

"Oh no, no, stay, my dear! Don't go . . ."

She wraps herself in the folds of her long black coat, drops her purse, catches it in the air, glances furtively and fearfully at the closed blinds.

"Don't go! Let Michelle sleep. Sleep is so good, Steeny. . . . My God!"

She stretches in the sun with a strange tremor. The light probes her miserable, tortured face; her painted lips shine weirdly. [p. 1356]

One would be tempted to dismiss this as melodrama, but more lurid than the behavior of the characters is the enigmatic relationship they embody, the odd compulsions they seem to obey. Queerly, with little explanation or warning, she insists that the boy follow her. The scene almost resembles a ballet of marionettes, but the outcome seems charged with meaning: "She stops again, looks right and left with her tracked animal's eyes, continues her strange dance. Steeny loses his breath following her. He could, of course, put an end to it by slipping quietly through the bushes, but he prefers to think that fate has willed that he spend the whole day with this absurd creature" (p. 1357).

The two bizarre exchanges that have been cited—Steeny and

Miss, Steeny and Jambe-de-Laine—are thrust upon the reader in all their incomprehensible urgency and immediacy. In each case, Bernanos follows up with background information, a network of events from the past in which the purely affective material can be situated and interpreted. The first instance is the evocation of Steeny's family: Michelle's absorbing, poisonous "sweetness," her fear and contempt for men, the obscure disappearance of Steeny's father, the disturbing signs that the boy embodies the same despotic, virile energy so abhorrent in the father. Likewise, Jambe-de-Laine's dramatic entry is followed by a brief account of her pariah status in Fenouille, her scandalous marriage with Anthelme (now dying), the presence of the retired professor, Monsieur Ouine, at their château. It terminates in pure Gothic melodrama: "Alas! It's been two years since Michelle has set foot at the Néréis château. Monsieur Anthelme is ill, perhaps mad; Monsieur Ouine invisible; Ginette sweeps across the country roads behind her huge mare, as if she were chased by ghosts" (p. 1359).

Steeny's visit to the Néréis château consists largely of his dialogue with Monsieur Ouine. It is a strange conversation, composed of the boy's insolence, his yearning for an authority figure, and the professor's appalling combination of lucidity, hunger, and passivity; it is punctuated by Steeny's blackouts, occasioned by wine and nervous tension. After Bernanos has depicted, in the experiential style, the boy falling asleep, then waking up alone and dropping off again with an urgent sense of promise, the following "chapter" is ushered in by still another strange relationship:

"I gave my word of honor,"[2] repeats Steeny again.
The same heavy rain, without any breeze, was falling on the smoking earth. Very far to the east, as if at the edge of another

---

[2] The French is significantly ambiguous: "Je lui ai donné ma parole d'honneur." "Lui" can obviously mean either him or her, and the reader has no way of knowing.

world, stormy dawn slowly formed its mists through the fine rain.

"O.K., O.K." said the little cripple Guillaume. "I understood, but don't talk so loud, Philippe. He came back this morning covered with mud, his ear almost pulled off, his gun lost. The police chased him from Dugy to Théroigne. Ah! If you'd seen him swallow the whole mug of beer in one gulp. What thirst. Occasionally, still breathing hard, he'd stop drinking, and I could hear him biting the clay, moaning. . . . My God, my God, Philippe, will I ever be able to love him?"

"You'd do as well to kill him," said Steeny gravely. And then, he burst out laughing and took the hand of his friend.

"Don't laugh!" begged the cripple. "You really frighten me, Philippe. I'm not afraid of anybody, not even of that horrible bastard[3]; but sometimes . . . you seem to be pulling on me with all your strength; I'm going to fall; I'm all hollow."

"All right then. Let go of me, friend. I can fall all by myself."

"Never," said the child in a muffled voice. "Never!"

From whom, which ancestor, which fierce master did he inherit that small savage face, with its mongolian cheeks, the deep hollow of the eyes under the double frontal arc, the imperious, almost wild mouth, the black brows? [pp. 1375–1376]

Everything in the above extract is jolting. Instead of picking up the elements of the conversation with Monsieur Ouine, this exchange mentions a promise that we haven't witnessed, introduces Guillaume and his own odd relationship to Steeny, and gives an elliptic account of some individual's mysterious arrival in the early morning. *Later* we will realize that the "horrible bastard" is Eugène and that his strange return home is a key element in the murder, a murder that we significantly know nothing of at the moment. (One usually doesn't, with the real thing.) Once again the dialogue closes with a much-needed evocation of Guillaume's background. We thus learn

[3] In French "bâtard" is a neutral descriptive term for an illegitimate child, but the English counterpart is unfortunately either charged with feeling (connotatively) or almost archaic (denotatively).

about his grandfather and still another turbulent family drama: the old man derives his pride and fortitude from a "might-have-been" version of the nobility of his ancestors; this exaggerated sense of dignity heightens his disgust at the marriage of his daughter Hélène with the irresponsible, seductive woodsman, Eugène.

The lengthy passages that have been quoted should give a fairly clear indication of Bernanos' technique: sensuous or affective immersion followed by clarifying information. The encounters are frequently frantic and brutal; conduct seems urgent. The reasons appear only later in the narrative, and as the past begins to surface, we can begin to see patterns in the explosive behavior of the characters. There is, first of all, a need for some principle of honor or stature according to which one might live. The grandfather's nostalgia for the myth of his ancestry (and the concomitant rejection of his children's disorder), the dying Anthelme's confession to Philippe that his father is still alive, and the boy's hunger to make of Monsieur Ouine a mentor—these needs are richly and suggestively interwoven by the narrative technique itself. The reader's confusion is desired, for the separate stories are interrelated. The second pattern is related to the first, but still more obsessive and more unifying: the injuries suffered by children.[4] It is a hallmark of Bernanos' work, and all the enigmatic behavior of *Monsieur Ouine* can, in some sense, be traced to it. Miss's treatment of Steeny is less gratuitous after we learn about her miserable childhood; Maman's sugary form of suffocation in dealing with her son is a result of early experiences; the priest describes his own lonely youth; and Monsieur Ouine's need to appropriate others can be somewhat understood as the result of his pitiable childhood and the homosex-

---

[4] The theme of injured children is, of course, central in the two novels about Mouchette, but it is also sounded in Bernanos' concept of the priest-characters themselves.

ual perversion of his instinct for love. Whereas the adults exhibit in retrospect the scars of childhood, it is to Steeny, the boy on the verge of manhood, that we must look for full embodiment of this theme. If Steeny seems to be all open-ended passion, it is because he has all the promise and vulnerability of childhood. Much of the reader's jolting discomfort comes from sharing the violent, uncontrolled, affective response that he brings to experience. In Steeny there is both hunger for life and desire for order; Bernanos' repeated, lyrical use of the *Route* motif—the path that leads away from frustration and injury toward promise and fulfillment—well expresses both those dimensions of the childlike appetite. Philippe explains to Guillaume that "our life must not be an objective, but a catch. And not only one, but thousands upon thousands of catches, as many as there are hours. What counts is getting them all, right up to the last one, the last of all, the one that always gets away—bam! Something moves, and you pounce on it" (p. 1386). Bernanos has a strange compassion for this kind of hunger, even though it may lead his characters into destruction. Ouine himself is moved and fascinated by the fragility of youth: "a young human life, all ignorance and daring, the truly perishable part of the universe. . . . When everything changes, decays, returns to the original clay, youth alone dies, knows death" (p. 1369). The work of Bernanos is haunted by this mixture of innocence, vulnerability, and passion. In the Preface to *Les Grands Cimetières sous la lune* we are told that the novels are, above all, an attempt to recapture the childhood consciousness:

Of course, my life is filled with the dead. But the deadest of the dead is the little boy that I was. However, when the hour comes, it is he who will take his place at the head of my life, gather together my poor years right up to the last, and, like a young officer putting his veteran troops into order, he will be the first to enter the Father's House. After all, I should have the right to speak in his name; but that is the point: one cannot speak for childhood, for we would have to speak its language. And it is that forgotten language, that language which I foolishly seek in book after book, as if such a language could be written, had ever been written.[5]

The narrative strategy of *Monsieur Ouine*, with its emphasis on the affective, is meant to express the childlike vision and its dangers—those which beset it and those of which it is capable. Such urgency has little to do with traditional morality, and the child may, in his hunger, brush aside any sense of purpose or order and plunge into pure sensuous experience. In that light, Eugène, graceful and cunning, is a purely animal version of the more complex drives that control Philippe. Bernanos' argument—presented late in the book and to which I shall return—is that religion created an image of man that acknowledged and even directed these extreme passions and compulsions so visible in the child, repressed and thwarted in most adults. *Monsieur Ouine* assaults the reader with the immediacy of such feelings. This accounts for the undefined character relationships. The fierce interactions between Steeny and Miss, Steeny and Jambe-de-Laine, Steeny and Monsieur Ouine, are depicted point-blank, at such close range that our vision is blurred. One senses a world of emotional absolutes, a system of spiritual and visceral forces that is operative behind the façade of conventional character roles. The world view is cogent and imperious, but it wrestles fitfully with traditional labels. The upshot is often bewildering, consisting of enigmatic, puppetlike, spasmodic behavior patterns.

After a number of violent exchanges, we finally reach a chapter that is quite different. The first sentence reads: "They have carried the small corpse into the room in the town hall, on the table whose green cloth had been quickly removed"

[5] Georges Bernanos, *Les Grands Cimetières sous la lune* (Paris Livre de poche, 1962), pp. 8–9. My translation.

(p. 1392). Our book now becomes a detective story, and a rather strange one since the crime will never be "solved."

At this point the narrative strategy of withheld information, ambiguity, and enigma is seen to be doubly effective. The affective power of such a presentation has already been assessed; as the explanations order the experiential exchanges and the background material situates the actors, we may register a progressive movement toward clarity. On a quite literal level, we learn how to read the novel, to get the names and characters straight, to acquire an image of the whole parish at Fenouille; we should have some notions about the guilty party. And now we face the inevitable answer: it could have been anybody. Monsieur Ouine is the prime suspect, of course (after all, he gives the title to the book); there is explicit mention of his going out to meet the cowherd (the dead child), and his curiosity could well lead him to murder. But there is also considerable internal evidence against others. Eugène will be accused of it, and that is feasible, given his life style. Jambe-de-Laine has been shown in one near-murder attempt against Steeny, and the unpredictable nature of her behavior has been emphasized. The mayor himself is so obsessed with human filth and guilt that he is not wholly free of suspicion. Finally —and I shall spend a moment with this—Philippe has an alarming propensity to violence and to blackouts, an unfortunate combination in these circumstances. Bernanos renders these moments with immediacy. Consider, for example, the boy's fury at Jambe-de-Laine's great mare: "He sees only the beaten animal; he senses only the raw hurried breathing, a tempo of terror, the cracking of sweat-soaked leather; he gasps furiously an odor so hot and alive that it seems like blood. Everything in him that normally judges, reasons, accepts or rejects—withdraws. *God knows how many times in the last weeks he felt something in him stretched to the breaking point, something monstrous about to happen*" (p. 1391; my italics). The book opens with Miss's attack on Steeny, but we are treated to a number of aggressive scenes where the boy—blindly—takes the initiative:

> "Philippe! Steeny."
> He had just lunged forward, blindly, or rather he gets up, escapes, and already he feels the blond neck bend under his fingers. The supple softness of the hips attracts and repels him, like the glance, with its astonishing speed. [p. 1446]

As in the scenes of fatigue or shock, Bernanos obliges us to share in these attacks:

> "Enough said!" he says in a hoarse voice that he hardly recognizes, and immediately he feels the furious rush of the blood in his neck. His eyes weigh in the sockets like little lead marbles.
> "Do you think you scare me, *you sniveling, street urchin, sissy! You crazy loon, son of an idiot!*"[6]
> He thought it was the door knob he was shaking so violently, and he couldn't even get his stiff fingers together over it. The paralysis went up his arm to his shoulder, and for all the gold in the world, he couldn't move his neck. [p. 1450]

Bernanos is not trying to outdo Agatha Christie by cleverly intimating that the boy is the real murderer. But he is showing, in the fury, infirmity, or madness of the separate character relationships, the murder impulse. At the center of these chaotic entanglements that seem to have only their violence in common—the private, rotten world of Miss, Michelle, and Steeny; the isolation and discord between Eugène, Hélène, the old man and his family history; the bizarre, urgent nature of Guillaume's relation to Steeny; the obscure corruption in the Néréis château involving Anthelme, Jambe-de-Laine, and Monsieur Ouine; the tragicomic story of the mayor and his guilt; the central but undefined relations between Steeny and

[6] The italicized words are given in English in the French text. Bernanos seems to be underscoring the possibility of insanity, as well as violence, in Philippe's conditioning.

Jambe-de-Laine, Steeny and Monsieur Ouine—lies an action concealed by the novelist but fatally uniting the characters: the murder of the cowherd. This isolated act of violence, emblematic of the vulnerability of childhood, is not shown, but we experience in its place, as a furious, lyrical echo, the reign of chaos or the death of spirit in every character relationship.

The scenes in the church and the cemetery are the climax of the novel: epistemological clarity for the detective story and chaos (acknowledgment of mass guilt) for the spiritual tale that embodies it. In realizing that the murder of the cowherd is the very crystallization of the moral decay in Fenouille, the priest, in effect, solves the mystery: " 'I should bless this poor dead child? What good would that do? He was the innocent cause of your downfall; it is the sin of all of you; I will not bless your sin' " (p. 1490).

Because this act has been concealed and bears the seal of no one character, it serves as a fitting common denominator for the violence of the parish. In announcing to his congregation that they are all guilty of the murder, the priest clarifies and transcends the preceding ambiguities. He both symbolically solves the murder and grotesquely restores his dead parish to life, unifying into a collective holocaust the isolated eruptions of violence that we have hitherto witnessed. As the blacksmith later remarked:

"In fact, for days the village had been wallowing in its crime; every man for himself, each looking out for his own, everything would have gradually worked out. But it was the will of fate that all of us should go to that Mass, all at the same time, all together. It was like everybody's head getting fogged up. I tell you, when the priest spoke, there was no air to breathe, sir, word of honor. The air was hot and oily, like our bake-house when I kill my pig." [pp. 1483–1484]

Jambe-de-Laine's arrival at the cemetery serves as the necessary catalyst and precipitates the final mass murder (her own) which we and everybody else witness this time.

It has now become apparent that the gradual clarification of ambiguities and the outbreak of communal violence are bound together in causality. The solving of the small murder was the stimulus for the large one. The unseen act—recreated through style and content in the entire first half of the novel—is indeed the core of the book. As the layers of ambiguity and enigma are peeled away, the reader approaches the heart of the dilemma. In the church the priest removes the final veil, and the reality of the murder—if not the "ownership" of it—is at last assumed by the congregation. The realistic story of an isolated, unseen murder and the symbolic presentation of a town's spiritual death become one in the transition from individual crime to mass chaos, from church to cemetery.

Now the violence is over. The style of the rest of the novel is essentially lucid. The role of Arsène, the mayor, becomes particularly significant at this juncture. As the mayor, the elected representative of the parish, he is exemplary of its decay, a kind of moral barometer and living symbol of the breakdown at Fenouille. Equipped with a spectacular nose (which apparently did duty as a quasisexual organ in the mayor's youthful escapades), Arsène is consumed by guilt and choked by the filth of being human. He vainly tries to explain this condition to his wife, Malvina:

"You don't understand," he said with horrible sadness. "I scrub and scrub myself, naked under the pump, and it may look crazy. But so what. And to explain it? Try to explain light to a blind person. A pin prick would make you jump, but a bad smell is like Greek to you. Modern man has an atrophied sense of smell, that's certain; you can check with the doctor. You can't smell odors any more than you can see the dead; but if you did see the dead crawling around everywhere, you'd have to stop eating. Moreover, everything stinks, men, women, animals, earth, water, the air I breathe, everything—all of life stinks. Sometimes in the summer when the days never end, when they get mushy and stretched out, like dough, you'd think that time stinks too. You'll say that we can clean, rinse, scrub, what the devil! And there may be some cause in my case too, O.K. But the odor I'm talking about is not really a smell, it comes from further away, from something deeper, from our memory, our soul, who knows? Water doesn't get rid of it; we need something else." [pp. 1439–1440]

Perhaps nowhere is the cleft between the two levels—the physical and spiritual, the realistic story and the moral allegory—more poignant than in that passage. Notice the creative dimension of Arsène's anguish, the awesome richness of his perception, including the vision of the dead, the reek of time, the threatening malleability of appearances, the reality of spirit. The community staunchly resists him by casting him in the archetypal role of the scapegoat: insane. In attempting to explain this "madness," each character posits, in effect, his interpretation of all the disorder in the novel. The individual efforts to understand, to explain, constitute the last phase of the novel's progression.

Malvina's explanation is a simple one: " 'All men are going crazy,' she said with a deep sigh. 'Like they said, there must be something in the air, maybe a poison or something. You see, Doctor, in my day—I'm talking about my youth, of course—the old people didn't have half as many vices as they do now. As far as I'm concerned, that's the problem. The world is falling apart because of the old people' " (p. 1511).

The doctor is more rational. Earlier, he comforted Arsène by reminding him: " 'You're getting moral, my friend, as most old sinners do when they turn sixty. In short, something's wrong down there, in the pit of the stomach, right? Maybe a little lower, if you want, in the plexus, sure, the seat of the soul' " (p. 1400). The realistic man of science refuses to see in the entire situation anything more transcendent than physiological or psychic disturbances. Arsène is merely neurotic; his illness is a "bizarre tumor of the mind."

The priest recognizes in Arsène symptoms of a disease which must necessarily befall a society that has renounced God: " 'Yes, the hour is coming (maybe it has already come), when our need for purity, which we think we've locked up in our conscience and divested of its very name, that need is going to burst its sepulcher. And if no other outlet is available, it will find one in our flesh and our blood—yes—you will see it appear in unexpected forms, hideous, horrible forms, I tell you' " (p. 1509). The violence of the image, the breakthrough of chaos and monstrosity, in short, the world of spirit in physical forms, all this contrasts vividly with any form of realism, narrative or otherwise. The priest's view and the doctor's explanation illuminate a dialectic that is central to Bernanos' work. Only in *Monsieur Ouine,* however, does the contrast between the scientific, psychological mode and the spiritual vision of God affect the very form of the novel. Bernanos has sought means to suggest the awful power and impact of such transformations prophesied by the priest. Rather than recording veritable metamorphoses or vying with Hieronymous Bosch, Bernanos has attempted to convey the intensity of such a vision: he has depicted characters buffeted by forces, performing enigmatic acts, attracted to and repelled by one another as if in fits of seizure. Therefore, it can be said that the perspectives of the priest and the doctor imply two aesthetics as well as two world views. Bernanos has *presented* his story to implement the optic of the priest.

For the final interpretation we must now consider the only character other than the priest interested in the whole picture: Monsieur Ouine. If the priest and the professor are the only two concerned with the causes and forces that underlie behavior, their kinds of understanding are radically different. Ouine had, from the outset, explained to Steeny the frightening penetrability of others:

"I protected these people against themselves; so you decide whether I know them or not. Not a single cranny in these rooms that doesn't evoke an effort, a struggle, some pitiful lie stepped on by chance, like a bug. The task is over now, alas!—nothing left to kill. Their secrets are lying about everywhere. Oh, don't misunderstand: they don't care; they come and go, as before; they repeat continuously the same stories but they forget that the chest is emptied. At the last stage of vilification, a man loses his truth forever—they would step on theirs without recognizing it." [p. 1364]

Exemplary of the scrutinizing posture seen in Balzac, dramatized in James, Ouine observes and ferrets out secrets. As we saw in Balzac, that part of opacity and mystery that a person harbors may well be his integrity; the analytic study of people can be a deadly, emptying process. Such scrutiny is particularly inimical and parasitic when disinterested. Jambe-de-Laine warns Steeny of the vampirish nature of the professor: " 'I'll tell you, my dear: just as some people radiate warmth, our friend absorbs all rays, all heat. Monsieur Ouine's essence, you see, is the cold!' " (p. 1423). In a novel filled with bewildering emotive exchanges, the professor's account of his activities is given with the clarity of a rhetorical exposition. The conclusion is lucid, even pedagogical:

"Their Creator has not known them better than I have; no possession of love is comparable to that infallible control, which does not disturb the patient, leaves him intact but wholly at our mercy, prisoner but retaining his most delicate nuances, all the iridescences and transparencies of life. Such were those souls. That is what I did to Néréis, the poor fool. That is what I did to Jambe-de-Laine, in that old house which will preserve my memory, whose every stone is redolent of my pleasure." [p. 1559]

Although an appropriately "chilling" explanation, it is, on the face of it, somewhat less than satisfying, and many critics have noted the strange inadequacy of Ouine as villain or as character. It is through style, in particular our distinction between the rational-scientific and the experiential-spiritual mode, that we may best account for the retired professor. The contrastive reactions of the doctor and the priest enable us to discern a hierarchy of responses in *Monsieur Ouine*. It is no surprise that the Observer does not usually fare well with Bernanos.[7] The obstacles to understanding in *Monsieur Ouine*—immediacy, irrationality, opacity—suggest that Bernanos has given serious treatment to Sartre's *boutade* that omniscient writing à la Mauriac can only come from God. To be sure, there is omniscience in Bernanos' novels. But, in recognizing the problematic, exploitative dimension of observation and analytic writing, Bernanos faces the dilemma of conveying the intimate workings of individual consciousness and, at the same time, honoring the sanctity of the human heart. Although a retired professor, Ouine is the very image of the ironic, psychological novelist. The detached, poisonous, and ultimately sinful *knowledge* of Monsieur Ouine is an indictment against fiction itself; it also illustrates a particularly modern spiritual malady: the absence of compassion and the desire to observe, understand, and manipulate other human beings. Ouine tries to usurp the lucidness and power of God.

[7] Consider the writer Saint-Martin in *Sous le soleil de Satan*. A clear statement of Bernanos' distrust of observation can also be found in the Preface to *Les Grands Cimetières sous la lune*, p. 6:

"I am not a writer. Merely the sight of a blank piece of paper unsettles me. The kind of physical withdrawal necessary for such work is so odious to me that I avoid it as much as I can. I write in cafés at the risk of passing for a drunkard, and perhaps I would be one if the powerful Republics didn't pitilessly tax alcoholic beverages. Lacking them, I drink sweetish coffee with cream all day long. I write on café tables because I cannot, for any period of time, do without the human face and voice of which I have tried to write nobly. Let the cynics, in their language, claim that I 'observe.' I observe nothing at all. Observation doesn't take you very far."

However, the final enigma in Bernanos is always death, and that supreme agony constitutes the worth and tally of a man's life. Death is the infinite conclusion, the unfathomable experience that terminates the *Route*, provides a final outlet. Bernanos' suffering characters embrace death when it comes. In this crucial instance Ouine's vision falters, and he can experience only hunger and emptiness. The marrow of other lives that he has absorbed no longer sustains him; the precious secrets "resemble those old wines, without flavor or color, which, before dying, have devoured the cork and eaten into the walls of the bottle" (p. 1553).

It does not seem fanciful to emphasize the connection between Monsieur Ouine's stance in life and the manner in which Bernanos has told his story. The scientific image of man is inadequate because it cannot account for the deepest, most obscure forces that haunt us and dictate our conduct. Merely to observe or study human lives is, for Bernanos, sinful; such vision must come out of love if the childlike consciousness is to be hallowed rather than violated. The immediacy of experience—even when harmful or destructive—and the mystery of passion may yield a more authentic picture than the ravenous, often inhuman appetite for clarity. The living parish, like the balanced life, must acknowledge the affective and spiritual needs of the individual, while at the same time preserving some sense of form, harmony, and community. The community is threatened when passion becomes self-gratification, when selflessness and purity are forgotten, and the twin reign of violence and abstraction stamps out love. *Monsieur Ouine* is about such a breakdown. The author has used mystery and suspense to draw the reader into this decaying world. The detective story is predicated on hidden guilt and communal ignorance; Bernanos has brilliantly utilized this art form to evoke the emerging chaos of modern life and to convey to the reader a "living" feeling of a dead parish.

The extreme critical scrutiny which *The Sound and the Fury* has received and the countless displays of myth, symbol, psychology, and history that have been squeezed from it have well revealed the ambiguities of its themes and the suggestiveness of its structure. The critics have succeeded in tracking down all of the allusions, carefully rearranging the entire sequence of events, painstakingly filling in each and every ellipsis, and then throwing the explicated remains, the "story," open to interpretations ranging from Freudian paradigm to Southern decadence. Rather than quarrel with any one interpretation, my effort will be to perceive the novel in its wholeness and thereby to gauge the remarkable affective power that Faulkner's narrative strategy has endowed it with. If anything, the novel has been overexplained, and the effort to discern its meaning has led to a neglect of its mode. As Hyatt Waggoner long ago suggested, the "story" in *The Sound and the Fury* fits nicely in the nineteenth-century tradition of the decline of a family.[8] It is the presentation, the form, and the contours of the Compson story that are startling, and any valid account of the novel must fully assess its narrative brilliance, if we are to appreciate the work itself and not merely speculate about its implied meanings.

As with *Monsieur Ouine*, the affective thrust of *The Sound and the Fury* is best revealed by examining the onslaught the book makes against the reader. Let us begin where Faulkner does:

Through the fence, between the curling flower spaces, I could see them hitting. They were coming toward where the flag was and I went along the fence. Luster was hunting in the grass by the flower tree. They took the flag out, and they were hitting. Then they put the flag back and they went to the table, and he hit and

[8] Hyatt Waggoner, *William Faulkner: From Jefferson to the World* (Lexington, Ky.: University of Kentucky Press, 1959).

the other hit. Then they went on, and I went along the fence. Luster came away from the flower tree and we went along the fence and they stopped and we stopped and I looked through the fence while Luster was hunting in the grass.

"Here, caddie." He hit. They went away across the pasture. I held to the fence and watched them going away.

"Listen at you, now," Luster said. "Aint you something, thirty-three years old, going on that way. After I done went all the way to town to buy you that cake. Hush up that moaning."[9]

This is an example of the sensuous, nonintellective vision through which Benjy sees reality, and through which we are obliged to perceive his story. Little effort is required to realize that the scene describes a golf course, but the character's inability to make that deduction seems strange. The jerky, bizarre actions of the people described (stressed by the extremely simple, repetitive phrases) and the uncomprehending description illuminate the calm and routine violence ("hitting" or "hit" is used five times) of this scene, a violence altogether camouflaged by the label "golf course" and altogether unnoticed by the normal observer of any golf match. The idiot knows no abstractions, no semantic short cuts, and his perception forces us to encounter experience without labels or blinders; the upshot is an unsettling revelation of the way life, shorn of "meaning," confronts and engages our senses.

If it seems odd that the character is incapable of deducing "golf course" from the scene, it is more disquieting that he is moaning and equally unable to tell us that fact (it must come from Luster). If we interrogate the narrative for the cause of Benjy's pain, we must infer that the words, "Here, caddie," possess meaning and even anguish beyond what we can perceive. Of course, once the reader has read further in the novel, he knows that Caddy is the name of Benjy's beloved sister.

[9] William Faulkner, *The Sound and the Fury* (New York: Modern Library College ed., n.d.), p. 1. Subsequent quotations are from this edition.

Likewise, the reference to the "golf course" as pasture will become clear when we learn that it *was* the Compson pasture, that Benjy used to wait there daily for Caddy's return from school, that it was sold and converted into a golf course in order to finance the Harvard education of Benjy's brother Quentin, long (it will be learned in the next section) dead now. Finally we learn that Benjy has been castrated, and it may not be fanciful to assign some value to those golf balls as well. Thus, the moaning is quite justifiable; Faulkner merely gives us the reasons later. Why?

We saw in the opening passage of *Monsieur Ouine* a comparable instance of unlabeled emotion. There, however, the sensation—fear, suffocation, fascination—was unambiguously described, although the causes were unknown. Faulkner has gone further by rendering the emotion itself—the moaning—enigmatic, and unnamed. Benjy reports his sensations, and it is for us to name them: pain, pleasure. In each writer, however, there is an implicit challenge to the reader's response to feeling. We are accustomed to taking the printed word whole. The reader may reflect, ponder, disbelieve, endorse, reject, embrace, or even become furious as he responds to the literary statement; he does not, however, usually tamper with that statement because it does not need tampering. His response is to a finished product. Faulkner and Bernanos give us an art that is radically incomplete and truncated. They present fragments of "raw" feeling, enigmatic emotional exchanges, and the burden of interpretation and response lies heavily on the reader. It is a heavy burden because we are not accustomed to fiction making such demands on our sensibilities. The demands of James and Conrad are as mysterious and considerably more subtle, but those of Faulkner and Bernanos rest on the assumption that we—"knowing" nothing—care. It is an immense assumption. We must be not only curious, but, in some sense, outraged and threatened by the child's anguish in *Monsieur Ouine* and the idiot's moaning in *The Sound and the*

Fury. That anguish and that moaning both antedate the situations that embody them and establish the tone—one might say, the medium—of the two novels. The affective core of experience which fiction clothes in stories, characters, descriptions, and events is often blurred and even ignored because those stories, characters, descriptions, and events take on paramount importance for us as readers and critics. Faulkner and Bernanos have removed the fictional scaffolding, the intellective framework that "situates" and frequently palliates that affective core, and the result is stripped, impersonal, generic. Later in the novel, once all antecedents and grids have emerged, Faulkner will say of Benjy's wailing: "It was nothing. Just sound. It might have been all time and injustice and sorrow become vocal for an instant by a conjunction of planets" (p. 359). The test to the reader's humanity resides in his response to that unadorned, unintelligible sound. It implies, perhaps, an old-fashioned mode of reading, requiring an openness, sensitivity, and commitment to feeling rather than cognitive pattern. Because the two initial scenes are shorn of intellective footholds, they give the reader no rational leeway, while pressing him hard for attention. Comprehension, in the sense of perceiving the cogency of what is presented, seems denied; but the scene is nonetheless there, being read and inevitably responded to in some fashion. What is at stake is the appeal and intelligibility of feeling. The priority given to the unframed affections bespeaks a different kind of logic, a visceral, emotive order that baffles our critical attitude of rationality and objectivity. (If the tone of this argument seems truculent, it is because so much modern literary criticism seeks to be as "professional" and clinical as possible. It is no accident that such postures and values do not fare well in the work of Faulkner and Bernanos. Their art hallows the intuitive, the imaginative, and the affective, and their experiments in narrative form not only express but also demand from the reader comparable qualities.)

The art of emotive immersion and associational logic is common enough in poetry, but altogether more radical in the novel, where a story, a complex sequence of events, is to be apprehended sensorially rather than rationally or progressively. There are not many instances of such works in modern fiction. Certainly one might add the names of Woolf, Hesse, and Proust as novelists preoccupied with imagination and sensation, but few novels can claim such a compelling, almost despotic affective technique as *Monsieur Ouine* and *The Sound and the Fury*. The earlier conjectural realism of Conrad and Ford, as well as the pronounced intellectuality—encyclopedic or ironic or fantastic or playful or solipsistic—of many modern practitioners (Joyce, Beckett, Borges, Nabokov, Barth, the French New Novel), neither place a comparable value on the intensity of feeling nor make the same appeal to the visceral response of the reader.

The Benjy section illustrates the extreme form such sensory realism attains. Consider, for example, Benjy's bout with "sassprilluh":

I wasn't crying, but I couldn't stop. I wasn't crying, but the ground wasn't still, and then I was crying. The ground kept sloping up and the cows ran up the hill. T. P. tried to get up. He fell down again and the cows ran down the hill. Quentin held my arm and we went toward the barn. Then the barn wasn't there and we had to wait until it came back. I didn't see it come back. It came behind us and Quentin set me down in the trough where the cows ate. I held on to it. It was going away too, and I held to it. The cows ran down the hill again, across the door. I couldn't stop. [p. 24]

This kind of roller-coaster realism is quite similar to what we saw in Bernanos: here too the result is spasmodic, helpless, puppetlike behavior. However, Faulkner is not only interested in rendering action; he also wants to depict thought, particularly memory, the weight of the past. In Benjy, Faulkner has a character who "justifiably" cannot distinguish between past and present; such a character is invaluable if one wants to render a story of loss. There is no sequence for Benjy, no time for healing, forgetting, or adapting. He lives the family tragedy as a continuum, always fresh, like a never-closing wound. We saw on the opening page his ritual of waiting for Caddy at the fence bordering the "pasture." What time has done to him—no Caddy, just caddies, a golf course, and castration—is expressed at the outset by his moaning but "understood" by the reader only gradually. In depicting Benjy's consciousness, Faulkner is able to yoke together what time has drawn apart, and his narrative presents with simultaneity what logic and discursive prose can only tediously construct. Consider the following passage involving Benjy's relation to Caddy and her daughter:

"You, Benjy." T. P. said in the house. "Where you hiding. You slipping off. I knows it."
Luster came back. Wait, he said. Here. Dont go over there. Miss Quentin and her beau in the swing yonder. You come on this way. Come back here, Benjy.
It was dark under the trees. Dan wouldn't come. He stayed in the moonlight. Then I could see the swing and I began to cry.
Come away from there, Benjy, Luster said. You know Miss Quentin going to get mad.
It was two now, and then one in the swing. Caddy came fast, white in the darkness.
"Benjy," she said. "How did you slip out. Where's Versh."
She put her arms around me and I hushed and held to her dress and tried to pull her away. [pp. 56–57]

The sequence is completed with an account of Caddy struggling with her boy friend, leaving him in order to comfort Benjy, washing her mouth with soap, and finally "smelling like trees" again. We then have Quentin's performance:

I kept a telling you to stay away from there, Luster said. They sat up in the swing, quick. Quentin had her hands on her hair. He had a red tie.

You crazy old loon, Quentin said. I'm going to tell Dilsey about the way you let him follow everywhere I go. I'm going to make her whip you good. [p. 58]

Although the juxtaposition reveals the parallel sexual appetites in Caddy and Quentin, it illuminates, above all, their differences: Caddy's tenderness and shame as opposed to Quentin's callousness and vulgarity. Such simultaneous comparison evokes with poignance what Benjy has lost. There will be no commentary within the narrative: just the two images of a girl in a swing.

Most critics account for the sequence of the four narratives by stressing the childhood character of Benjy's memories. Thus Quentin's section would be adolescence, Jason's adulthood, and Dilsey's some larger, overall view. Whereas such a progression is indeed evident, it might be more appropriate to view Benjy's section as a purely sensuous entry into the story, a primordial, preconscious rendering of the themes to be developed. We must learn to understand Benjy's language, to know what it means when Caddy smells like trees, to see that he moans because Caddy has lost her virginity, or Damuddy is dead. Faulkner has entrusted the contours and values of his story to Benjy's perceptions, and the result is not so much "primitive" as a strange, intensely physical encounter with a world that, for most of us, has disappeared behind its array of meanings and labels. To read Benjy's monologue does not entail experiencing the sensations of an idiot, but rather living in a highly simplified and coherent world of pure sensation, a world totally structured by association. Benjy's experience is not complex (by comparison with actual mental processes); it is simply untempered by ratiocination. However, and herein lies its inestimable value, through Benjy, because he is incapable of reasoning, we partake of the sensuous immediacy of the Compson experience. He, the idiot, forces us, the "thinking" readers, to feel—and only to feel—the impressions of his life. Faulkner is not interested in our voluntary judgments nor even in our like or dislike of any of his characters. He wants to move us *into* the story, to make us grasp his story affectively or sensuously rather than abstractly. As Walter Slatoff has said, his presentation is designed to prevent us "from substituting language and 'mind's reasons' for the actual experiences he is trying to suggest."[10]

Once the primacy of associational structure is established over cause-effect, the resultant dislocation of a traditional, linear time scheme is obvious. As Faulkner has said, time for him is "a fluid condition which has no existence except in the momentary avatars of individual people. There is no such thing as *was*—only *is*."[11] The classical juxtaposition of *nebeneinander* in painting and *nacheinander* in literature which Lessing formulated in his *Laokoön* is grounded in the nature of the two media. All possible experimentation on Faulkner's part will not achieve the simultaneity in language that pictorial art enjoys. Words must follow each other, and there must be sequence, even if effect precedes cause. His goal, however, is not to achieve a oneness of cause and effect, but to prolong the effect indefinitely in the reader. Underlying Faulkner's aesthetic is the fear that rational, sequential discourse deadens experience, prevents it from being as moving—in both senses of the word—as he wants it to be. When asked at West Point why *The Sound and the Fury* was so difficult to complete, he replied that his goal was "to make it on paper as startling, as comic, anyway as moving, as true, as important as it seems in the imagination."[12] The same explanation was invariably given

[10] Walter Slatoff, *Quest for Failure: A Study of William Faulkner* (Ithaca, N.Y.: Cornell University Press, 1960), p. 241.

[11] "William Faulkner: An Interview," in *William Faulkner: Three Decades of Criticism*, eds. Frederick J. Hoffman and Olga W. Vickery (New York: Harbinger paperback, 1963), p. 82.

[12] *Faulkner at West Point*, eds. Joseph L. Fant, III, and Robert Ashley (New York: Vintage Books, 1964), p. 112.

when he was questioned about matters of style and technique. The rationale of immersing before informing is consonant with the denial of chronology; in a very precise and literal way, Faulkner endorses Mr. Compson's statement: "Only when the clock stops does time come to life" (p. 104). Faulkner seeks not so much to *depict* the moment, as Hemingway does, for that would be an act of paralysis, finality; he wants, rather, to prolong it, to keep it flowing and resonant, to transfer it alive to the reader.

A moving example of the tension between words and experience can be seen in Benjy's abortive attempt at love. Still waiting at the gate for Caddy to come with the only tenderness he knows, Benjy sees daily the young girls on their way home from school:

> I could hear them talking. I went out the door and I couldn't hear them, and I went down to the gate, where the girls passed with their booksatchels. They looked at me, walking fast, with their heads turned. I tried to say, but they went on, and I went along the fence, trying to say, and they went faster. Then they were running and I came to the corner of the fence and I couldn't go any further, and I held to the fence, looking after them and trying to say. [p. 63]

One day, however, the gate is not locked, and the need for love is very nearly gratified as his feelings erupt:

> They came on. I opened the gate and they stopped, turning. I was trying to say, and I caught her, trying to say, and she screamed and I was trying to say and trying and the bright shapes began to stop and I tried to get out. I tried to get it off my face, but the bright shapes were going again. They were going up the hill to where it fell away and I tried to cry. But when I breathed in, I couldn't breathe out again to cry, and I tried to keep from falling off the hill and I fell off the hill into the bright, whirling shapes. [p. 64]

As the attempted sexual expression merges into the anesthesia for the castration, we can measure the final blow that life has dealt to Benjy, the final and definitive denial of love. The entire novel is about the loss of love, and one can argue that the narrative technique is Faulkner's way of "trying to say." The need for love, for touch, is central in Faulkner's major work; it attains, at times, an urgency and grandeur that dwarf and seize the individual characters. In *The Sound and the Fury* the loss of Caddy, mirrored in the monologues of her three brothers, creates the vital center, the emotive source of the work, to and from which all actions can be traced. *Absalom, Absalom!* emphasizes familial continuity, and the flowing, coursing "blood" will serve as the communion or bridge that the characters must acknowledge. In *As I Lay Dying* and "Old Man," we sense an elemental realm of feeling (quite comparable to the affective core that informs the world of *Monsieur Ouine*) that assumes its true mythic identity: the River. The convict's struggle with the flood and the Bundrens' archetypal immersion and initiation into the swollen waters constitute a paradigm of the special Faulknerian baptism: the confrontation between the self-imprisoned individual and the larger, more primordial forces that nourish and control him. Benjy's intellect is arrested, and the surgeon effectively prevents any form of consummated love. Yet his desire remains whole, and, like the Grecian urn which haunts Faulkner's fiction,[13] only unconsummated passion endures. It is the wholeness of his narrative, the sensuous affective fullness unvitiated by reason or abstraction, that brings that light of magic suggestiveness to the old, old words.

[13] See the urnlike imagery in *Light in August* (New York: Modern Library ed., 1950), p. 6, the vaselike motif and allusions to Keats's poem in *Sartoris* (New York: Signet Classic, 1964), pp. 154, 208, 303, and the illuminating Afterword of Lawrance Thompson (pp. 304–316). See, in a different context, the explicit discussion of Keats's poem in "The Bear," *Go Down Moses* (New York: Modern Library ed., n.d.), pp. 296–297.

In contrast to the limpid, elemental diction and vision of Benjy, Quentin's section is tortured, self-conscious, abstract, and painfully intellectual. It is generally agreed that his monologue partakes of a remembered rather than a relived quality. Benjy immerses us blindly and sensuously in the story; at the close of his monologue the raw events reverberate in our mind. Quentin reveals not so much the happenings themselves as their effect on him. Whereas the impact of the past on Benjy was made graphically clear at the outset, it is revealed analytically, or by gradual disclosure, in Quentin's monologue. However, we are still far from the traditional declarative mode; here, as in the first section, Faulkner presents the story elliptically, gives effects without causes. But the results differ greatly from those of the Benjy chapter. Benjy urgently calls upon us to organize: we must deduce logically from the sensory material he uncomprehendingly reports. Our role in Quentin's chapter is reduced to witnessing (although a considerable amount of reconstruction is required to maintain our vantage point) what might be called a duel between past and present. Quentin's consciousness mirrors the dynamics of repression. As certain decisive events are gradually disclosed, we seem to sift through layers of effect before arriving at the central cause. The inevitable character of this revelation, like all analytic tragedy (for example, the Oedipus story), suggests a kind of fatalism: once what must be known is known, there is nothing more to be done.

If Benjy lives in a fluid continuum, Quentin is wracked by a state of tension in which past menaces, encroaches on present. No one has better described this condition than Sartre: "The past here gains a surrealistic quality; its outline is hard, clear and immutable. The indefinable and elusive present is helpless before it; it is full of holes through which past things, fixed, motionless and silent, invade it. Faulkner's soliloquies make us think of plane flights made rough by air pockets; at

every point the consciousness of the hero 'falls into the past.' "[14]
The gradual accumulation of invading fragments of the past
literally undermines Quentin's stability and condemns him to
death. Our role is to experience, as Quentin does, the effect of
the past—progressively and fatally.

Although there is a good bit of controlled or recalled past
(Father said, and so on), the decisive disclosures come unbid-
den and force themselves upon Quentin's present. For our
orientation Faulkner usually places them in italics. Quentin's
monologue is ordered by the resulting tension between his activities on June 2, 1910, his *controlled* recollection of events
and conversations from the past, and, on the other hand, issuing from the deeper reaches of his mind and forming a fatal
pattern, the fragments of events which condemn him. These
uncalled images represent, *are* a past which is not and cannot
be assimilated. Increasing in scope and usurping more and
more of Quentin's stability, they give both meaning and urgency to the preoccupations and gestures of the present.

The first fragments from the past, evoking Caddy's marriage, are disquieting: the reader is able to piece together the
event, but not Quentin's attitude toward it. As Caddy's marriage to Herbert takes on flesh, we learn about Herbert's un-
savory character, Benjy's anguish at the wedding, Quentin's
contempt for Herbert, and the growing suspicion that the
wedding is, in every sense, a façade—covering not only Caddy's
pregnancy but also disturbing Quentin in obscure ways that
the narrative has concealed.

After the honeysuckle motif is initiated and more direct
reference to Caddy's promiscuity is made, the extent of Quentin's involvement begins to emerge. The relation between
past and present becomes less haphazard: Gerald Bland is increasingly juxtaposed with Dalton Ames and Herbert Head.

[14] Jean-Paul Sartre, "Time in Faulkner: *The Sound and the Fury,*"
in *Three Decades,* p. 228.

Finally, the exchange between Quentin and Herbert before the wedding paves the way for Quentin's confrontation with Caddy and the disclosure of her "sickness." At this point Caddy becomes the sole subject of Quentin's memories. Herbert disappears; Benjy is hardly mentioned again. Although there is obviously a gradual, inexorable movement throughout the whole chapter toward dissolution (the revelation of a fatal "wound" in the past and its concomitant, death, in the present), one is nonetheless tempted to say that only here does Quentin commence to flounder. Admittedly, he has made his decision for suicide long before this day: the flatirons and letters testify to premeditation. However, until the open treatment of Caddy occurs, Quentin is outwardly composed and apparently still in some control over the resurging images of the past. Despite the shadow and clock motifs, his Harvard day has retained some semblance of authority; present has resisted past. Now the Caddy themes—sexuality and Quentin's fear of it, promiscuity and Quentin's sense of honor—can no longer be treated obliquely. The past with its secret causes now begins to surge forth, illuminating the gestures and events which have seemed unclear. Above all, there is a change in the emotional tenor, a change indirectly but powerfully registered in the broken leg episode. Although Quentin has recalled Benjy's bellowing, he has on no instance spoken of his own anguish. For the first time there is acknowledged pain: *"told me the bone would have to be broken again and inside me it began to say Ah Ah Ah and I began to sweat . . . and my jaw-muscles getting numb and my mouth saying Wait Wait just a minute through the sweat ah ah ah behind my teeth"* (p. 132). Occurring at the initiation of the sexuality theme, this passage serves as the "objective correlative" of the suffering which Caddy has caused and which he can no longer repress.

An element of urgency now enters into the fragmentary memories. The long talk between Quentin and Caddy is revealed over a ten-page section, and the central themes of

Caddy's pregnancy, Quentin's desire to flee with her to "a hell beyond that," and the threatening disintegration of the family come to the surface. The tenor of the *recalled* events is also menacing and pointed: Versh's tale of mutilation and Mr. Compson's thoughts on virginity. Only the present scene appears to offer some refuge in the idyllic episode of the three boys fishing.

As the condemning evidence from the past accumulates—the sale of the pasture to send him to Harvard, his father's weak health and drinking, the futile attempt to dissuade Caddy from marrying Herbert—the narration of the present leads Quentin into a bakery and places him before "a little dirty child with eyes like a toy bear's and two patentleather pig-tails," to whom he says "hello, sister" (p. 155). At this point one almost expects to hear a whirring noise as the infernal machine begins, or something like the French custom of the three knocks which indicate that—for better or worse—the play has begun. The conjunction between times past and present has clicked and is in focus. This encounter is a small masterpiece of suggestivity, of childlike naiveté and nightmarish undertones. The crucial elements of Quentin's childhood which condemn him are ironically and grotesquely recast into the present. The authority of the past—always operative but hitherto veiled—now shapes the very stuff of the present, extends its reign, usurps the whole pitiful area of Quentin's life. The emerging pattern of impotence fills the story on all levels, leaving no room for the relief of the Deacon, the speculations on Negroes, the memory of Louis Hatcher's possum hunting.

Quentin's kindnesses to the girl are larded with ambiguity, and Faulkner describes the "innocent" episode in terms and images fraught with sexual significance. The description of the child's fingers, "damp and hot, like worms" (p. 157) clutching the bread that is "wearing slowly out of the paper" (p. 166), "fraying out of the newspaper" (p. 167) is highly equivocal. The two walk around looking for the girl's house, frequently in view of a hanging "garment of vivid pink" (p. 163), with the "nose of the loaf naked" (p. 168), as Quentin thinks of the stifling honeysuckle "all mixed up in it as though it were not enough without that, not unbearable enough" (p. 166) and desires only peace. The scene with the girl reaches its muffled crescendo with the sound of a bird, "a sound meaningless and profound, inflexionless, ceasing as though cut off with the blow of a knife, and again, and that sense of water swift and peaceful above secret places, felt, not seen nor heard" (pp. 168–169). At this point Quentin says "Oh, hell, sister" and we read, "about half the paper hung limp" (p. 169). The nature of these descriptions blends in so powerfully with the adjacent tale of mutilation, the haunting remarks about purity, virginity, and menstruation, and the stifling odor of honeysuckle that the texture of the story, ominous with suggestiveness and gathered energy, virtually expels the memories which now appear and alone explain Quentin. We now see beyond the wedding scene into the origins of his trouble:

. . . What did you let him for kiss kiss

I didn't let him I made him watching me getting mad What do you think of that? Red print of my hand coming up through her face like turning a light on under your hand . . .

. . . What do you think of that scouring her head into the. Grass sticks crisscrossed into the flesh tingling scouring her head. Say calf rope say it

I didnt kiss a dirty girl like Natalie anyway . . .

. . . It was raining we could hear it on the roof, sighing through the high sweet emptiness of the barn.

There? touching her

Not there

There? not raining hard but we couldn't hear anything but the roof and as if it was my blood or her blood . . .

. . . It's like dancing sitting down did you ever dance sitting down? . . . How do you hold to dance do you hold like this

Oh

*I used to hold like this you thought I wasnt strong enough
didn't you*
  Oh Oh Oh Oh . . .
    *. . . She stood in the door looking at us her hands on her
hips . . .*
      *. . . I jumped hard as I could into the hogwallow and mud
yellowed up to my waist stinking I kept on plunging until I fell
down and rolled over in it . . . She had her back turned I went
around in front of her the rain creeping into the mud flatting her
bodice through her dress it smelled horrible. I was hugging her
that's what I was doing. . . .*
  I dont give a damn what you were doing
  *You dont you dont I'll make you I'll make you give a damn.
She hit my hands away I smeared mud on her with the other
hand I couldn't feel the wet smacking of her hand I wiped mud
from my legs smeared it on her wet hard turning body hearing
her fingers going into my face.* [pp. 166–170]

This scene has been quoted at length so that its essentially non-elliptic nature and explanatory role might be apparent. Coming, as it does, interspersed over five pages, the episode requires a minimal amount of reconstruction. Nevertheless, the fragments follow each other so closely, and the completed picture is so revealing, that the interweaving of past and present yields a kind of breathless tempo that both reveals Quentin's frame of mind and jerkily sweeps the reader along. When this traumatic childhood experience with sex is juxtaposed with the climax of the little girl episode where Julio attacks Quentin and accuses him of molesting his sister, the ironies and parallels with the Caddy situation are painfully obvious.

In a manner somewhat like hemorrhaging, this memory soon triggers a still larger, more corrosive sequence. Shreve, Spoade, Gerald, and Mrs. Bland—the emissaries from the present—are now on the scene. These characters with their nicely defined personalities, the two young ladies slightly shocked by Quentin's appearance, the very atmosphere of youth and bantering

and college activities, even the parody of Mrs. Bland—all
strikes us as weightless and even dreamlike, so palpably the
spell of the past has been evoked, the overwhelming reality of
its ghosts, the urgency of its dictates. No longer through elliptic glimpses and spurts, the final revelation now comes to us
with crushing and imperious finality. In this last encounter the
present completely vanishes, and we witness the most direct
and moving confrontation between Quentin and Caddy. Here
Caddy outspokenly asserts her sexuality and love for Dalton
Ames as well as the willingness to grant Quentin whatever he
may ask of her; Quentin, stifled by the honeysuckle, is powerless to carry out the incest, to commit suicide, or to defend
the Compson honor against Caddy's lover. The scene is far too
long to permit quotation, and its very length is an index of its
paralyzing and enduring hold on Quentin. The merciless authority of the past, now full-born and unrepressed, consumes
everything. There is little in fiction comparable to this utterly
graphic struggle for life; to be sure, we "know," from the
letters and the flatirons, that he will commit suicide, but we
see him die, go under as he vainly tries to redeem the Compson honor by striking out at Dalton Ames—and hitting Gerald
Bland.

Our analysis of Quentin's section as the disclosure of a fatal
past sheds a strange light on the final remembered exchange
where we see the boy struggling against the nihilistic "temporary" philosophy of his father.[15] It is clear that Quentin's

---

[15] Because this passage is well known and lengthy, I shall quote it
here rather than in the text:

"... you are not thinking of finitude you are contemplating an
apotheosis in which a temporary state of mind will become sym-
metrical above the flesh and aware both of itself and of the flesh
it will not quite discard you will not even be dead and i temporary and he you cannot bear to think that someday it will no
longer hurt you like this now ... you won't do it under these
conditions it will be a gamble ... no man ever does that under

past makes his present intolerable; it seems equally clear that he has not *yet* begun to regard his feelings for Caddy as temporary. Moreover, there is no indication in the story that these sentiments will change, or that Quentin even harbors such a fear; on the contrary, the structural logic of the monologue insists on the wholeness and vividness of that relationship. We must conclude then that his suicide is an act of affirmation—the only affirmation of which he is capable. In taking his life, Quentin proves that his feelings, crippling though they may be, are absolute; and that death is preferable to an existence where those feelings, never diminishing, can bring only pain.

In a study of affective techniques, Jason's interest is that of a foil. The monologues of Benjy and Quentin make use of suspense and suspension. Although one is a fluid continuum and the other a tension-filled confrontation, both may be seen as a commitment to feeling, a cry of loss. It would thus seem appropriate that, following these affective and obscurely private

---

the first fury of despair or remorse or bereavement he does it only when he has realised that even the despair or remorse or bereavement is not particularly important to the dark diceman and i temporary and he it is hard believing to think that a love or a sorrow is a bond purchased without design and which matures willynilly and is recalled without warning to be replaced by whatever issue the gods happen to be floating at the time no you will not do that until you come to believe that even she was not quite worth despair perhaps and i i will never do that nobody knows what i know and he i think youd better go on up to cambridge right away . . . and i suppose i realise what you believe i will realise up there next week or next month and he then you will remember that for you to go to harvard has been your mothers dream since you were born and no compson has ever disappointed a lady and i temporary it will be better for me for all of us and he every man is the arbiter of his own virtues but let no man prescribe for another mans wellbeing and i temporary and he was the saddest word of all there is nothing else in the world its not despair until time and its not even time until it was" (pp. 220–222).

narratives, Jason—self-styled as the first sane Compson—should order the Compson story, constitute its rational, clarifying moment. To be sure, Jason regards the Compsons as crazy. He resolutely lives in the present. Where his brothers have lost love, he has lost a job. Finally, his story is legible; his arrangements with Lorraine are ordered and contractual (as contrasted with Benjy's "trying to say" and Quentin's suicide); his narrative and his life are outfitted with the signs and syntax of sanity.

Yet, Jason fails abysmally as *raisonneur*. His story may not be as forbiddingly private as that of his brothers, but the ubiquitous "I says" indicates an egomania of some proportions. As the practical man of affairs, Jason is somewhat less than a success: his ventures in the stock market are a disaster; after embezzling $50 a month for fifteen years from Caddy, he has saved slightly less than $3000 for Quentin to steal; he is a man who spends the money intended for part ownership in the business on a car which, when he drives it, gives him vicious headaches; finally, Jason's balanced, sane image of himself does not fit the harried little man we see, running back and forth from business to bank to home and back, overcome by violent spells of anger and mistrust toward his family and acquaintances. The full extent of Jason's blindness, of the inadequacy of his "rationality" can be seen in his outraged pursuit of Quentin and her beau (who wears the very symbol of irrationality, a red tie). Jason is able to find (and insult) only a little old man in a pullman car, but it is enough to trigger the long-expected reversal: " 'You bastard,' the other shrieked, scrabbling at the table. Jason tried to grasp him in both arms, trying to prison the puny fury of him. The man's body felt so old, so frail, yet so fatally single-purposed that for the first time Jason saw clear and unshadowed the disaster toward which he rushed" (p. 386).

In Jason's story we are inevitably *informed* about much that we have experientially encountered in Benjy's tale. Benjy has moaned at the golf balls, has reported how he was "trying to say" at the gate; Jason translates for us, tells us about the "Great American Gelding" and how "they never started soon enough with their cutting" (pp. 328–329). The contrasts and implications of these two modes of narration express fundamentally different responses to experience. The order which Jason brings to the book is wholly without moral insight and ungraced by imagination. He prolongs the dissensions within the family, and the vindictive fury which animates him and informs his narrative is radically different from the "slant" or "disorder" which characterize Benjy's and Quentin's stories. The first two chapters make us "feel" the story before perceiving its configurations or origins; Jason's is, as it were, a closed account, a magnificent character portrait if you will, but one which neither invites nor rewards reader immersion. The pattern of retribution which is finally enacted with regard to Jason (Quentin's theft) is significantly ironic, haphazard. Instead of resolution or insight, we have only "poetic" justice. If the Compson story is to be ordered, its madness and waste evaluated or redeemed, it is to Dilsey that we must turn.

After the claustrophobic intimacy of the three brothers' monologues, Dilsey's section inaugurates the movement toward a broader vision. The narrative is presented in the third person, and we finally see, from the outside now, what people look like. It is an odd feeling, after having lived with their thoughts and obsessions, to confront these characters physically. The effect is one of shock, like that of suddenly restored sight, as we see Luster enter the room

followed by a big man who appeared to have been shaped of some substance whose particles would not or did not cohere to one another or to the frame which supported it. His skin was dead looking and hairless; dropsical too, he moved with a shambling gait like a trained bear. His hair was pale and fine. It had been brushed smoothly down upon his brow like that of children in daguerreotypes. His eyes were clear, of the pale sweet blue of cornflowers, his thick mouth hung open, drooling a little. [p. 342]

The meticulous "objective" description should not deceive us, however, for the real thrust of the final section is that of transcendence, of going beyond the world of facts and surfaces. The initial descriptions of Dilsey indicate how "her skeleton rose," "now only the indomitable skeleton was left rising like a ruin or a landmark above the somnolent and impervious guts" (p. 331). The chords of rebirth and resurrection are already sounding. Dilsey is the life principle, that endurance that alone redeems suffering and loss; the description of her breathing life into the Compson household on Easter morning is one of the most beautiful passages in Faulkner's work:

Dilsey prepared to make biscuit. As she ground the sifter steadily above the bread board, she sang, to herself at first, something without particular tune or words, repetitive, mournful and plaintive, austere, as she ground a faint, steady snowing of flour onto the bread board. The stove had begun to heat the room and to fill it with murmurous minors of the fire, and presently she was singing louder, as if her voice too had been thawed out by the growing warmth, and then Mrs. Compson called her name again from within the house. Dilsey raised her face as if her eyes could and did penetrate the walls and ceiling and saw the old woman in her quilted dressing gown at the head of the stairs, calling her name with machinelike regularity. [p. 336]

The contrast between Dilsey's selfless labor and the Compson egoism is emphasized by juxtaposing the old woman's "machinelike regularity" with the grace of Dilsey's acts and vision (that "could and did penetrate the walls and ceiling"). That vision is most fully embodied in the Easter sermon.

In a manner reminiscent of *Monsieur Ouine*, the events at the weathered church with its "crazy steeple" constitute the moment of order and light in the Compson story. The much-acclaimed Reverend Shegog "fum Saint Looey" is at first a disappointment, with his "wizened black face like a small, aged monkey" and his white man's oratorical but passionless virtuosity. Then the voice changes: "Brethren." This time the sound is dark and sad and timbrous, and it reverberates in the hearts of the congregation. "Brethren and sisteren." "I got the recollection and the blood of the Lamb." With no need for words or logic, the language of feeling touches the congregation, breaks down their individual walls, and welds them into a community: "And the congregation seemed to watch with its own eyes while the voice consumed him, until he was nothing and they were nothing and there was not even a voice but instead their hearts were speaking to one another in chanting measures beyond the need for words" (p. 367).

Against this backdrop of "soul," of "giving" rather than possessive love, we can evaluate the Compson story. The now Negroid intonation, "Breddren en sistuhn," encompasses the Compson brothers and sister as well as the black congregation. And the story of their pain and loss is transcended by the larger Passion and Redemption celebrated at Easter. Amid the congregation, Dilsey sits "bolt upright, her hand on Ben's knee," as the Reverend evokes the Christ tragedy and creates the communion of spirits through the intensity of vision:

"Listen, breddren! I sees de day. Ma'y settin in de do' wid Jesus on her lap, de little Jesus. Like dem chillen dar, de little Jesus. I hears de angels singin de peaceful songs en de glory; I sees de closin eyes; sees Mary jump up, sees de sojer face: We gwine to kill! We gwine to kill! We gwine to kill yo little Jesus! I hears de weepin en de lamentation of de po mammy widout de salvation en de word of God!"

"Mmmmmmmmmmmmmmmmmmmmmmmm! Jesus! little Jesus!" and another voice, rising:

"I sees, O Jesus! Oh I sees!" and still another, without words, like bubbles rising in water.

"I sees hit, breddren! I sees hit! Sees de blastin, blindin sight!

I sees Calvary, wid de sacred trees, sees de thief en de murderer en de least of dese; I hears de boasting en de braggin: Ef you be Jesus, lif up yo tree en walk! I hears de wailin of women en de evenin lamentation; I hears de weepin en de crying en de turnt-away face of God: dey done kilt Jesus; dey done kilt my Son!"

"Mmmmmmmmmmmm. Jesus! I sees, O Jesus!"

"O blind sinner! Breddren, I tells you; sistuhn, I says to you, when de Lawd did turn His mighty face, say, Aint gwine over-load heaven! I can see de widowed God shet His do'; I sees de whelmin flood roll between; I sees de darkness en de death ever-lastin upon de generations. Den, lo! Breddren! Yes, breddren! Whut I see? Whut I see, O sinner? I sees de resurrection en de light; sees de meek Jesus sayin Dey kilt Me dat ye shall live again; I died dat dem whut sees en believes shall never die. Breddren, O breddren! I sees de doom crack en hears de golden horns shoutin down de glory, en de arisen dead whut got de blood en de rick-lickshun of de Lamb!" [pp. 369–370]

It is an epiphany, a radiant moment of light which orders the Compson story. Much like the effort of the priest in *Monsieur Ouine*, the Easter sermon breaks through the imprisoned egos of the individual characters, illuminating their defects. The stories of Benjy, Quentin, and Jason have in common not only their response to the loss of Caddy, but their cruelty and parasitic exploitation of others. In Jason's case, his treatment of Quentin, Luster, Caddy, Benjy, and Dilsey makes the charge self-evident. But it is equally true that Benjy and Quentin have devoured Caddy with their merciless love; they have relentlessly taken from her, tried to prevent her growth into maturity and pleasure, attempted to possess her in any manner possible. The black congregation "sees de blastin, blindin sight," but the Compsons have been blind. Caddy's eyes "gone dead," Ben's empty gaze, the empty eyes of the Confederate soldier in the Square, the metal tube screwed in the face of the watch-repair man, and the eye which Jason should keep on Mottson; all indicate a vision that is palpably wrong, that is a mirror of the self's appetites rather than an awareness of others.[16]

The extreme dissimilarity in the monologues not only illustrates that life varies according to the viewer; we also acutely sense the gulf between the stories, between the brothers, the intensely self-centered, almost tyrannical nature of their desires, the stifling narrowness in which they function. As Robert Penn Warren pointed out, their subjectivity *is* their doom.[17] The selfless communion at the Easter sermon is a liberation; it opens a larger, harmonious realm beyond the tortured individual consciousness of the Compsons. Beyond logic and beyond the individual, it is a celebration of life and of the community. Bernanos' priest broke through the walls of his characters to reunite them in a ritual of murder. Faulkner's parish is not dead; the genteel white Southerners are doomed, but, in the black church, the integrity of feeling survives, against which his fragmented story of loss can be ordered.

Whereas conflicting interpretations follow in the wake of communal violence in *Monsieur Ouine*, the burden of explanation remains on the reader's shoulders in *The Sound and the Fury*. The meaning of the four sections is ultimately a matter of vision, of the reader's ability to understand the novel's sensory language, to feel with its suffering characters, to grasp the inner truth and arrive at the knowledge which Dilsey takes from the Easter sermon:[18]

[16] For a discussion of vision in *The Sound and the Fury*, see Walton Litz, "William Faulkner's Moral Vision," *Southwest Review*, XXXVII (Summer 1952), 200–209.

[17] See Robert Penn Warren, "Faulkner: The South, the Negro, and Time," *Selected Essays* (New York: Random House, 1958).

[18] Faulkner is concerned with vision, our vision. It has been pointed out that Cash Bundren's ultimate awareness of the meaning of his family's pilgrimage is disappointingly slight; similarly it is a critical commonplace to discuss Sutpen's blindness and the questionable value of what Quentin has learned (questionable, at least, to Quentin).

"I've seed de first en de last," Dilsey said. "Never you mind me."

"First en last whut?" Frony said.

"Never you mind," Dilsey said. "I seed de beginnin, en now I sees de endin." [p. 371]

Despite the different cultural and literary backgrounds from which they issue, *Monsieur Ouine* and *The Sound and the Fury* are curiously similar novels. In each case, techniques of ellipsis, experiential immersion, and interior monologue are used to present the chaotic inner picture of individuals caught up by forces beyond their control. In both novels the effort to go beyond the fragmented and destructive private vision takes the shape of a church sermon. There is little harmony in either work: a surface order settles on the village of Fenouille after the mass violence has erupted and Monsieur Ouine dies; the last image of the Compson family is not one of Dilsey and Benjy at the Easter sermon, but the grotesque suffering of the idiot as Luster drives him around the Square the wrong way. The sensuous immediacy of each novel, brought about by the radical departure from traditional storytelling, seems to be in the service of anguish, chaos. The reader is indeed immersed in the inchoate flow of experience, but the larger question as to whether such feeling can be converted into knowledge or healing—the possible *value* of the affective technique—is left open. To be sure, we cannot read *Monsieur Ouine* and *The Sound and the Fury* without penetrating (and being penetrated by) the sensory language of the characters; however, the reader, even when lessoned and "baptized" by the style,

---

Likewise, Joe Christmas says little about the peace he seems to discover before he is caught, and we have seen Dilsey sum it all up with "I seed de beginnin, en now I sees de endin." These are Faulkner's great visceral works, and we need merely think of the didacticism, the oracular loquaciousness of so much of the later work to appreciate the eloquence and power of the affective technique.

can do little other than watch the fatal events transpire and merely project some hypothetical realm where the gained insights might be put to use.

Absalom, Absalom! takes place almost entirely within that hypothetical realm. The conjectural, malleable form of the Sutpen story is forged, not once but several times, during the course of the novel. This reconstructive activity has distinct parallels with the aesthetic of Conrad, Ford, and James; however, Faulkner transforms the imaginative act into a gesture of passionate identification. The primacy of feeling and touch, seen as the useless, bittersweet lesson emerging from the claustrophobic relationships of *Monsieur Ouine* and *The Sound and the Fury*, is at the heart of *Absalom, Absalom!*, informing its theme and its technique. Whereas the presentation in the first two novels dramatizes the priority and the power of the affective, *Absalom* harnesses that power, gauges the full, spectacular extent of its fictional and epistemological dimension. *Absalom* is about the intensity of loving and caring. It is Faulkner's emotive version of Jamesian refinement: matter, evidence, the givens remain recalcitrant until—like alchemy— the heat of passion has penetrated and liberated their mystery and riches.

Absalom, Absalom! gives definitive form to the central paradigm of this book: the distance between sight and insight. We see a world of evidence, matter, bodies, colors, printed words. We need to see a world of meaning, pattern, thought, feeling. Literature invariably mediates between these two realms, but the books under discussion here illuminate an evolving interest in the unseen, in those patterns of order that, not readily visible, must be perceived or forged by the character or reader. The mystery story is predicated precisely on that exploration of the unseen. Rastignac and Pip, caught in the conflict between human bonds and social codes, initiate a search for meaning; the process of interrogation shapes the work of James, Conrad, and Ford as the ambiguities of appearances and the subjective biases of vision hinder or prevent any definitive grasp of truth. The characteristic form of Faulkner's fiction derives from the attempt to comprehend some mysterious or extraordinary event: the significance of the Sutpen story, the events behind the death of Joanna Burden and the emerging story of Joe Christmas, the reporter's fanatic efforts to assimilate the three flyers in *Pylon*. In other Faulkner books the amazed reaction, the attempt to understand, is simply a component rather than the subject of the novel: the "outsiders' " reaction to the Bundren pilgrimage; the attitude of the older doctor and his wife toward Harry and Charlotte at the opening of *The Wild Palms*. Indirectly expressive of the same rhythm are the convict's agonizing efforts to "understand," to cope with the flood; the Bundrens' coming to grips with their "natural" trials; the experience of Ratliff and Gavin Stevens in coping with the Snopes; Chick Mallison's adventures in solving a murder. This act of comprehension—be it characterized by amazement, outrage, ironic query, or passionate commitment—structures Faulkner's major fiction and brings forth an imaginative involvement from the reader. As we have seen in Bernanos' *Monsieur Ouine* and Faulkner's portrait of the Compson family, comprehension is defined in terms of feeling. The inescapable infirmities of the private vision are honestly acknowledged, but there is an effort toward community. The value of selfless commitment and the embracing, creating vision of love are asserted against the claims of logic, evidence, and appearances.

Such an art challenges the authority of the entire scientific tradition with its postulates of objectivity and distance. As Marshall McLuhan has pointed out, reading itself is firmly lodged within *that* tradition: the reading experience is solitary; the living human content has been transformed into letters, words, and phrases appearing on a page; we are taught (a glance at the methods used in literature courses or, as finished product, literary criticism itself, will bear this out) to read lucidly, knowledgeably, impassively. Faulkner's attempt is all the more remarkable, therefore, in *Absalom, Absalom!*, to overcome the logical categories of language and discourse, to go beyond the generic blindness that all of us experience with regard to the living thoughts of others. To the inevitable personal limitations of one consciousness trying to understand another, Faulkner adds the barriers of time and death. The Sutpen story is from another era, and Quentin and Shreve are trying to bring history to life. The traditional voice of the historian is the product of meticulous research and rational methods of deduction; the novelist who interprets the past usually tempers his respect for the facts with a controlled dosage of imagination. Faulkner's solution differs sharply from both.

The initial entry into the Sutpen saga is anything but clear. Rosa Coldfield grimly, indomitably, and elliptically forces upon Quentin the story of the man whose ghost she seeks to evoke. There is no background, no preparation for this "man-horse-demon" who abrupts out of quiet thunderclap, overseeing his "band of wild niggers" and harried French architect, violating the wilderness with his intentions, "creating the Sutpen's Hundred, the *Be Sutpen's Hundred* like the olden-time *Be Light*."[19] The Sutpen story emerges early in a skeletal, strangely lyrical form that announces the facts but conceals the motives:

It seems that this demon—his name was Sutpen—(Colonel Sutpen) —Colonel Sutpen. Who came out of nowhere and without warning upon the land with a band of strange niggers and built a plantation—(Tore violently a plantation, Miss Rosa Coldfield says)—tore violently. And married her sister Ellen and begot a son and a daughter which (without gentleness begot, Miss Rosa Coldfield says)—without gentleness. Which should have been the jewels of his pride and the shield and comfort of his old age, only—(only they destroyed him or something or he destroyed

[19] William Faulkner, *Absalom, Absalom!* (New York: Modern Library ed., 1951), p. 9. Subsequent quotations are from this edition.

them or something. And died)—and died. Without regret, Miss
Rosa Coldfield says—(Save by her) Yes, save by her. (And by
Quentin Compson) Yes. And by Quentin Compson. [p. 9]

The mythic, folk-tale dimension of Sutpen's life seems to
defy analysis, but as the refrain closes and we see the involvement of Rosa and Quentin, the effort to make human sense of
the monolithic past is begun. Rosa's story is impaired for lack
of essential facts: she does not know about Sutpen's childhood
or his first marriage; she is able to say and believe that Judith's
marriage was "forbidden without rhyme or reason or shadow
of excuse." However, the old lady has suffered a great deal at
the hands of critics not because her facts are wrong, but because her vision is jaundiced. Rosa is that sad specimen: the
unreliable narrator. Her vitriolic, outraged tale of demons and
ogres is simply not believed. Her own life is so entwined with
Sutpen's fate that we are warned to decode and decipher her
narrative before trusting it. One wonders what the concept of
reliability has to do with consciousness, isn't Iago *really* "hon
est Iago"—to Othello? Rosa Coldfield is, to some extent, what
Sutpen has made her; the wildest details of her Gothic account
are relevant to an understanding of either of them. Her rage,
like Benjy's anguish, becomes a medium through which the
story is told.

Faulkner does not disdain rage as a means of perceiving
truth. The balanced, urbane narrative of Mr. Compson, with
its telling emphasis on role-playing and inauthenticity, falls
short precisely because of his detachment, his irony. His attempt to account for the murder of Charles Bon on the basis
of the morganatic wedding, Henry's Mississippi, homespun
Puritanism in conflict with Charles's European, Catholic sen-
sualism, is subtle and elegant storytelling. But it is inadequate:

It's just incredible. It just does not explain. Or perhaps that's it:
they dont explain and we are not supposed to know. We have a
few old mouth-to-mouth tales; we exhume from old trunks and

boxes and drawers letters without salutation or signature, in which men and women who once lived and breathed are now merely initials or nicknames out of some now incomprehensible affection which sound to us like Sanskrit or Chocktaw; we see dimly people, the people in whose living blood and seed we ourselves lay dormant and waiting, in this shadowy attenuation of time possessing now heroic proportions, performing their acts of simple passion and simple violence, impervious to time and inexplicable—Yes, Judith, Bon, Henry, Sutpen: all of them. They are there, yet something is missing; they are like a chemical formula exhumed along with the letters from that forgotten chest, carefully, the paper old and faded and falling to pieces, the writing faded, almost indecipherable, yet meaningful, familiar in shape and sense, the name and presence of volatile and sentient forces; you bring them together in the proportions called for, but nothing happens; you reread, tedious and intent, poring, making sure that you have forgotten nothing, made no miscalculation; you bring them together again and again nothing happens: just the words, the symbols, the shapes themselves, shadowy inscrutable and serene, against that turgid background of a horrible and bloody mischancing of human affairs. [pp. 100–101]

The scientific, chemical nature of Mr. Compson's enterprise should not be overlooked: understanding the human truth behind the configurations of the past is more than a matter of aligning them together carefully.

The fifth chapter, entirely in italics and devoted to the thoughts and feelings of Rosa Coldfield, is both literally and figuratively the center of the novel. Rosa's story, told in the most turgid, yet rhapsodic prose Faulkner ever wrote, is an homage to pure sentience. It is the antipode of Mr. Compson's measured narrative, for it goes beyond an arrangement of facts, speaking of what "they cannot have told" Quentin, of the wholly imagined, invisible inner world that flaunts evidence and beggars reality, the "might-have-been which is more true than truth" (p. 143). Rosa, called by Shreve "the little dream woman," evokes the precious and extravagant dreams of her youth, the pitiful, unrecorded sense of magic and promise that was intimated but never fulfilled by reality: *"Once there was (they cannot have told you this either) a summer of wistaria. It was a pervading everywhere of wistaria (I was fourteen then) as though of all springs yet to capitulate condensed into one spring, one summer"* (pp. 143–144). The grim, embattled spinster, first introduced to the reader in her "eternal black" clothes and her tomblike, airless room, insists on the desire for life and love that she felt when she became a woman. The images of the seed, the hungry plant, the urge for light, are interwoven with the themes of love, sexual fulfillment, and the fairy-tale realm which is true, even if unrealized. In that vintage year, the *"sweet conjunction of root bloom and urge and hour and weather,"* the small, unfeminine child makes no claims for bloom or leaf, but does insist on root and urge, *"for had I not heired too from all the unsistered Eves since the Snake? Yes, urge I do: warped chrysalis of what blind perfect seed: for who shall say what gnarled forgotten root might not bloom yet with some globed concentrate more globed and concentrate and heady-perfect because the neglected root was planted warped and lay not dead but merely slept forgot?"* (p. 144). The poverty of her experience is offset by the grandeur of her imagination, as the fourteen-year-old girl celebrates passion, delivers her dense, heady dithyramb to the primacy of love: *"I who had learned nothing of love, not even parents' love—that fond dear constant violation of privacy, that stultification of the burgeoning and incorrigible I which is the meed and due of all mammalian meat, became not mistress, not beloved, but more than even love; I became all polymath love's androgynous advocate"* (p. 146). Rosa never even saw Charles Bon, but in the one unsuccessful visit he paid her, *"there must have been some seed he left, to cause a child's vacant fairy-tale to come alive in that garden"* (p. 146). Rosa's vision is of a *"world filled with living marriage,"* and out of that belief come her two magnificent, aborted creations: the love between Charles and Judith, and her own love for Sutpen. Again, the garden is there, as Rosa fancies herself Sutpen's light:

And then one afternoon (I was in the garden with a hoe, where the path came up from the stable lot) I looked up and saw him looking at me . . . looking at me with something curious and strange in his face as if the barn lot, the path at the instant when he came in sight of me had been a swamp out of which he had emerged without having been forewarned that he was about to enter light. [pp. 162–163]

"Love" is altogether too narrow and personal a term to apply to this reverence for attraction, this devotion to the forces of life:

I was that sun, who believed that he (after that evening in Judith's room) was not oblivious of me but only unconscious and receptive like the swamp-freed pilgrim feeling earth and tasting sun and light again and aware of neither but only of darkness' and morass' lack—who did believe there was that magic in unkin blood which we call by the pallid name of love that would be, might be sun for him. [p. 167]

The wizened caricature whom we met at the outset of the book, who goes to waste after being spurned by Sutpen, would be seen by the town, *"before sun-up gathering greens along garden fences, pulling them through the fence since she had no garden of her own, no seed to plant one with, no tools to work it with herself"* (p. 170).

Rosa, reliable or not, defines the hierarchy of values in the novel. Her posture in life—be it the earlier commitment to love or the later one to rage—asserts the primacy of the affective over the rational. The Western tradition of the vulnerable inferior flesh and the unique inviolate mind is sharply reversed:

Because there is something in the touch of flesh with flesh which abrogates, cuts sharp and straight across the devious intricate channels of decorous ordering, which enemies as well as lovers know because it makes them both—touch and touch of that which is the citadel of the central I-Am's private own: not spirit, soul; the liquorish and ungirdled mind is anyone's to take in any darkened hallway of this earthly tenement. But let flesh touch with flesh, and watch the fall of all the eggshell shibboleth of caste and color too. [p. 139]

The final scene in which Quentin accompanies Rosa to Sutpen's Hundred is a climax, sexually as well as narratively, to the story. We are told that Rosa "climbed into the buggy with a kind of clumsy and fumbling eagerness," and Quentin repeatedly hears her panting, trembling, whimpering, "not talking, not saying words, yet producing a steady whimpering, almost a moaning sound" (p. 366). Like Benjy's moaning and "trying to say," Rosa's whimpering is not only a desire for touch and consummation but also a language, a mode of expression and perception. Quentin and Shreve will learn her language of love.

In this light we can see that the final narrative thrust, the story jointly imagined by the two boys, is, in every sense, a labor of love. Faulkner does not minimize the obstacles between them: "Tell me about the South. What's it like there. What do they do there. Why do they live there. Why do they live at all" (p. 174). Shreve's sophomoric irony, his transformation of Mr. Compson's heroic tale into mock heroic (Rosa finding "instead of a widowed Agamemnon to her Cassandra an ancient stiff-jointed Pyramus to her eager though untried Thisbe" [p. 177]) must gradually yield to a sense of active and then inspired participation. The growing intimacy between the two boys, shown physically and even sexually as they prepare for bed, Shreve half naked with his "smooth Cupid-fleshed forearm," more fully revealed by the growing harmony in their dual narratives, their ability to understand each other *à demi-mot*, finally achieves mythic overtones of national unity and healing:

the two of them not moving except to breathe, both young, both born within the same year: the one in Alberta, the other in Mississippi; born half a continent apart yet joined, connected after a fashion in a sort of geographical transubstantiation by the Continental Trough, that River which runs not only through the physical land of which it is the geological umbilical, not only runs through the spiritual lives of the beings within its scope, but is very Environment itself which laughs at degrees of latitude and temperature. [p. 258]

The two youths effect a ritual of storytelling, and their intimacy, paralleling the frankly sexual attitude of Rosa to the story, adumbrates that "world of living marriage" that seemed to be only a childhood dream.

The story forged by Quentin and Shreve, unlike the demonic tale of Rosa or the classical one of Mr. Compson, focuses essentially on Bon and posits love in each essential, undefined relationship: love between Bon and Judith, Bon and Henry, and, above all, Bon and Sutpen. Their Bon, discovering to his amazement that he can still feel, desperately wants recognition, wants to touch his father. Quentin and Shreve do not merely speculate about such a need; they experience its urgency, and through their straining, creative reach into the past, achieve gratification: communion with the ghosts, liberation from their prisonlike "earthly tenement":

It did not matter to them (Quentin and Shreve) anyway, who could without moving, as free now of flesh as the father who decreed and forbade, the son who denied and repudiated, the lover who acquiesced, the beloved who was not bereaved, and with no tedious transition from hearth and garden to saddle, who could be already clattering over the frozen ruts of that December night and that Christmas dawn, that day of peace and cheer, of holly and goodwill and logs on the hearth; not two of them there and then either but four of them riding the two horses through the iron darkness, and that not mattering either: what faces and what names they called themselves and were called by so long as the blood coursed—the blood, the immortal brief recent intransient blood which could hold honor above slothy unregret and love above fat and easy shame. [p. 295]

The mythic, generic nature of the communion, the liberation from the limitations of time and personality, is emphasized by the mobility of the scene: the coursing blood and the affective continuum it represents, as well as the four boys on two horses. That core of feeling, always present in Faulkner's work, can be brought to illuminate the Sutpen story only after Quentin and Shreve have experienced it themselves:

"And now," Shreve said, "we're going to talk about love." But he didn't need to say that either, any more than he had needed to specify which he meant by he, since neither of them had been thinking about anything else; all that had gone before just so much that had to be overpassed and none else present to overpass it but them, as someone always has to rake the leaves up before you can have the bonfire. That was why it did not matter to either of them which one did the talking, since it was not the talking alone which did it, performed and accomplished the over-passing, but some happy marriage of speaking and hearing wherein each before the demand, the requirement, forgave con-doned and forgot the faulting of the other—faultings both in the creating of this shade whom they discussed (rather, existed in) and in the hearing and sifting and discarding the false and con-serving what seemed true, or fit the preconceived—in order to overpass to love, where there might be paradox and inconsistency, but nothing fault or false. [p. 316]

This is Faulkner's credo. Sufficiently the modernist and heir of the Jamesian tradition to acknowledge the collapse (at least aesthetically) of any viable omniscient, or even agreed-upon world view, Faulkner nonetheless moves beyond the frag-mented private view and its concomitant rule of arbitrariness. The kinds of truth and order posited by the scientific tradition may have little bearing in the realm of human values and human actions. There is no grid that can be imposed, no guaranteed Cartesian method for understanding or interpreting experience. The truth about people (the only truth of interest to literature) is often undefined, contingent on subjective complications. Since the world is (unfortunately) opaque, our reasoning and measuring powers are frequently better at describing than penetrating. Within the human maze that we inhabit, it may well be the unscientific integrity of feeling and keenness of response that best orient us. Human truths are better tested by the intensity of our needs than by the logic of our evidence: "What was it the old dame, the Aunt Rosa, told you about how there are some things that just have to be whether they are or not, have to be a damn sight more than some other things that maybe are and it dont matter a damn whether they are or not" (p. 322). Let us not confuse this inner, forged sense of truth with a casual reliance on "gut" feelings. There is necessity and urgency in Rosa's philosophy; love must be there first, if we are to achieve the insight and the overpass.

We have seen in the studies of *Monsieur Ouine* and *The Sound and the Fury* that the techniques of ellipsis, effects before causes, sensory immersion, make fluid and resonant the core of feeling that informs the story. In *Absalom* we see the extreme version of such an aesthetic. The delayed disclosures make us attend to "the story" (for example, live with Rosa's outrage) before acquiring an understanding of it. The widespread use of alternative suggestions,[20] of "not this . . . but

[20] Warren Beck's penetrating discussion of Faulkner's style (*Three Decades*, pp. 143–156) deals with this dimension of his writing. Beck points out the clothes left behind by Rosa Coldfield's eloping aunt in "kindness or haste or oversight." More telling and extravagant in its multiplicity is the description of Flem Snopes's nose in *The Hamlet*:

". . . a broad still face containing a tight seam of mouth stained slightly at the corners with tobacco, and eyes the color of stag-

that" clauses, forces the reader to ponder the "might-have-beens," to play with, in his own mind, the potential and tangential stories that the Sutpen saga contains. More grandly, there are three full-blown versions of Sutpen's life and motives, each filled with false leads. All the false leads, the little ones and the big ones, "count"; words remain on pages and in readers' minds. Erroneous interpretations, in fiction as in life, are real; they may be discredited, but they cannot be erased. The style itself is a protest against verbal enclosure, an attempt to extend the confines of the fictional statement. Not only those long, unending sentences with their hosts of present participles, but also the circling, weaving account of specific events is designed to keep them reverberating. The crucial episode concerning Sutpen's childhood "innocence" illustrates the technique. The child's curiosity about the big house, the rifle parallel, the innocence are described at length. Then the boy, unaware of "status," goes to the door of the stately mansion. But when he actually reaches the door, we read, "he told Grandfather how, before the monkey nigger who came to the door *had finished saying what he said* [my italics], he seemed to dissolve and a part of him turn and rush back through the two years they had lived there" (pp. 229–230). We do not learn what the boy heard, for thereupon Faulkner *seems* to drop the thread, gives us two pages of flashbacks, focusing on the boy's retrospective awareness of his condition as white trash, his father's unquestioning resentment of the blacks (expressed through the extraordinary toy balloon-laughing face

nant water, and projecting from among the other features in startling and sudden paradox, a tiny predatory nose like the beak of a small hawk. It was as though the original nose had been left off by the original designer or craftsman and the unfinished job taken over someone of a radically different school or perhaps by some viciously maniacal humorist or perhaps by one who had only time to clap into the center of the face a frantic and desperate warning" (quoted by Beck, pp. 151–152).

metaphor). Then on page 232 the boy before the door reappears and Faulkner casually, almost backhandedly writes "and he never even remembered what the nigger said, how it was the nigger told him, even before he had had time to say what he came for, never to come back to that front door again but to go around to the back." Those words (themselves holding back their meaning until the very end) are deft and stinging, but their real weight derives from the amount of experience and feeling Faulkner has crammed in between the first mention of the door and the final statement. In like manner we have a letter of Mr. Compson split over half the book, a statement by Wash Jones divided by a chapter.

The most moving example of delayed disclosure is the meeting between Quentin and the ghostlike Henry Sutpen. As Quentin sees Rosa descend the stairs like a sleepwalker, he says to himself, " 'I should go with her' and then, 'But I must see too now. I will have to. Maybe I shall be sorry tomorrow, but I must see.' So when he came back down the stairs . . ." (pp. 370–371); and the meeting is "by-passed." We read of Quentin going to the carriage, taking Rosa home, and trying to sleep. And then—the "wasted yellow face" and the words break through:

And you are—?
Henry Sutpen.
And you have been here—?
Four years.
And you came home—?
To die. Yes.
To die?
Yes. To die.
And you have been here—?
Four years.
And you are—?
Henry Sutpen. [p. 373]

Hyatt Waggoner has written pertinently about the language of this scene:

Everything before this has been hearsay, rumor, conjecture, hypothesis, or, at best, based on accounts of matters of fact. Here we are in the presence of something that we know "really happened," the terrible culmination of the Sutpen story. We are in position to understand and to respond emotionally and imaginatively. Quentin does not need to theorize, or even to create an atmosphere. The bare, elliptical, subjective record, the fragmentary memory of what happened that night is enough. Without what has preceded the record would be meaningless.[21]

We have something quite similar to Dilsey's "I seed de beginnin and now I sees de endin"; these moments have been prepared by the techniques of immersion, and Faulkner will not overly verbalize them. It should also be emphasized that this key scene does not need to be recounted in the past, as memory: it takes place after, and is the indirect subject of, the opening scene between Quentin and Rosa. Yet, Faulkner has purposely delayed its "telling"; he has held it off until the very end, so that the human tragedy contained in those few lines might be as real on paper as it was in his imagination.

The affective technique elicits a response from the reader, forcing him to attend to material before interpreting it, to identify—as Quentin and Shreve must—with the story. Such a way of writing reveals the author's reliance on feeling as knowledge and his distrust of discursive prose to convey those feelings. There is no seam between presentation and substance because selfless love affords Quentin and Shreve both an entry into the Sutpen story and the knowledge of its tragic defect. Wholly at one with the dead youths, Quentin and Shreve imagine the full, melodramatic past of Bon, "where there might be paradox and inconsistency but nothing fault or

[21] Waggoner, *Faulkner*, p. 162.

false." In attributing to Bon a need for love, they illuminate Sutpen's tragic blindness. Sutpen's refusal to acknowledge his son, his efforts to discourage Bon by sending "a message like you send a command by a nigger servant to a beggar or a tramp to clear out" repeat all too clearly the pattern of his own determining childhood injury. Sutpen's grand design is born of his hurt, and its success—shown graphically in the cold abstractions used to describe it[22]—depends on ignoring the invisible, unpredictable inner integrity of people: "that innocence which believed that the ingredients of morality were like the ingredients of pie or cake and once you had measured them and balanced them and mixed them and put them into the oven it was all finished and nothing but pie or cake could come out" (p. 263). Such a method—calling to mind Mr. Compson's chemical formulas—cannot cope with the secrets of human behavior.

All of the closed doors in *Absalom, Absalom!*, ranging from Rosa's childhood ventures "from one closed forbidden door to the next" (p. 145) to Clytie's warding her off, "standing calmly in a gingham dress before a closed door which she would not allow me to enter" (p. 149), to Quentin's obsessive sense that "there was also something which he too could not pass" (p. 172), to the fundamental experience of exclusion that marked Sutpen and Charles Bon: "telling Grandfather that the boy-symbol at the door wasn't it because the boy-symbol was just the figment of the amazed and desperate child; that now he would take that boy in where he would never again need to stand on the outside of a white door and knock at it" (p. 261), these doors are the enclosures of blindness, the structures in which we live, walled off from life and others. They are also the doors of codes, of evidence, of fear.

[22] Sutpen explains his dilemma in the following way to Grandfather Compson: "I found that she was not and could never be, through no fault of her own, adjunctive or incremental to the design which I had in mind, so I provided for her and put her aside" (p. 240).

They are visible. Only the overpass to love can go beyond them.

Absalom, Absalom! is about the effort to open up the closed past, closed doors, and closed minds. Such enclosure is, unfortunately, the natural condition of the finite, circumscribed human being who is himself and no one else. Proust once said that the value of literature was in its magic ability to convey to us the experiences of other minds, experiences that are accessible to us only through art. Yet, the act of writing about the feelings of another is immensely questionable. How does the writer *know?* It is a question whose moral dimensions plagued James and Bernanos. Faulkner's art, with its interior monologues and flashbacks, seems to revel in the inner knowledge of others. But *Absalom, Absalom!* dramatizes the awesome cost of such knowledge by asserting that the Past, the world of Others, can come alive for us, yield its secrets to us, only by an act of love. In the final, imagined scene between Henry and Charles, the scene where the miscegenation charge is finally brought forth, we see the fruits of Quentin's and Shreve's collective labor. It is true that the close of the novel, like the close of the Compson story, is one of discord and despair,[23] but the vision of the past, a vision rich in knowledge

---

[23] The most powerful case for discord in Faulkner has been made by Slatoff. He argues that Faulkner, through his particular stylistic and formal devices such as oxymoron, false alternatives, and imagery of tension, creates a great many unresolved tensions, is engaged in what Slatoff calls a quest for failure. Needless to say, *Absalom* is a virtual test case for such lack of resolution. After quoting both Shreve's cruel taunt concerning the future Jim Bonds to come and Quentin's closing cry ("'I dont hate it,' Quentin said, quickly, at once, immediately; 'I dont hate it,' he said. *I dont hate it* he thought, panting in the cold air, the iron New England dark; *I dont! I dont! I dont hate it! I dont hate it!*" [p. 378]), Slatoff makes the following commentary:

> "It is difficult to conceive of an 'ending' which would provide less ordering and resolution. For not only is there no resolution

for the present, has—even if ephemerally—been born. Let us conclude this chapter by quoting merely the "birth" of that scene, the modest but miraculous passage from a Harvard dormitory to bivouac fires in Carolina; here the seam between present and past, regular print and italics, is so right and—after the labor—effortless, that the fundamental fiction of literature, its claim to tell us about Others, is overpassed:

Shreve ceased again. It was just as well, since he had no listener. Perhaps he was aware of it. Then he had no talker either, though possibly he was not aware of this. Because now neither of them were there. They were both in Carolina and the time was forty-six years ago, and it was not even four now but compounded still further, since now both of them were Henry Sutpen and both of them were Bon, compounded each of both yet either neither, smelling the very smoke which had blown and faded away forty-six years ago from the *bivouac fires burning in a pure grove, the gaunt and ragged men sitting or lying about them, talking not about the war yet all curiously enough (or perhaps not*

on a cognitive level, but we are also confronted with the differing tones of the four 'commentaries,' and the terrible ambivalence of Quentin's final outburst. We 'end,' then, with a psychological oxymoron of simultaneous love and hate, with internal conflict and self-contradiction. It is an intense and powerful ending, and a proper one to seal off and preserve the complex suspension of elements the book has presented. But it is also a pitiful ending. It is pitiful in that Shreve and Quentin seem to have been so little instructed by their immense labor of imagination. It is pitiful (and among many other things, perhaps, Faulkner is saying this too) in its varied assertions that so much energy, effort, and pain have come to so little: to a lone idiot, an ironic letter, a brutally flippant commentary and act of cruelty to a roommate, and a bewildered cry of pain. It is, above all, pitiful because by it, Faulkner again demonstrates his unwillingness to step beyond the sanctuary of the paradox, to make himself, as do a number of his characters, the clarifying 'gesture,' which might enable him and us to move beyond that bewildered cry of pain" (*Three Decades*, pp. 191–192).

curiously at all) facing the South where further on in the darkness pickets stood. [p. 351]

The vision has been opened, and its darkness may be our light. It may be hoped that the affective identification necessary for such insight could generate a recognition of humanity making the presence of those men sitting at the bivouac fires unnecessary, a senseless, blind mistake, senseless because blind. In a time of structured, parliamentary-run committees to study violence, to end wars, to save the children, where the extent of our feeling is measured by the numbers on a check, Faulkner's appeal to our senses and our empathy may indeed, like the Greek catharsis, prove to be valid ethically as well as aesthetically.

4 | Eclipse: Kafka, Joyce, and Michel Butor

In the works studied in the earlier chapters, the theme of blindness and the narrative forms needed to convey that blindness have been emphasized. Yet, the framework of those novels was still essentially individualistic, in that the focus was upon the rightness or wrongness of a particular vision, but not really upon the observed world itself. However much Balzac thought himself the historian-zoologist of Parisian life, one senses, even within the broad panorama of those Parisian scenes, the economy and discipline of a plot that is fitted to the needs and fate of Rastignac himself. A comparable connivance between character and event is operative in *Great Expectations*. In each case, of course, the protagonist must learn to see right, to grasp the fundamental laws at work behind the appearances. Yet, the two novels are tailor-made for the two characters, and the mystery of the scene is ultimately absorbed into the knowledge of the protagonist.

As we have seen, the mysteries are considerably less resolved in James, Conrad, and Ford. But even where insights are wholly lacking and ambiguities rule the scene, the story is still that of an individual's quandary or of the difficulty in perceiving the pattern or meaning of any single person's life. In Bernanos and Faulkner the vision is deepened so that it may be broadened. Their works hallow the inchoate experience of the individual, but emphasize transcendence, that "overpass to love" which would redeem the private picture and place it in a larger communal framework. The compelling and arduous narrative forms chosen by Bernanos and Faulkner, forcing a sensory-emotive apprehension of the stories and mirroring in terms of technique the distrust of reason and logic that the novels deal with thematically, give ample evidence that the way to community is through feeling, not design. *Absalom, Absalom!* stands at the extreme limit of such an aesthetic, with its combined allegiance to the fragmented private picture and faith in the integrity of feeling as a kind of knowledge in a world of enclosed consciousness.

But the visceral art of Bernanos and Faulkner is, despite its nostalgia for community, as individualist in its conception as the work of the writers discussed earlier. That process of absorption by which we suck in the outside world, mold it into our reality, is still essential in their works. The human center of gravity has not been displaced; the centrality of the characters' needs within the framework of the fictional world has not been challenged. In that sense their work may be distinguished from the modernist ventures in formal design or nonanthropocentric descriptions that will be dealt with in the last chapter; those writers—Borges, Claude Simon, Robbe-Grillet—are like one another and different from Bernanos and Faulkner precisely in their implicit assumption that literature is no longer largely defined by its individualist charge, its allegiance to human pattern and consciousness. The growing split between the (human) subject matter and the medium of the novel, still yoked together by the writers studied thus far, becomes no longer bridgeable. How do such developments come to pass, and where do they happen?

Ortega's account of the dehumanization of art is helpful in this respect.[1] The changes emphasized by Ortega—formal experimentation for its own sake, the death of illusion, the ero-

[1] José Ortega y Gasset, *The Dehumanization of Art* (Garden City, N.Y.: Doubleday Anchor Book, 1956).

sion caused by irony, the appeal to a purely aesthetic response —are discernible enough, but my focus is conversely on the increased burden of empathy and insight that such an art places on the reader. My contention is that narrative experimentation follows the strained course of vision in a world that is increasingly opaque and alien. The modern age cannot easily countenance an art form that grants primacy and authority to the individual; too much has happened, in terms of science, industrialization, wars, adherence to monolithic systems. On the other hand, the writer's medium—language—has been virtually rediscovered as an entity of its own, possessing its own laws and its own genius, frequently harnessed into humanistic service, but intrinsically loyal only to itself.

The final chapter takes up the issue of how one writes and reads fiction that is liberated from the charge of vision, but at issue in this chapter are the last antics of the individual on stage. There is obviously no strict or chronological development from Balzac's reliable depth to Faulkner's overpass and then to Robbe-Grillet's geometry. Beliefs do not die uniformly, or according to any schedule. But the impulse toward knowledge and education, at the core of the works reviewed in the first three chapters, is either not dominant or not successful in most of the major contemporary novelists. Therefore, my focus is no longer on mere personal blindness, but on the inadequacy of the individual as an integer, as a unit of consciousness or means of rendering the world. In the works of two of the most seminal writers of our age, Kafka and Joyce, we can best measure how the workings of the individual and his vision—intense and subtle as that may be—are eclipsed. The two are different. Kafka's heroes are enmeshed in a vast labyrinth of doors, corridors, offices, protocol, and unattainable, incomprehensible authorities. Joyce's Bloom is the everyday man afloat in the astounding linguistic, literary, mythological, historical, religious continuum of his life-in-Dublin. Without undue exaggeration, we may say that the

literature of alienation springs from Kafka, and the encyclopedic aesthetic of pure design begins with Joyce; yet each has
in common the plight of the individual consciousness grap-
pling with a world that dwarfs it. It is their sense of imbalance,
the cleft between the myopic human concerns and the richly
diverse fictional world, that alter the course of vision in the
modern novel.

Perhaps the most extraordinary characteristic of Kafka's
fiction is his characters' calm and unquestioning acceptance of
the grotesque. A man, arrested one morning by an authority
he knows nothing of for a crime he knows nothing about,
gradually loses himself in the labyrinthine working of the
Court and the Law. Another man arrives at a village and demands contact with the Castle; finally failing even as school
janitor, he will become increasingly lost in a mazelike network
of authorities. The complex system of relationships and priorities between individual and the Law, village and the Castle,
becomes a marsh in which he sinks further and further. One
accepts. However, among the things to be accepted are phenomena more bizarre than arrests or communication failures.
In *The Castle*, K. frequently encounters surprises like the following: "K. was awakened during the night by some noise or
other, and in his first vague sleepy state felt for Frieda; he
found that, instead of Frieda, one of the assistants was lying
beside him."[2] The clear exposition reminds us even in the
wording of the unforgettably understated beginning of "The
Metamorphosis": "As Gregor Samsa awoke one morning from
uneasy dreams he found himself transformed in his bed into a
gigantic insect."[3] Kafka's protagonists are almost systemati-

[2] Franz Kafka, *The Castle*, tr. Willa and Edwin Muir (New York:
Knopf, 1959), p. 166. Subsequent quotations are from this edition.
[3] "The Metamorphosis," tr. Willa and Edwin Muir in *Franz Kafka:
The Complete Stories*, ed. Nahum N. Glatzer (New York: Schocken
Books, 1971), p. 89. The English translations, however, do not retain

cally victimized by monstrous transformations, when not in their own bodies, then in the circumstances surrounding them. The country doctor examines the sick child and is reassured by what he sees: "the boy was quite sound, something a little wrong with his circulation, saturated with coffee by his solicitous mother, but sound and best turned out of bed with one shove."[4] A moment later, however, ready to take his leave, the doctor discovers that the situation has changed:

> This time I discovered that the boy was indeed ill. In his right side, near the hip, was an open wound as big as the palm of my hand, rose-red, in many variations of shade, dark in the hollows, lighter at the edges, softly granulated, with irregular clots of blood, open as a surface mine to the daylight. That was how it looked from a distance. But on a closer inspection there was another complication. I could not help a low whistle of surprise. Worms, as thick and as long as my little finger, themselves rose-red and blood-spotted as well, were wriggling from their fastness in the interior of the wound toward the light, with small white heads and many little legs. [p. 223]

Metamorphosis is an activity that characterizes the scene of much of Kafka's fiction. Virtually by definition, the setting in

---

the syntactical parallels—a syntax devised to render shock—in the two German passages:

> "Als K. in der Nacht durch irgendein Geräusch erwachte und in der ersten unsicheren Schlafbewegung nach Frieda tastete, merkte er, dass statt Friedas ein Gehilfe neben ihm lag" (*Das Schloss*, Frankfurt: Fischer Bücherei, 1968, p. 110).
> "Als Gregor Samsa eines Morgens aus unruhigen Träumen erwachte, fand er sich in seinem Bett zu einem ungeheuren Ungeziefer verwandelt" ("Die Verwandlung," *Das Urteil und andere Erzählungen* [Frankfurt: Fischer Bücherei, 1952], p. 23).

Subsequent quotations from the *Stories* are from the Glatzer edition.

[4] "A Country Doctor," tr. Willa and Edwin Muir, *The Complete Stories*, p. 222.

which the hero finds himself is unstable in human terms though doubtless in accord with other suspected, never identified or understood, awesome principles. Much has been written about the cause of the grotesque in Kafka, *why* Joseph K. is arrested or Gregor Samsa transformed into a bug. Rather than speculate about the possible rationale behind the work, let us examine its visible rhythms and patterns.

First we note that quite simply everything, for the Kafka protagonist, has become problematic. The slightest events, the most minimal assertions are plagued with ambiguities and difficulties. If one is a bug without teeth, how does one unlock and open a door? If one is a fifteen-year-old foreigner in a New York country house without electricity, at night, how does one find one's way? If one wishes to act decisively and effectively against an enigmatic arrest, how does one find the courtroom? If one is finally in the presence of an Official ready, even eager to cut through the bureaucratic channels and take up one's cause, how does one stay awake? The Kafka hero is generically unable to cope with these situations because any situation, studied with adequate scrutiny, is a labyrinth. Kafka has the imagination of a simpler organism observing the habits of more complex ones. His is an anatomical appreciation of behavior, wherein the simplest gestures, such as tying a shoelace or buttoning a shirt, take on terrifying proportions in their complicated array of cooperating nerve impulses and bone structures. Consider the plight of the man from the country who wants to know the Law. The situation becomes nightmarish as we observe the geometric progression of difficulties:

"If you are so strongly tempted, try to get in without my permission. But note that I am powerful. And I am only the lowest doorkeeper. From hall to hall, keepers stand at every door, one more powerful than the other. And the sight of the third man is already more than even I can stand." These are difficulties which the man from the country has not expected to meet, the Law, he thinks, should be accessible to every man and at all times.[5]

We see him waste his life, trying in vain to gain entrance, learning upon death that this entry to the Law was destined for him alone. The sense of paralysis, of insuperable difficulties between oneself and the simplest, most essential goals, is heightened by the extraordinary blend of casuistry and desperate logic as K. and the priest alternately try to interpret the parable. Like Kafka's work in general, the interpretations are infinite, but one is struck by the inevitable recourse to logical argument and its inexhaustible supply of intelligent, futile meanings.

Here we approach the central impulse in Kafka's work: the stubborn, heroic-insane use of logic in situations where it can be of no avail. Gregor Samsa does not waste one word bewailing his metaphysical condition as bug; he devises innumerable plans, however, with almost joyous energy, to get his many-legged body off the bed so that he can catch the train in time to get to work. The reasoning process in Kafka reminds one of that dark vein in James, where the most brilliant interpretations are rife with their own futility. Yet, one feels that even the narrator of *The Sacred Fount* is closer to some kind of truth, creates at least a version of events that is as plausible as anything else. The Jamesian propensity for refined speculation is somehow proper; in Kafka the indefatigable logical forays are hopelessly beside the point, do not begin to solve or even face the problems confronted by the protagonist. James's work is, despite the ambiguities, a tribute to intelligence and perception. Kafka—like his literary descendants, Beckett and Robbe-Grillet—presides over the declining status of reason. The Renaissance ideal and the Cartesian dream of man asserting his authority over the world through his reason-

[5] *The Trial*, tr. Willa and Edwin Muir (New York: Vintage Books, 1969), pp. 267–268. Subsequent quotations are from this edition.

ing powers have become a mockery in Kafka's endless dialectical debates about the intricacies of court procedure or the devious ways of reaching Klamm. The genius for argument that each Kafka character possesses serves merely to confuse issues still further, to put up a smokescreen of rational obfuscation before the immense, stark facts of existence. Orientation is impossible. Not only is Karl Rossmann lost in America or K. bewildered by the complexities of the chancery, but interpretation of events produces no inroads. The dazzling stories of the Barnabas shame or Pepi's brief moment of glory as waitress in *The Castle* are—like the parable of the man before the Law—perfectly inscrutable. Stories and actions have no handles; the seemingly well child suddenly has a worm-filled gash in him; the seeming majesty of Barnabas becomes threadbare and vulgar once he removes his coat; the weak, aged father in "The Judgment" is suddenly quite able to defy and destroy his son; the family of Gregor Samsa is metamorphosed into a strong, independent, heartless working unit through the sufferings of their son.

In this constant process of transformation and monstrous surprises, the Kafka hero resolutely keeps his head to the ground and argues. And one can almost see him sink further into the quagmire as the hypotheses and stratagems mount up. Gregor Samsa, issuing frantic, guttural reassurances through the door that all is well, that he can still make the next train, then anxiously pondering how to go about getting the door open, is Kafka's *homo sapiens*. This utter, and utterly unsuccessful, dependence on rational analysis and methodological approach is inextricably linked to another major concern in his work: the concept of Business. Crudely put, logical argument and rational programming are the tools, one might say the religion, of the modern business ethic. The malady in Kafka is spiritual, and the healing resources are merely clinical. The country doctor states the dilemma that informs most of Kafka's work: "Always expecting the impossible from the doctor. They have lost their ancient beliefs; the parson sits at home and unravels his vestments, one after another; but the doctor is supposed to be omnipotent with his merciful surgeon's hands" (p. 224). This conflict of values reminds one of the dialectic in Bernanos, but whereas *Monsieur Ouine* is told from the affective, spiritual point of view, Kafka relentlessly narrates from the myopic, rational perspective.

The setting in Kafka is well known for its mechanized bureaucratic structures which do not acknowledge the human element. The realistic description of the Uncle's business and the automatonlike functions of the hotel porters in *Amerika* reveal the same dehumanization that Joseph K. discovers in the court procedures and K. in the Castle's relations with the village. The classic expression of the loss of humanity incurred in such a mechanistic scheme is to be found in the remark of the man thrashing Joseph K.'s guards: "I am hired to whip people, and whip them I shall" (p. 107).[6] If at first Kafka's description of Judgment and Grace in the form of Austrian bureaucracy seems outlandish, we must notice that the attitude of the characters thrown into that maze is consistently bureaucratic as well. The world depicted in Kafka's fiction may be filled with metaphysical horrors, but one would never know it from the thoughts and words of the characters. The major quality we associate (wrongly) with his work, *Angst*, is never felt or acknowledged within the work. The emotive human response to Kafka's disorders is given no place in the scheme of things; there is remarkably little weeping or laughing, little love and still less hate.

It is the emotional sterility of Kafka's characters, the human cost for the unswerving, myopic intellectual energy, that provides a clue to the mysterious configuration of his work. Let us consider Joseph K. He is, at the moment of his arrest,

6 This is my translation. Muir renders "Ich bin zum Prügeln angestellt," as "I am here to whip people," and I feel that he does not capture the bureaucratic function implicit in "angestellt."

strong, energetic, secure in his business position, confirmed in
his innocence—so unlike what we know of Kafka.[7] As we
read, we begin to measure the cost of Joseph K.'s success: his
overbearing treatment of others, his ignorance and indifference about the lives of those around him (Miss Bürstner, for
example), his mistrust of emotion (his embarrassment over the
lawyer's pledge of friendship). The scene where Leni examines the picture of Joseph K.'s mistress, makes numerous
comparisons, and finally surprises K. with the question: "But
would she be capable of sacrificing herself for you?" elicits
a telling response: " 'No,' said K. 'She is neither soft nor kind,
nor would she be capable of sacrificing herself for me. And
up till now I have demanded neither the one thing nor the
other from her. In fact I've never even examined this photograph as carefully as you have.' " Leni's reaction tells us more
about K. than he himself knows: " 'So she doesn't mean so
very much to you,' said Leni. 'She isn't your sweetheart after
all' " (pp. 136–137) The same mixture of business success and
human failure is evident in K.'s inclination to regard his trial
as another business venture, a matter of shrewdness and strategy, not of guilt and commitment:

Yet there was no need for exaggerated anxiety at the moment.
In a relatively short time he had managed to work himself up to
his present high position in the Bank and to maintain himself in
that position and win recognition from everybody; surely if the
abilities which had made this possible were to be applied to the
unraveling of his own case, there was no doubt that it would go
well. Above all, if he were to achieve anything, it was essential
that he should banish from his mind once and for all the idea of
possible guilt. There was no such guilt. This legal action was
nothing more than a business deal. [pp. 158–159]

The abyss between the spiritual and the material is again
illuminated in the words of the priest in the Cathedral:

[7] See, especially, "Brief an den Vater," *Das Kafka-Buch*, ed. Heinz
Politzer (Frankfurt: Fischer Bücherei, 1965), pp. 13–51.

"I am the prison chaplain." "Indeed," said K. "I had you summoned here," said the priest, "to have a talk with you." "I didn't know that," said K. "I came here to show an Italian around the Cathedral." "That is beside the point," said the priest. "What is that in your hand? Is it a prayer book?" "No," replied K., "it is an album of sights worth seeing in the town." [pp. 263–264]

K.'s fatal inability to perceive the ethical dimension of his dilemma, of his life, may be described as the business syndrome. It is ubiquitous in Kafka's work and helps to account for the configuration of the bureaucratic labyrinth itself. In this light, the scene between the exhausted K. and the Officer Bürgel in *The Castle* takes on its full significance. Bürgel, awakened by mistake by K. in the middle of the night, points to the Achilles heel of the whole bureaucratic framework: the Officer, caught by surprise, touched, can drop his official inhuman role and intercede:

The never beheld, always expected applicant, truly thirstingly expected and always reasonably regarded as out of reach—there this applicant sits. By his mute presence, if by nothing else, he constitutes an invitation to penetrate into his poor life, to look around there as in one's own property and there to suffer with him under the weight of his futile demands. This invitation in the silent night is beguiling. One gives way to it, and now one has actually ceased to function in one's official capacity. It is a situation in which it very soon becomes impossible to refuse to do a favor. To put it precisely, one is desperate; to put it still more precisely, one is very happy. Desperate, for the defenseless position in which one sits here waiting for the applicant to utter his plea and knowing that once it is uttered one must grant it, even if, at least in so far as one has oneself a general view of the situation, it positively tears the official organization to shreds. [p. 348]

Bürgel's declaration is of immense importance, for it establishes—even if ironically and hedgingly—the primacy of personal relations and human needs over the seemingly invisible Organization. K. could, if he were awake and made his re-

quest, free himself from the maze. But K., ordinarily so assidu-
ous and even brutal in pursuing his claim, has yielded to sleep
and, awakened, leaves Bürgel with a "sense of the utter use-
lessness of staying any longer in this room." What Bürgel has
offered K. is nothing less than Kafka's peculiar version of an
overpass to love, and K. cannot grasp it, because he, somewhat
like Sutpen, has ever regarded other people as pawns in his
design, means to accede to the Castle. Admittedly less imperious than his counterpart in *The Trial*, K. nonetheless, as
Frieda points out, exploits others and, above all, proceeds by
reason alone through his existential labyrinth. It is true that he
defends Frieda and asserts the importance of the individual,
but his actual relationships are ungraced by feelings of joy or
sorrow. To have Frieda or to lose her is merely part of the
larger dialectic of storming the Castle. The fundamental reason for his presence, for his need to be recognized, remains obscure and, one is tempted to say, beyond the reach of K. himself. He is the typical Kafka protagonist, bent on rectifying a
situation through reason and force, whereas the dilemma, to
some extent, originates from the abuse of reason and force.

Bürgel's proffered grace is met by sleep not merely because
K. does not merit redemption, but also quite simply because
the body has needs and logic of its own that are quite different
from the running commentary and argumentation furnished
by the characters themselves. Fatigue, such as K.'s in the presence of Bürgel or Joseph K.'s in the chancery, is one of the
signs that man does not live by reason alone. Bodies are interesting in Kafka, for the breakdown of the rational system
occurs through them. In *Monsieur Ouine*, Bernanos wrote
that the forces of the spirit, if denied for too long, will issue
forth in the flesh in monstrous forms. Kafka had already
dramatized such a vision literally in the case of Gregor Samsa;
with Joseph K. and K. the body is not transformed, but it
betrays and sabotages their carefully wrought plans. If we
look at the activity of Kafka's protagonists, we see them

mocked by themselves as well as by circumstances, forever sidetracked and wasting their energies. Love, even more than fatigue, epitomizes the inadequacy of the rational program. Joseph K.'s sudden desire for Miss Bürstner and his highly inappropriate lovemaking with Leni are depicted as both irresistible and irrelevant, even harmful, to his design. K.'s frenzied lovemaking with Frieda has positively no place in his scheme of things, but he is nonetheless overwhelmed by its urgency. In such ways Kafka reveals the terrible discrepancy between the hero's visceral necessities and the stubborn, radically insufficient use of logic he brings to bear on events. The gulf between the protagonist's narrow vision and the immense, unilluminated stage he occupies, accounts for the unresolved tensions and the residual, haunting opaqueness of Kafka's novels. In these novels emerge, definitively and prophetically, the imagery of labyrinths and the thematics of orientation. The characters enact a drama that dwarfs their reasoning, and beneath the steady, unemotional, unceasing flow of argumentation is the feeling, never articulated, that they are eclipsed. Thus we have the great hunger in Kafka, the hunger of K. and Frieda:

She was seeking and he was seeking, they raged and contorted their faces and bored their heads into each other's bosom in the urgency of seeking something, and their embraces and their tossing limbs did not avail to make them forget, but only reminded them of what they sought; like dogs desperately tearing up the ground, they tore at each other's body, and often, helplessly baffled, in a final effort to attain happiness they nuzzled and tongued each other's face. [p. 60]

It is the hunger for something beyond the reach of logic or even flesh that Gregor Samsa feels as he starves to death, that Kafka has given permanent form to in the parable of the Hunger Artist who fasted solely because he never found the food he might have liked.

Kafka's art, because it is relentlessly and futilely logical, because it is sparse and incomplete, embodies this hunger. It depicts a quest for nourishment, for which the bureaucratic framework and the tools of reason are a foil. Knowledge in Kafka is as close to pain as clarity, and the interminable verbal discussions must yield to a kind of visceral illumination, a kind of *Verklärung* like that of the tortured prisoners in the penal colony who have *bodily* experienced Grace, "*auf dem Leib erfahren.*"

On the face of it, the Wandering Jew of Dublin has only the remotest affinities with Kafka's quest heroes. Many of the threads that are interwoven in this study—affective response, mystery, even vision—are not noticeably present in the work of Joyce. But no account of the individual in relation to the setting can afford to leave him out. The development so easily discernible in his work epitomizes the course of modern literature. From one point of view the distance from *Dubliners* to *Finnegans Wake* can be assessed in terms of naturalism and symbolism; but, for our purposes, the transition can best be described as the gradual emergence of a form principle, a way of looking at and organizing reality as well as a strategy for writing books. This form principle leads to eclipse.

The individual is submerged in Joyce. As the snow falls at the close of "The Dead," Gabriel Conroy is overwhelmed by mutuality, by unknown kinships and claims that mock the small, ordered picture he took to be his life. The snow falls on all of Ireland, on Michael Furey's grave, reminding Gabriel that he is an unwitting part of a larger drama, a dumb spectator to the passion of Greta and of Ireland itself, a mere player among the uncounted living and dead. The snow binds without distinction, but the solidarity it reveals is achieved through the extinction of the individual; his private cogency is gone, and his single vision is not long to be the center of gravity in Joyce's work. Even the *Portrait*, Joyce's most compact work dealing exclusively with the development of a single, autobiographical character, is marked by its accretive rhythm, its movement from simplicity to complexity so well expressed by Stephen's inscription on the flyleaf of his geography book:

Stephen Dedalus
Class of Elements
Clongowes Wood College
Sallins
County Kildare
Ireland
Europe
The World
The Universe[8]

Following Stephen's definitions of lyrical, epical, and dramatic forms, we are obliged to acknowledge that the *Portrait* is, of necessity, still allied to the lyrical, the personal expression. Yet there is little effort to give a rounded picture of Stephen's life; rather the novel depicts a progressive loosening of ties, a growing sense of liberation and alienation from the bonds that ordinarily betoken identity.

In *Finnegans Wake* the individual has wholly dissolved into the race. Richard Ellmann has stressed the dream dimension of the *Wake* in terms that recall the falling snow in "The Dead": "Sleep is the great democratizer: in their dreams people become one, and everything about them becomes one. Nationalities lose their borders, levels of discourse and society are no longer separable, time and space surrender their demarcations. All human activities begin to fuse into all other human activities, printing a book into bearing a baby, fighting a war into courting a woman."[9]

[8] James Joyce, *A Portrait of the Artist as a Young Man* (New York: Viking Press, 1956), p. 16.

[9] Richard Ellmann, *James Joyce* (New York: Oxford University Press paperback, 1965), p. 729.

The sameness of things obliterates the individual contours and threatens their specific meanings. In his mature work, Joyce seems more interested in discovering and forging new relations than in rendering already known phenomena. It has been said that all of his writings are supremely autobiographical, but never have the events and details of a life been so converted into the *materials* of literature, the necessary names and faces and places with which to create a world. Even the countless hatchet jobs in *Ulysses* (Gogarty as Mulligan, Sir Horace Rumbold as the hangman) have their own dramatic integrity and do not need to be "explained" by tracking down the allusions. Stephen's pronouncement (in the *Portrait*) that "the dramatic form is reached when the vitality which has flowed and eddied round each person fills every person with such vital force that he or she assumes a proper and intangible esthetic life" is essentially valid for all the works; the statement predicts the autonomy of detail and the forbidding, impenetrable integrity of specific characters in *Ulysses*. For, in the last analysis, Joyce's world is both excruciatingly private (necessitating, ideally, a specialized knowledge of his own life and the topography of Dublin) and, paradoxically, entirely surface. The facts that he culls from his own life are never keys to meaning, but rather the elements of a mosaic. This is not to say that Joyce's interest in Ireland, or Stephen's resemblance to himself, are purely superficial; but the enduring dimension of his art, as appears in *Ulysses*, is the malleability of meanings, the manipulation of phenomena into willfully contructed patterns, the unending transformation of details from the realms of fact, thought, and sensation into an aesthetic entity.

One can argue that all literature, all art, transforms the materials of life into aesthetic entities. But, in *Ulysses*, filled though it is with Dublin speech and names, Bloom's corporal presence, Stephen's intellectual queries, and Molly's reveries, the center of gravity is gradually displaced from the meaning of the book's elements to the configuration of those elements. It is a process of derealization and, as such, announces much that is to come in modern fiction. Ever since Eliot's essay on *Ulysses*, critics have argued as to the intent of Joyce's mythical method: parodistic, comic, tragic, what have you. The point here, however, is whether the integrity of character and/or plot in *Ulysses* survives the masterly treatment Joyce accords them. To what extent is *Ulysses* finally about Bloom, Stephen, and Molly? Surely, we must recognize that the pressures of selection and economy that any "story" imposes on its author are mocked by Joyce, and the Homeric girdle hardly gives a shape to such an inchoate mass of details. Joyce's grid is so large that we are no longer able to say what should or should not be included. His is the true "slice of life," in contrast to the excessive cogency and deterministic pattern of Zola's work. Total inclusion makes for single obliteration, however, and we may feel that the three main characters are mere integers in a panorama, vehicles for Joycean expression. *Ulysses* is not an "unsuccessful" Odysseus story in which recognition is not achieved, but rather a novel that is, in fact, not addressed to its ostensible subject.

Most critics account for the nonrecognition and failed relationships of *Ulysses* in terms of Joyce's toughness, his modernist refusal to pander to specious harmonies of the past. Stephen and Bloom urinating in the garden, passing by one another in the newspaper office, Bloom with his head at Molly's rump—such scenes of marginal contact are deemed honest or moving or possibly farcical, but always compelling and significant. Is it possible that their "humanness" did not interest Joyce very much? My contention is that the human potential of his story, the signifying connection between the characters and elements of his book, is largely the creation of literary critics. The business of criticism is to humanize, and it is a noble task. The most spectacular displays of formal virtuosity will eventually be harnessed into human categories; the most hermetic works will sooner or later be invaded by the humanist troops. There is vitality and purpose in such a critical posture, and a meaning-oriented inquiry is, in my opinion (as this book testifies), preferable to a criticism that dispenses with human reference. But there can be too much of a good thing; or, rather, criticism, inebriated by the subtlety of its own nets and anesthetized to the recalcitrance of the work, may blind us to what is really going on. Let us recall the Jamesian proclivity for speculation, for misreading and over-reading the signs; in the criticism of much modern fiction we see a widening gap between the work and the commentary it incites. Given such a warning, we may want to take a step back, to ask whether the book's rationale and its *modus vivendi* have, in fact, anything to do with the story it is presumably telling. And, if not, *how* do Bloom, Stephen, and Molly coexist with the author's design?

Such a claim may seem rash and overstated. Even critics who dislike the growing stylization of *Ulysses* insist on the human integrity of the first chapters. Walton Litz, who has convincingly documented the centrifugal, linguistic emphasis of Joyce's revisions in *Ulysses*, asserts that "fortunately the human forces of Bloom and Stephen, and the momentum established in the early chapters, kept the revisions of *Ulysses* from completely overshadowing the *données* of each episode."[10] The first part of the novel is unquestionably in the service of character: first Stephen, then Bloom. Joyce's use of stream of consciousness gives us a wealth of detail and psychic activity that makes his two characters overwhelmingly present. And yet, even in these human-bound, pithy chapters, one senses the economy of Joyce rather than the integrity of Stephen or Bloom. The allusions to the events of the *Portrait*, the innumerable literary motifs ("Lycidas," *The Tempest, Hamlet*),

[10] Walton Litz, *The Art of James Joyce* (New York: Oxford University Press paperback, 1964), p. 36.

the political and religious satire, the emphasis on usurpation, keys, the meditation on history, the foot and mouth disease, the refrain of "agenbite of inwit"; these are merely some of the *elements* aligned with and superimposed upon each other to render Stephen. Stephen is rendered quite compositely, but the author's arranging hand is felt; above all one feels that these are components, building blocks, used now to depict Stephen but ultimately designed for duty elsewhere as well. The parts do not so much coalesce as they extend outward, betoken things to come, suggest that their propriety is in the overall scheme of things rather than in the domestic organization of Stephen Dedalus. Likewise, Bloom seems more a locus for seemingly random sensory and mental impulses than a defined person. Obviously Joyce doesn't believe in "defined" characters, but there is something voracious and almost faceless in Bloom's recording activities. The purchasing and frying of the kidney, the perusal of pornography, the session in the outhouse, the clandestine correspondence, the reflections on Paddy Dignam's death, the observance of the Mass; all these details are wonderfully concrete, and they "get" Bloom unforgettably into the novel and the reader's mind. But there is a disquieting kind of equivalency among those events, more a panoramic survey than an inside picture, more a moving camera than a moving person. One waits for orientation, for emphases; it is clear that Bloom has a flavor all his own, but even his scattered insights and reflections merely contribute to the surface detail. Gradually, it becomes clear that Joyce is not going to *use* Leopold Bloom, as other characters have been used by their authors. Leopold Bloom's richness is, in some sense, gratuitous, the unavoidable by-product of Joyce's inclusiveness. Rastignac, Pip, Dowell, Sutpen, Quentin, even Joseph K. are presented in a certain way *so that* what happens will seem inevitable (or at least plausible); this fictional economy, this interplay of character and plot, no longer obtains for Joyce. Of course, one is always free to claim that everything happening in *Ulysses* constitutes a plot and happens to Bloom or Stephen. But is it true? What happens in the early part of the book is an onslaught of naturalistic detail, punctuated—sparsely and coyly—by reminders of a story: "agenbite of inwit," glimpses of Blazes Boylan heading to his assignation, chance and purely formal encounters between Bloom and Stephen.

Ulysses makes us realize that other books are about interaction; the impulse and center of gravity in Balzac, Dickens, Conrad, Ford, and James are unmistakably lodged in *relationship*. In those books the mystery form is used to generate a search for relation; there is cohesion between character and character, character and event, event and event. Such an art does not naively assert that "life out there" comes in packages or plots; but it does posit that the role of the artist (and, by extension, that of the protagonist and the reader) is, ultimately, to create an ordered picture—not necessarily a resolved or harmonious picture, but one whose elements cohere in such a way as to show us what we could not have seen without the work of art. It is in this light that we can gauge both the particular coherence and particular anarchy of *Ulysses*.

If we assume that life is amorphous, then all art cheats through arrangement and selection. My contention is that *Ulysses* cheats more than most works do, but—and this is quintessential—its pattern of selectivity is aesthetic rather than ethical. R. P. Blackmur has eloquently described this aspect of the novel:

No more orderly book of fiction was ever written, and no book in which the principles of order, unless taken aesthetically, seemed so frivolous or impotent. Dante is casual in comparison, for Dante has tried to put things in order only within reason and tradition, whereas Joyce went ahead anyway, presenting a kind of nihilism of unreasonable order. He had an overmastering predilection for order and a cultivated knowledge of many kinds of order, and their heresies, within the Graeco-Christian tradition, catholic, classic, historical, and aesthetic, but he had to treat them all, in fact, as if they were aesthetic, images or stresses rather than summaries or concepts of the actual. Thus the waywardness or high jinks in the book is order pushed, the chaos is order mixed, the disgust is order humiliated, the exile is order desiderated or invoked. Thus, too, the overt orders of the book—homeric, organic, stylistic—make obstacles, provoke challenges, not all of which are overcome; and also serve to get around (by forcing overflows, damming power) such psycho-ethical matters as motive in character, meaning in action, and purpose in sequence.[11]

Joyce, like Eliot and Pound, confronted a vast cultural breakdown and gave it form; unlike Eliot and Pound, Joyce was able to endow his mosaic with incredible human fullness in the portraits of Bloom, Stephen, and Molly. But they remain pieces of the mosaic, somehow lost and unauthoritative amid the bustle of thoughts and sensations they are transmitting. Not only is interaction absent (other than in purely formal terms, such as proximity or parallel or parallax), but the characters are astonishingly (and deviously) egocentric. Doubtless the stream-of-consciousness presentation itself (as we saw in *The Sound and the Fury*) carries a considerable dosage of narcissism with it. Customarily Stephen alone is taxed for self-indulgence and alienation, while Bloom and Molly are celebrated for their openness to life. But is that the case? Bloom's incessant, quasiprogressive chatter (viciously and acutely criticized by the narrative voice of *Cyclops*) is genuinely alert and bubbly, but it is, in every sense, small talk. His almost mechanical responses to all random stimuli (is there anything in Dublin that he does not perceive on that day?) show that the system is working, that it entertains countless minute speculations and queries of the "wonder what?" and "interesting"

[11] R. P. Blackmur, *Eleven Essays in the European Novel* (New York: Harcourt, Brace & World, 1964), p. 32.

variety, but can such a performance pass for vital interest or even intense curiosity? The bulk of his thoughts about Molly and Milly are undifferentiated from his musing about advertising and public transit. Is the human mind, even when daydreaming, as indiscriminate and uncommitted as that of Bloom? Should we look for a story, then we notice that the running commentary is occasionally punctuated with sentiments of fear (Boylan) or pathos (Rudy or his father), but most of it is secure in its surface banality. Only in *Circe* do the repressed or obscured affective bases of Bloom's life come to the fore, but even there they seem to be part of a larger carnival. Such a creation is unquestionably "lifelike," but, before Joyce, he would have been *used* in some fashion (consider, for example, the dramatic use of Homais in *Madame Bovary*). Joyce is, of course, under no obligation to show Bloom in crisis (to show us, in some sense, what his mettle "really" is), but we are correspondingly unable to do much with him. His sporadic moments of deep feeling and courage are buried under the flow of his ordinary, one-dimensional ruminations.

Let us see him as he really is: a man who gives and cares very little. He brings Molly breakfast, buys her books, and returns to her bed in the evening, but he appears strangely anesthetized; his thoughts concerning his marriage and his life are about as personal as a shopping list. His apparent interest in outside phenomena is appallingly routinized, short-winded, epidermal. Unlike Conrad's Jim, he is truly "one of us," but that should not blind us to his limits: far from penetrating or empathizing with the world around him, he sidles up to it, like a cat, and uses it for his pleasure. In this light, the episode with Gerty MacDowell is a paradigm for a man with modest needs, bent after small pleasures, content with what he can get. Gerty will do.

It is questionable how much fulfillment Bloom derives from Molly, but one may return home to a warm bed for a number of reasons, ranging from gratification to convenience. The point is that Joyce does not deal with those reasons; Bloom returns homeward as surely as Stephen heads into the void, but to call Molly an anchor or a center of gravity is to affirm more than the text warrants.

If Bloom is self-contained, Molly is self-adoring. The surge of life is admittedly there, and she is a tribute to the protean vitality of the flesh. But she denies relation even more staunchly than she affirms life. Molly's reverie is almost claustrophobic in its self-reference, and although "Poldy" is acknowledged (and even deemed quite special), one never senses that he means very much to her. Instead, we have petulancy and resentment toward the exploitative aims of all men and an intense awareness of herself as object of appetites. And those appetites include her own: "I bet he never saw a better pair of thighs than that look how white they are the smoothest place is right there between this bit here how soft like a peach easy God I wouldn't mind being a man and get up on a lovely woman" (p. 755). The beautiful series of "yes I said Yes I will Yes" which closes the book is significantly a memory of someone other than Bloom. Molly, like her husband, is faithful to her appetites, and the outside world is somewhat indiscriminately and insignificantly a source of pleasure. This husband and wife are stupendously successful literary creations, but the level of their consciousness which Joyce has tapped is so random and unengaged that they both appear uninvolved, like dazed spectators who strayed within the precincts of Joyce's book and did duty for him. Bloom's thin curiosity and Molly's plump sexuality lead neither to knowledge nor to relation; they are "there" as few characters in fiction are, but they are not in any meaningful way "there together."

To attempt to rewrite a book is foolish, particularly when it is nothing less than a verbal universe like *Ulysses;* but to idolize Joyce or to claim his work as a *summa* is to suggest a wholeness which is not there. Joyce made choices; he wrought magnificently, but there were losses too. Along with its achievements, *Ulysses* also registers a waste of human potential. The Stephen, Bloom, and Molly sections of the book are like ships veering in different directions, each circumscribed by its own waters, charting its own course, displaying its own style(s). To be sure, it can be shown that the characters are actually related in subtle and intricate ways, that various motifs are interwoven for the attention of the careful reader. But, in great art there is also something obvious, something for the not-so-careful, the nonprofessional. *Ulysses* is not niggardly; there is plenty of life there. But other views of human behavior are possible: Bloom might have seen in Stephen more than possible Italian lessons, in Molly more than a warm bed; Stephen might have felt more than fatigue in his association with Bloom; Molly might have claimed more than "spunk" for Poldy. Joyce might, without changing his view of human nature, have let them respond more to each other.

If the seemingly character-based chapters are anarchic, what is to be said of the more overtly stylized sections of the book? What is being furthered in *Aeolus?* Does the parody of *Nausicaa* outrun its dramatic function? The *Wandering Rocks* chapter well illustrates the principle of formal harmony replacing human cogency. We follow a number of Dubliners—Father Conmee, Corny Kelleher, the one-legged sailor, Katey and Boody Dedalus, Blazes Boylan, and many others, Bloom and Stephen among them—in a bird's-eye view of what they are doing at a particular moment in time. A few strands tie some of these people together, but it would be naive to assert that each character has a role to play in Bloom's story. Clearly, one of Joyce's points is that "stories" do not exist in reality; but what emerges from the juxtaposition of the chapter is the puppetlike utility of Joyce's materials (for they begin to strike us as only that), their human inanity, and their formal propriety. Consider the following: "On Newcomen bridge the very reverend John Conmee S.J. of Saint

Francis Xavier's church, upper Gardiner street, stepped on to an outward bound tram. Off an inward bound tram stepped the reverend Nicholas Dudley C.C. of Saint Agatha's church, north William street, on to Newcomen bridge."[12] Here we are looking at a diagram of vectors, not at people. The characters are crushed by the authoritative, relentless, controlling description of title, place, and motion. A kind of annihilation takes place in those paragraphs, and we cannot simply ascribe it to parody or planetary realism; there is comedy too, of course, of the mechanistic variety so often seen in Moliére and assessed by Bergson, but Joyce's tendency to depict people as forces in a magnetic field inevitably suggests dehumanization. It matters little that these are minor characters, and, as such, that they are the occupational hazards of all writers. The entire chapter is about minor characters—it makes everybody minor characters. The argument is frequently made that this chapter is not supposed to be about people, but about the random, pulsating activity of the city itself. But do we see life-in-the-city, or puppets caught in grids?

The penultimate chapter, *Ithaca*, with its impersonal, abstract, scientific, interrogatory style, gives us a final image of Bloom that is so distant that the threads of the story disappear in favor of an astronomical, zoological chart. The immensity of the stage, extending, like Pascal's famous dictum, to the infinite in both great and small, provides the narrative focus and effectively obliterates the thinking protagonist:[13]

[12] James Joyce, *Ulysses* (New York: Modern Library ed., 1934), pp. 218–219. Subsequent quotations are from this edition.

[13] Whereas Joyce is ironic, distant, and lyrical, Pascal is anguished and immediate:

"Car enfin qu'est-ce que l'homme dans la Nature? Un néant à l'égard de l'infini, un tout à l'égard du néant, un milieu entre rien et tout. Infiniment éloigné de comprendre les extrêmes, la fin des

With what meditations did Bloom accompany his demonstration to his companion of various constellations?

Meditations of evolution increasingly vaster: of the moon invisible in incipient lunation, approaching perigee: of the infinite lattiginous scintillating uncondensed milky way, discernible by daylight by an observer placed at the lower end of a cylindrical vertical shaft 5000 ft deep sunk from the surface towards the center of the earth: of Sirius (alpha in Canis Major) 10 light years (57,000,000,000,000 miles) distant and in volume 900 times the dimension of our planet: of Arcturus: of the precession of equinoxes: of Orion with belt and sextuple sun theta and nebula in which 100 of our solar systems could be contained: of moribund and of nascent new stars such as Nova in 1901: of our system plunging towards the constellation of Hercules: of the parallax or parallactic drift of socalled fixed stars, in reality evermoving from immeasurably remote eons to infinitely remote futures in comparison with which the years, threescore and ten, of allotted human life formed a parenthesis of infinitesimal brevity.

Were there obverse meditations of involution increasingly less vast?

Of the eons of geological periods recorded in the stratifications of the earth: of the myriad minute entomological organic existences concealed in cavities of the earth, beneath removable stones, in hives and mounds, of microbes, germs, bacteria, bacilli, spermatozoa: of the incalculable trillions of billions of millions of imperceptible molecules contained by cohesion of molecular affin-

---

choses et leur principe sont pour lui invinciblement cachés dans un secret impénétrable.

"Egalement incapable de voir le néant, d'où il est tiré, et l'infini, où il est englouti, que fera-t-il donc, sinon d'apercevoir quelque apparence au milieu des choses, dans un désespoir éternel de connaître ni leur principe ni leur fin? Toutes choses sont sorties du néant et portées jusqu'à l'infini. Qui suivra ces étonnantes demarches? L'auteur de ces merveilles les comprend; tout autre ne le peut faire" (Pensées, eds. Tourneur et Anzieu [Paris: Librairie Armand Colin, 1960], I, 142).

ity in a single pinhead: of the universe of human serum constellated with red and white bodies, themselves universes of void space constellated with other bodies, each, in continuity, its universe of divisible component bodies of which each was again divisible in divisions of redivisible component bodies, dividends and divisors ever diminishing without actual division till, if the progress were carried far enough, nought nowhere was never reached. [p. 683]

What is there to say about such a *tour de force?* As writing, it is magnificent, filled with puns, alliteration, and great rhetorical effects ("nought nowhere was never reached" is prodigious). But what is it doing? It nullifies the characters, calls into question its own metaphysical content by the weight of its style, effects (as does much of *Ulysses*) a rhetorical overkill. If we take such a framework seriously, individual gesture is inconceivable, for the generic alone prevails. Thus the story embodied in the Odysseus myth, of human trials, of wit and humor and cunning leading to survival and ultimate recognition and union, is transformed into graph. Stephen's "meeting" with Bloom is rendered as a virtual diagram. The discussion between the "father" and the "son" is not so much a failure of communication as a pretext for the real business at hand, the real order to be forged, the rhetorical and grammatical activity of the author:

What counterproposals were alternately advanced, accepted, modified, declined, restated in other terms, reaccepted, ratified, reconfirmed?

To inaugurate a prearranged course of Italian instruction, place the residence of the instructed. To inaugurate a course of vocal instruction, place the residence of the instructress. To inaugurate a series of static, semistatic and peripatetic intellectual dialogues, places the residence of both speakers (if both speakers were resident in the same place) the Ship hotel and tavern, 6 Lower Abbey street (W. and E. Connery, proprietors), the National Library of Ireland, 10 Kildare street, the National Maternity Hospital, 29,

30 and 31 Holles street, a public garden, the vicinity of a place of worship, a conjunction of two or more public thoroughfares, the point of bisection of a right line drawn between their residences (if both speakers were resident in different places). [p. 680]

One can always say that this is an honest, unromantic, unillusioned depiction of meeting and recognition, just as one can assert that the catechism form of *Ithaca* invites some kind of reader response. I would argue, however, that such interpretation involves wishful thinking, if not actual whistling in the dark; why must we, at all odds, humanize these vectors and abstractions, accept them as a valid picture of human relations? We often betray a willingness to validate the meanest abstractions, to embrace the most niggardly graphs and call them life. My argument is not that *Ithaca* depicts failed relations, but that it merely exploits the *forms* of relation, that its aesthetic claims both precede and undermine the ethical content it ostensibly bears. I contend, ultimately, that fiction has its own kind of law of conservation of energy, that one cannot therefore claim *Ulysses* to be both a novel and more than a novel. In being more than a novel, it effectively becomes less. There is a dialectic—and this appears with startling clarity in Claude Simon and Alain Robbe-Grillet—between the integrity and significance of character and the needs and authority of style. What you give to one, you may very well be taking away from the other, because they both share the same stage, and they exist in a symbiotic relationship. Or at least they did until Joyce. Even in the stylized art of a writer like Racine, one can argue that the aesthetic conventions serve the author's message; in *Ulysses* it seems that the priorities are reversed, that language itself, the *signifiant*, is energized, while the story, the *signifié*, limply follows. It is merely a change of emphasis, but the change is devastating in its implications. Let us compare Joyce's version of recognition and nonrecognition with the models we have seen thus far: Pip's inability to recognize Magwitch as his "father"; Jim's failure to recognize Brown; Dowell's disastrous misreading of his fellows; Sutpen's refusal to acknowledge Bon. Everything in the other books—style, structure, language—is in the service of that vision and that blindness. In the works of Conrad, Ford, and Faulkner, the formal innovations are far-reaching in their own right; but they enhance our apprehension of the human themes (the *signifié*); better still, they generate the vision by which we perceive those themes. It is against this backdrop that Joyce's formal achievement seems prodigiously self-serving and aloof to the presumed human subject matter. Thus, *Ulysses* actually becomes the kind of work that structuralist critics like Roland Barthes would claim as properly literary: "For literature . . . language can no longer be the convenient instrument or the superflous backcloth of a social, emotional or poetic 'reality' which pre-exists it, and which it is language's subsidiary responsibility to express, by means of submitting itself to a number of stylistic rules. Language is literature's Being, its very world; the whole of literature is contained in the act of writing, and no longer in those of 'thinking,' 'portraying,' 'telling,' or 'feeling.' "[14] My essay on Joyce is meant to delve into what happens humanly in such art.

Thus it seems most plausible to regard the style of *Ithaca* as merely another one of the brilliant guises Joyce can assume, a performance with no allegiances, done because Joyce can do it. In most of the other chapters, notably *Aeolus, Sirens, Nausicaa, Oxen of the Sun,* and *Circe,* the same voracious style impulse is evident; the rhetorical possibilities of the language seem to usurp Joyce's interest as the book continues, and we see the phenomenon of literature shrugging off its subject mat-

[14] Roland Barthes, "Science versus Literature," *Introduction to Structuralism,* ed. Michael Lane (New York: Basic Books, 1970), p. 411.

ter in celebration of its own *modus vivendi*.[15] The living pulse
of *Ulysses* is its style, for the pressures and demands of plot
and character have been superseded. The term "mosaic" has
been used to indicate the strange single-dimensional nature of
its texture. Nothing—the autobiographical details, the erudite
allusions, the intense sensory and auditory and visual realism—
commands authority by sole virtue of its meaning; all the components of the glittering surface, including the human ones,
share in stylistic equality. Notice the absolute parity in this
passage:

In the mirror of the giltbordered pier glass the undecorated
back of the dwarf tree regarded the upright back of the em-
balmed owl. Before the mirror the matrimonial gift of Alderman
John Hooper with a clear melancholy wise bright motionless
compassionate gaze regarded Bloom while Bloom with obscure
tranquil profound motionless compassionated gaze regarded the
matrimonial gift of Luke and Caroline Doyle. [p. 692]

The words themselves reign in Joyce, betokening sound
and allusion more urgently than meaning:

Eglintoneyes, quick with pleasure, looked up shybrightly. Gladly
glancing, a merry puritan, through the twisted eglantine. [p. 205]

Jog jig jogged stopped. Dandy tan shoe of dandy Boylan socks
skyblue clocks came light to earth. . . . One rapped on a door,
one tapped with a knock, did he knock Paul de Kock, with a

[15] Obviously the *vedette* in such a performance is the brilliant
pastiche of English writers, supposedly mirroring the birth of the
language and literature while ostensibly describing Bloom's visit to the
hospital and the birth of a child. Harry Levin (*James Joyce* [New
York: New Directions, 1960], pp. 105–106) has shrewdly assessed the
claims made for this chapter: "These parodies, we are admonished,
illustrate the principle of embryonic growth. We cannot take this
admonition very seriously. To call in so many irrelevant authors as
a middle term between the concepts of biology and the needs of the
present narrative is to reduce Joyce's cult of imitative form to a final
absurdity."

loud proud knocker, with a cock carracarracarra cock. Cockcock.
[p. 278]

Joyce's aim seems less the representational one of onomatopoeia
than a calculated loosening of language, a liberation from
single meanings and traditional structures. The actual sexual
transformation in the Nighttown chapter from masculine to
feminine that we see in Bloom and Bella Cohen, the granting
of voice and animus to all elements of the chapter—this is,
among other things, the logical (and morphological) extension of the Joycean principles of organization. The fixed dual-
ity of earlier literature, consisting in words as reasonably stable
counters for a world of depth, of meanings, is being exploded.
Joyce, concerned with the creative potential of the words
themselves, cares little for immovable meanings and priorities.
In *Finnegans Wake* the feat of total manipulation, the ultimate
verbal alchemy, is visible to all, but in *Ulysses*, it is somewhat
obscured by the Balzacian wealth of detail. But things can be
all things only at the cost of single identities. The visible world
and the unit of the word are exploded into a richly suggestive,
dazzling artifact, but the claims of a single story and the cogency and pre-eminence of the human personages in that
story are necessarily diminished.

The coherence of *Ulysses* derives from formal association.
It is a world composed solely of building materials, each asserting equal claims, each used for its formal aptness. Joyce's
encyclopedic mind delighted in bizarre comparisons and
purely figural resemblances. His work frequently offers startling harmonies that are wholly created, but such aesthetic
resolution is rarely in the service of human concerns. Consider,
again in the penultimate chapter, the affinities between the
moon and woman:

Her antiquity in preceding and surviving successive tellurian
generations: her nocturnal predominance: her satellitic depen-

dence: her luminary reflection: her constancy under all her phases, rising, and setting by her appointed times, waxing and waning: the forced invariability of her aspect: her indeterminate response to inaffirmative interrogation: her potency over effluent and refluent waters: her power to enamour, to mortify, to invest with beauty, to render insane, to incite to and aid delinquency: the tranquil inscrutability of her visage: the terribility of her isolated dominant implacable resplendent propinquity: her omens of tempest and calm: the stimulation of her light, her motion and her presence: the admonition of her craters, her arid seas, her silence: her splendour, when visible; her attraction, when invisible. [p. 686]

The *topos* is old, but the virtuosity of the Joycean treatment revivifies it. However, there is no corresponding effort to suggest some kind of harmony (or disharmony), relationship (or lack of relationship) between Molly Bloom and her husband. Joyce seems not to be interested. Perhaps a still more telling illustration of what Joyce is and is not doing can be seen in his treatment of water:

What in water did Bloom, waterlover, drawer of water, water-carrier returning to the range, admire?

Its universality: its democratic equality and constancy to its nature in seeking its own level: its vastness in the ocean of Mercator's projection: its unplumbed profundity in the Sundam trench of the Pacific exceeding 8,000 fathoms: the restlessness of its waves and surface particles visiting in turn all points of its seaboard: the independence of its units: the variabilty of states of sea: its hydrostatic quiescence in calm: its hydrokinetic turgidity in neap and spring tides: its subsidence after devastation: its sterility in the circumpolar icecaps, arctic and antarctic: its climatic and commercial significance: its preponderance of 3 to 1 over the dry land of the globe: its indisputable hegemony extending in square leagues over all the region below the subequatorial tropic of Capricorn: the multisecular stability of its primeval basin: its luteofulvous bed. . . .

Having set the halffilled kettle on the now burning coals, why did he return to the stillflowing tap?

To wash his soiled hands with a partially consumed tablet of Barrington's lemonflavoured soap, to which paper still adhered (bought thirteen hours previously for four pence and still unpaid for), in fresh cold neverchanging everchanging water and dry them, face and hands, in a long redbordered holland cloth passed over a wooden revolving roller.

What reason did Stephen give for declining Bloom's offer?

That he was hydrophobe, hating partial contact by immersion or total by submersion in cold water (his last bath having taken place in the month of October of the preceding year), disliking the aqueous substances of glass and crystal, distrusting aquacities of thought and language.

What impeded Bloom from giving Stephen counsels of hygiene and prophylactic to which should be added suggestions concerning a preliminary wetting of the head and contraction of the muscles with rapid splashing of the face and neck and thoracic and epigastric region in case of sea or river bathing, the parts of the human anatomy most sensitive to cold being the nape, stomach, and thenar or sole of foot?

The incompatibility of aquacity with the erratic originality of genius. [pp. 655–657]

The passage is much longer than what has been quoted, including a lovely description of the circuitous route of water between the reservoir and Bloom's tap. Undeniably, such writing vigorously expands our vision of the world. Yet, like the woman-moon comparison, the theme of water *could* have a profound bearing on the story of Bloom and Stephen. Given Stephen's fear of water, the "snot green sea" as contrasted with the wine-dark sea, the "scrotumtightening sea," the drowning of Icarus and Lycidas, the perversion by the "seachange" evidenced in the "bag of corpsegas" seen in *Proteus*, we have come to attribute a great deal of reverberating meaning to the cluster: Stephen and water. In contrast to this, inviting and even demanding comparison from any writer other than Joyce, is the cluster: Bloom and water.[16] Bloom's naturalness, his acceptance of the body, his fluid ease, are beautifully rendered in *Lotus eaters:*

> Enjoy a bath now: clean trough of water, cool enamel, the gentle tepid stream. This is my body.
> He foresaw his pale body reclined in it at full, naked, in a womb of warmth, oiled by scented melting soap, softly laved. He saw his trunk and limbs riprippled over and sustained, buoyed lightly upward, lemonyellow: his navel, bud of flesh: and saw the dark tangled curls of his bush floating, floating hair of the stream around the limp father of thousands, a languid floating flower. [p. 85]

One can argue that the two responses to water are, in fact, developed contrapuntally by Joyce in *Proteus* and *Lotus eaters.* But the initiated motif and the resonant chords are ignored in *Ithaca;* their rich, thematic, character-based fullness is neither emphasized nor acknowledged because the encyclopedism of the chapter uses Stephen and Bloom as integers, not as subject matter.

Critics have agreed that there is little assertion in *Ulysses.* To survive, to get on in the modern world is already a great deal, and Bloom—like his mythical counterpart—manages to hang on and return home. Aside from these ethical concerns, however, I am arguing that there are formal constraints that effectively diminish the authority and scope of Stephen, Bloom, and Molly. The examples mentioned in the *Ithaca* chapter point up the priority Joyce gives to the aesthetic potential of his material: meeting and recognition interest Joyce as forms, and his book does not genuinely explore them as themes. Thus, the human story tends to be crowded out of the novel; despite their undeniable fullness, the three characters

---

[16] I am indebted to Philip M. Weinstein for the comparison of water motifs in Joyce's treatment of Stephen and Bloom.

are afloat and isolated—not only from one another, but often from their "own" reporting and recording. Robert Scholes has argued that "the technological and scientific perspectives of *Ithaca* extend Bloom and Stephen to new dimensions without aggrandizing them. (And without dwarfing them as is sometimes contended.) . . . At the end of this chapter, after a day of anxiety, Bloom rearrives at an equilibrium which is not merely that of a body at rest but that of a self-regulated system operating in harmony with other systems larger than itself."[17] Foremost among those systems is the formal determinism of *Ulysses*. Bloom survives, but the fullness he might have brought to bear on his story goes wasted. There is equilibrium, but such harmony also spells out manipulation and eclipse.

Richard Ellmann has given us an interesting insight into the formal, associational nature of Joyce's thinking:

> Bloom consoles himself with the thought that every betrayal is only one of infinite series; if someone mentioned a new atrocity to Joyce, he at once pointed out some equally horrible old atrocity, such as an act of the Inquisition in Holland. He was interested also in variation and sameness in space, in the cubist method of establishing differing relations among aspects of a single thing, and he asked a friend to do some research for him in the possible permutations of an object. That the picture of Cork in his Paris flat should have, as he emphasized to Frank O'Connor, a cork frame, was a deliberate, if half-humorous, indication of this notion of the world, where unexpected simultaneities are the rule.[18]

Joyce's genius at uncovering hidden affinities and creating new resemblances is never more apparent than in the innumerable limericks he wrote all during his life. The meanings of words are sabotaged by their sound or allusive potential. Similarly, when assisting his translators, Joyce invariably insisted

[17] Robert Scholes, "*Ulysses*: A Structuralist Perspective," *James Joyce Quarterly* (Winter 1973), 170.
[18] Ellmann, *Joyce*, p. 563.

upon the primacy of sound and rhythm over meaning. The principle of associational logic, if carried to its fullest extension, yields a vision of complete parity, wherein priorities and distinctions of time, space, matter, and identity are wiped out. Such a vista is most fully achieved in the *Wake,* but it is adumbrated throughout *Ulysses.* But there are threats involved for human life when such a vision is operative on an individual level. We may glimpse the risks inherent in such freedom by considering one anecdote concerning Joyce's daughter, Lucia. It would be rash and vulgar to equate Lucia's mental condition with the qualities of vision implicit in her father's work, but Ellmann recounts one episode that is perhaps worthy of comparison. On September 15, 1934, Lucia, under the attention of Dr. Forel at Les Rives de Prangin, started a fire in her room in four places and nearly burned it up. When pressed for explanations, she was silent, but "remarked later to a nurse, however, that her father's complexion was very red and so was fire."[19] The free connective principle, linking together "disparate" elements such as a painting of Cork and a cork frame, or a red complexion and fire, creates new, unsuspected harmonies, but does so at a risk. Humanism is a privileged stance, perhaps a fictive, even limiting scheme of things, replete with hierarchies, distinctions, and large areas that don't count at all. If those distinctions of meaning and depth (the familiar humanist ploy) are replaced by harmonies of a different order (be they verbal, visual, or what-have-you), our universe is expanded, but that taut spring, the centripetal force between things and us, between the spectacle and its meaning, snaps. The result is a kind of weightlessness, a realm of pure vision and liberated, open-ended, value-free, meaning-free gesture dictated by form alone. The human

[19] Ellmann, *Joyce,* p. 688. Needless to say, Lucia's remark can be explained in elemental psychological terms as the desire to inflict damage on her father by setting fire to the room. But the analogical principle itself is ultimately more destructive than the emotional content it may support.

being, shorn of protective categories and priorities, is freed from the anthropomorphic blinders. In such a context, "humanism" becomes a specious term.

For its fullness of character and place, for its flavor of felt experience, *Ulysses* probably has no match in the literature of our age. In formal prowess, nothing (other than *Finnegans Wake*) approaches its overwhelming autonomy, its existence as man-made universe. But—and Joyce typifies our dispossessed age in this—there is a chasm between those two achievements. Not only are the human and the formal dimensions separated, but, as I have tried to show, they are antagonistic and, ultimately, nullifying. *Ulysses*, supposedly the story of *l'homme moyen sensuel*, indeed announces a form of wholly egalitarian vision and opens the twentieth-century debate about the possibility of literature.

The legacy of Kafka and Joyce is so overwhelming and diffuse that one could not possibly chart all of the forms it assumes. For our purposes, however, their works embody the notion of eclipse in two fundamental ways. In Kafka the protagonist is dwarfed by the labyrinthine setting, and his efforts at rational orientation are grotesque failures. Joyce tends to transform the human dimension of his work into pattern, replacing the cogency of plot and the interaction of character with harmonies of a purely verbal order.

The work of Michel Butor, particularly *Passing Time*, can be seen as the convergence of the strands dealt with in Kafka and Joyce. The protagonist is pitted against an overwhelming alien setting, and his task is to make some valid order of it. The order that finally emerges, however, involves a sacrifice of the private psychological schemes in favor of a larger, impersonal series of coordinates, relegating the human actor to the background. The notion "eclipse" has been used to characterize these three writers because each records—overtly in Kafka and Butor, implicitly in Joyce—the conflict between human needs and exigencies of a larger, nonhuman order. This tension itself testifies to the continuing authority of a human reference, of a need for meaning and cogency which the novel depicts and serves.

Michel Butor's novels are marked by their didactic character, their commitment to the expansion of man's knowledge about his surroundings. In one of his early essays, "The Novel as Research," Butor stresses the exploratory and epistemological role of fiction. As an art form, however, the novel has not kept pace with the changing structures of modern life: "Now it is clear that the world in which we live is being transformed with great rapidity. Traditional narrative techniques are incapable of integrating all the new relations thus created. There results a perpetual uneasiness; it is impossible for our consciousness to organize all the information which assails it, because it lacks adequate tools."[20]

Passing Time and *Change of Heart,* in contrast to most of the *nouveaux romans,* are "situated" geographically and historically; to a significant degree they are respectively about life in an English industrial city, the meaning today of Paris and Rome. *Degrees* reflects the efforts of Pierre Vernier to assign all the temporal and spatial coordinates of a day in a Parisian school. Later works such as *Mobile, Réseau aérien,* and *Description of San Marco,* while exploding the limitations of the novel form, are clearly a continuation of the major theme embodied in the novels: orientation and exploration. Butor in no way rejects tradition. Like Eliot, Joyce, Pound, and Faulkner, he seeks to create an art that can render the present scene with fidelity while also honoring deeper, less visible ties with tradition and the past.

Butor's faith in art as a means of knowledge is also illustrated by his interest in the novel's affective potential. In ad-

---

[20] Michel Butor, *Inventory* (New York: Simon & Schuster, 1968), p. 28. This essay is translated by Richard Howard.

dition to queries about the effect of different narrative voices, Butor probes the material properties of the novel. A book is something we physically apprehend; its composition and appearance, the layout of its pages and printing, the sequential mode of reading itself, not only can but must influence our understanding. Every aspect of the book is expressive, and its proper use is as guidebook or even talisman for the reader. Not the least of the book's privileges is its structure: unlike records and films, it can be turned back to specific pages of interest; it can be consulted like an index or dictionary; it can, of course, be read more than once. Now it is obvious that these ideas tell us much about the kind of story Michel Butor is going to write: one that realizes and exhausts its potential in book form, that serves as a guidebook, that needs to be opened again and again at certain pages.

Passing Time is such a book. It is, however, more. The first-person narrative grants it a lyrical and emotional intensity absent from Butor's other works; the richness of description and mythological allusion, far less restrained than that of *Change of Heart*, creates an atmosphere of overripeness, of haunting but specious parallels. Butor assures us of having drawn up charts and blueprints for his time scheme,[21] but our interest is in what that architecture *does*, not how it looks on paper. Butor has told us that a book can be read discontinuously, that certain pages may be referred to several times, but such theories mean little until we realize that Jacques Revel's experience (and our own as well) can be told in no other way. Butor's major concerns—the relation between agent and setting, the attempt to order experience, the problematic efforts to relate that experience—make of *Passing Time* a powerful example of the novel as research.

As most critics have noted, the story is meager. Jacques Revel comes to Bleston (Manchester) to work at Matthews

[21] Interview with Madeleine Chapsal in *Les Ecrivains en personne* (Paris: Julliard, 1960), p. 64.

and Sons on October 1. At the end of seven months' struggle
with the city, he begins a diary to relate his experience: we
learn of his purchase of a map and novel about Bleston for
means of orientation; we are informed of his acquaintances
and friends, his romantic interests, his various visits (to the
museum, the two cathedrals, various restaurants, and fairs).
Revel loses his two girls to his two friends, is perhaps cause of
a mysterious "accident" concerning the author of the novel he
bought, is unable to cover all twelve months in his diary, and
leaves September 30, one year later. To describe Butor's novel
in such terms is to extract whole eggs out of the omelette, but
reconstruction is both the subject and method of *Passing
Time*, and Butor wants us to piece together this story, if we
can.

The first thing Butor makes us notice is the elemental dishonesty of first-person writing and the time-honored convention of ignoring that dishonesty. Revel's problems come from
certain basic questions. How can the narrator be unaware of
the present as he relates the past? Does time not exist for the
writer as well as the events he recounts? Does this effect of
time alter the episodes past? In May, Jacques Revel begins
narrating his October arrival. Much that happened in October
makes sense only because of what Jacques has learned during
the intervening months. In June, Jacques is obligated to tell us
what was happening to him in May while he was narrating
about October. Things are never over for Revel because he
does not stop living while he is writing. An incident in August may bring something from October back into play, neces-
situating revisions and reinterpretations. There is no stability.
For Butor, all time is lost time, since we are always "situated"
and never able to gain a final perspective, to effect a definitive
reconstruction. Herein, as Jean Pouillon has shown, Butor is
the anti-Proust:

Where, ultimately, is Proust? "For a long time I used to go to bed early." Who is this "I"? The person who used to go to bed early? The one who remembers it? But when and why? Both, obviously, that is, this elusive tightrope walker who glides where he wishes, in all directions, on the wires of time. For Butor, on the other hand, the essential thing is the present, and if he has to re-examine his past, he does so to understand how he got where he is. The narrator doesn't stroll haphazardly in time; he is caught by his present; in writing his story, he must yield to those laws of passing time that the novelist generally observes only for his characters while ignoring them for himself.[22]

This dissolving perspective has a definite effect on the reader; he sees the same incidents at different moments in time and is at a loss to evaluate their respective interpretations. Progressive revelation means progressive destruction.

Let us consider the first mention of Jacques's betrayal of George William Burton. The narration follows the event by only one day. At the Baileys, Ann returns *The Murder of Bleston* (Burton's novel about Bleston) to Jacques who, be-wildered, confesses that he knows the author and finally divulges the name to Rose. Several points are to be made. First, the pattern of narrating only the events of the "past" (October or November) is disrupted, and time breaks in upon the narra-tive focus. Second, *we* know next to nothing of this novel, whereas it obviously has had some importance for the char-acters (precisely during those months that Revel has not had time to relate). This significance is rendered all the more troubling by the ambivalent remarks concerning parallels in the murder story and the "real" situation—parallels that only Jacques seems to notice. After revealing the identity of the author, Jacques realizes that he may have endangered Burton's life, but he lamely hopes nothing will come of it. The entry closes with these words: "Then why did I take such a risk,

---

[22] Jean Pouillon, "Les règles du 'je,'" *Les Temps modernes*, No. 134 (April 1957), 1954. My translation.

when it would have been so easy, even supposing all this is
true, to ensure perfect safety for George Burton behind his
protective *nom de plume*, J. C. Hamilton, having neither face
nor address, no civil status, no biography and no other
works?"[23] The reader is so busy trying to sort out all the new
information, to grasp how and why this material is important
(the narrator, at least, seems to think so), that he scarcely
heeds Jacques's rhetorical question. However, this betrayal—
which, almost camouflaged by the device of the first-person
narrator, will be Jacques's crime, perhaps *the* crime of the
novel—begins to plague Jacques. He explicitly questions his
motives several times and, finally, the confession comes two
months later: Jacques betrayed Burton to please Rose, to
erase a moment we have seen, but paid no attention to: Jacques's
fall on the steps leading to the cathedral, his dirtying himself
in the presence of a young girl descending the steps. Later,
much later, the event is recalled with a full sense of Jacques's
inadequacy, of what the humiliating scene meant for him and
what it, therefore, led him to do: "I felt increasingly afraid
that she [the girl on the steps, 'presumably' Rose Bailey]
might remember something of that deplorable encounter, that
she might have identified me, even if only subconsciously,
with that loathesome mud-stained figure, as pitiful as an epi-
leptic in his trance, so repellent that she had instinctively taken
flight; and I could not bear the thought, and I felt impelled to
counteract it by some word or action that would enhance my
prestige in her eyes" (p. 179). Thus, the betrayal has been
motivated; we merely learn about it later, and we do so because Jacques understood it only later. One cannot speak of
reliable or unreliable narrators in such an instance; it is rather
a case of "truth" being retrospective. There is, as Revel recognizes, ignorance and complicity in our dealings with ourselves,

---

[23] Michel Butor, *Passing Time*, tr. Jean Stewart (New York: Simon
& Schuster, 1960), p. 62. Subsequent quotations are from this edition.

ignorance because we do not yet know, complicity because we do not want to know: "Last night, then, I read that account which I had written myself, but which appeared to me more and more like the scrupulous work of another to whom I had confided only a portion of my secrets, through lack of time, through incapacity to distinguish as yet what was important, and also, I must admit, through a desire to deceive that other, to deceive myself" (p. 177).

As the narration continues we meet phrases like "I see only too well now . . ." and "I wasn't fully aware then . . ." Often the reader is ahead of Jacques; we recognize the "black Morris" and suspect James of the attempted murder (after all, in a detective story, how can it be a mere accident?); we remember the name of Richard Tenn while Jacques must look it up; we see the disturbing frequency of James's visits with Ann; we note that Lucien is described as a ladies' man. In short, we play the game marvelously, trying to follow the parallels, fill in the ellipses, solve the crime.

That does not quite happen, however. If anything, the novel becomes more complex. For each new discernible pattern, there are additional troubling details; for each clarification gained by the present, something else in the past becomes "significant" or something happens to the narrator, implicating him and his story in time, adding to his diary. In the form of a chart, Butor's analysis of *Passing Time* as a progressive series of references is clear; in the reading experience of the book, these interrelations are overwhelmingly chaotic. The following sentence ties together so many moments in time that it defies both analysis and digestion:

I deposited on the livid green eiderdown the *Evening News*—which in its general layout was just like the copy I have bought this evening from the same paper-seller in front of the chemist's, although every line of the text is different—the red square plan of bus routes, which still lies today, soiled, crumpled and dog-eared, among my other papers on the left corner of my table in this pleasanter room to which I only moved to month later—and that long rectangular booklet the colour of milky tea, the big map, identical with the new clean copy which I have bought since, at the same newsagent's, from the same Ann Bailey, and which I am now turning over between the fingers of my left hand to check my statements and make them more precise; and I sat for a long time on the chair, the one chair, with its upright wooden back, staring at them, smoking the last cigarettes out of a packet of Churchman's, waiting for my strength of mind to come back. [p. 40]

This passage may look like a parody of Proust's opening page,[24] but the juxtaposition of different moments of time and the aimless, fruitless interrogation of the objects described belong to an enterprise quite different from that of Proust. These unending phrases are functional, for they translate both the attempt to order events through parallel and analogy, and the futility of such an effort. There is no synthesis for Revel, no illumination coming from these series: just a long chain (see, especially, the French version) with countless links which, although forged by the narrator, seems to control and suffocate him. It is an inventory, a process of surface knowledge and arrangement, uninformed by knowledge or insight.

The technique of delayed meanings is matched by the corresponding device of referring to events which have happened to Jacques but have not been narrated in his journal (Lucien is there before we know how he got there; the discussion of Burton's novel is "loaded," but we don't know why). There

---

[24] It is, of course, in the French that we discern the stylistic parallels. Butor's endless sentence begins with "Longtemps, après avoir déposé sur l'édredon vert livide l'*Evening News* semblable, dans son aspect général, à celui que j'ai acheté ce soir. . . ." (*L'Emploi du temps* [Paris: Ed. de Minuit, 1957], p. 43); compare with Proust's celebrated opening line: "Longtemps, je me suis couché de bonne heure."

is no such thing as a neatly ordered first-person story, and the reader is obliged to manage as best he can each time the web of past events is broken by intrusions from the present. In an important essay on "The Bear," Butor stresses this particular feature of Faulkner's art:

The reader must always be on the inside, that is, he must always be treated as if he himself belonged to the story that is being revealed. The facts must, in so far as possible, appear to him as they appear to the characters within the work. Thus we will always be thrown in the midst of events, and from the very first lines, a great number of things will be mentioned that we are supposed to know, and which will only gradually become clear to us as we continue our reading. We are supposed to know those basic facts which, in truth, we only acquire in reading the work, and afterwards still more information is given to us, just as it is given to the characters within the story. This deepening of the Jamesian notion of point of view represents, as far as realism in the novel is concerned, a remarkable achievement.[25]

The process of scrutinizing the past in search of its value illustrates the retrospective nature of all knowledge. Our consciousness is filled with unappraised data, faces, and facts that clutter our minds but have yet to receive meaning and priority in our scheme of things. The novelistic convention of labeling all events with their significance from the outset is avoided, but the resultant free-floating structure is, in every sense, unsettling. In *Passing Time* this mobility of meanings is explicitly compared to the detective story. As Revel tries to keep up with his experience, to interpret past by present and vice versa, he finds Burton's theories regarding this genre enticing:

in the best of such works the novel acquires, as it were, a new dimension, since not only are the characters and their relations transformed under the eye of the reader but so, too, is his knowl-

[25] Michel Butor, "Les relations de parenté dans 'l'Ours,' " *Répertoire* (Paris: Ed. de Minuit, 1960), pp. 251–252. My translation.

edge of those relations and of the story itself; the final definitive aspect of that story . . . revealed after, and through, a number of other aspects, so that the narrative is not merely the projection on a flat surface of a series of events, it rebuilds these as it were spatially, since they appear differently according to the position occupied by the detective or by the narrator. [p. 147]

Moreover, such an exercise can be given form in only one genre: the novel, or even more broadly, the *book*, whose material properties permit constant reshuffling, realignment, revisions, and rereadings. Revel is not oblivious to the bearing such an aesthetic has on his own situation:

in detective fiction the story goes against the stream, beginning with the crime, the climax of all the dramatic events which the detective has to rediscover gradually, and . . . this is in many respects more natural than a narrative proceeding without a backward look, where the first day of the story is followed by the second and then by subsequent days in their calendar order, as I myself at that time had been describing my October experiences; in detective fiction the narrative gradually explores events anterior to the event with which it begins, and this, though it may disconcert some readers, is quite natural, since obviously in real life it is only after having met somebody that we take an interest in his previous actions, and only too often it is not until some disaster has struck our lives that we wake up enough to trace its origins. [pp. 155–156]

The detective story form serves Butor well, for it is an ideal reflection of our efforts to apprehend and order experience. Determining which factors are relevant, discerning pattern in the preceding events, solving a crime is a pedagogical exercise. Most of our waking (and sleeping) moments constitute a quest for order, and Butor has tapped the resources of the detective story to express—and to elicit from his readers—this elemental search for patterns.

As a structural principle, as a method, the theories of George Burton fit the situation of Jacques Revel. Moreover,

200 / Vision and Response in Modern Fiction

since *The Murder of Bleston* does describe the actual city, why not utilize it for orientation, along with the map? But what about the story itself, the "fictional" murder case? It has been pointed out that many *nouveaux romans* are styled on the "*roman en abîme*" mentioned by Gide in his Journal.[26] In varying degrees we encounter this phenomenon in Nathalie Sarraute's *Portrait of a Man Unknown*, Claude Simon's *Flanders Road*, Robbe-Grillet's *Jealousy* and *In the Labyrinth*, and Butor's *Change of Heart*. But *The Murder of Bleston* seems at once the most intricately related to the narrative and the most specious (whence its didactic value); its true function is to be unreliable literally, but to be valid as method. As soon as Revel mentions the novel and its author to the Baileys, we "know" there is some hidden significance. From then on, the patterns begin to accumulate, to lure us in: the book is seen to be considerably more than an index of streets and sites. The symbolic relevancy of the Old Cathedral and the scorn for the New Cathedral, the mysterious parallel with Richard Tenn, the strange animosity of James Jenkins and his mother toward the author, the tempting echoes of each meal in the Oriental Bamboo restaurant: all this provides a bristling network of resemblances that woos both narrator and reader. Is there evidence that the Bleston murder is real, that Jacques is both reconstructing and reliving many of its episodes? Is the detective story a structural principle or is it the magic key to Jacques's experience? These are the distinctions on which Butor's novel is based. *Passing Time* is about the possibility of order, and *The Murder of Bleston* is the temptation, the ready-made meaning package:

Through a newspaper poster I had discovered J. C. Hamilton's

[26] For a discussion of the "roman en abîme" and its relevancy for the *nouveau roman*, see Bruce Morrissette, "De Stendhal à Robbe-Grillet: Modalités du 'point de vue,'" *Cahiers de l'Association Internationale d'Etudes Françaises*, No. 14 (March 1962), 158–161.

detective story *The Bleston Murder;*[27] through reading this I had discovered the Murderer's Window, which in its turn had given rise to this conversation with its closing words of advice to visit the New Cathedral. It was as though a trail had been laid for me, at each stage of which I was allowed to see the end of the next stage, a trail which was to lead me hopelessly astray. [p. 75]

Butor presents these insinuations and hints in such a fragmentary, disjointed fashion that the reader, like Revel, eagerly seizes them, is all too anxious to accept the parallels. Thus we plague ourselves about the meals at the Oriental Bamboo which *seem* to echo the fateful events of Burton's novel; we too are intrigued by the reactions of James Jenkins and his mother to *The Murder of Bleston.* Ultimately, however—and this is surely the point of Butor's novel—*The Murder of Bleston* is shown to be, if taken too literally, a false lead, a blinder. Like Léon Delmont in *Change of Heart* who outfitted the people in his train compartment with imagined names and situations, Jacques Revel has fabricated a spurious order, has erected a house of cards. Anxious to discern patterns, and to find those patterns meaningful, Revel endows the slightest events or reactions with portentous meanings. Sensing a similarity between the statue in the New Cathedral and Mrs. Jenkins, Jacques needs little stimulus to make the connection:

after taking James to lunch at the Oriental Pearl I had paused with him in front of the porches where the statues of the Arts and Sciences stood, streaming with rain, and I had watched him watching me; to my casual remark, "What an amazing likeness!" he had merely replied, "Yes, isn't it?" and then gone on to suggest a visit to the cinema to warm ourselves; which had proved to me that he had perfectly well understood me, that I was on the right track, and that he encouraged my researches. [p. 163]

Later Revel will simply call her the daughter of E. C. Douglas.

[27] I prefer to translate *Le Meurtre de Bleston* as *The Murder of Bleston* so that the ambiguity of Bleston as place or victim remains.

Likewise, Horace Buck will quickly be assumed responsible for some of the fires in Bleston. Burton's "accident" is, for Jacques, "doubtless an unsuccessful murder." These beguiling patterns are necessarily endorsed by the reader (whose optic is that of Jacques), and it is a jolt to realize that the reality does not fit the proposed form. While scrutinizing such reactions as that of James Jenkins to Burton's novel or the presence of a fly above Burton's head, Revel ignores other, less esoteric patterns such as the relationships between Lucien and Rose, James and Ann, and the significance of the New Cathedral.

The most striking source of order and pattern in *Passing Time* is, however, the use of myth. Butor, who has written on Joyce and Pound, uses what Eliot has termed the "mythical method." But whereas Leopold Bloom can be seen by the reader as a modern Ulysses, Jacques Revel hungrily watches himself enact the myths of Theseus, Cain, and even Oedipus. If the profuseness of the references does not alert us, the fact that Revel is directed to them by Burton's novel should dispel any doubts. Armed to the teeth with Greek myths and Biblical echoes, Revel is ready to "tag" all events, large and small. Ann and Rose are, of course, Ariadne and Phaedra, and Jacques relies on each for love and guidance in the mazelike Bleston; unfortunately, Theseus-Revel loses both himself and the girls. Cain, the archetypal murderer, the founder of the city, of the arts, is also a convenient reference, and Revel occasionally identifies with him too. And Oedipus is the ideal detective, both blinded and cast out of the city.

How are we to judge these myths? It would seem that they have an ambivalent function comparable to that of the detective story. They are archetypal symbols for certain human experiences, and Revel's situation in Bleston is labyrinthine. Moreover, they undeniably give scope and body to Revel's plight and provide a lush, lyrical form of expression for his anguish. On the other hand, they must not be taken literally, as Jacques does, as a plug-in code to his uncharted experiences.

Revel abuses the myths, just as he does the detective story. The artifice of the Greek references is emphasized by the films on Crete and Greece which Jacques sees solely as means of escape from Bleston into ancient myth, himself into archetype, his experience into pattern; such a transformation would change his senseless misery into significant doom. The myths, like the detective story, are seductive and unreliable.

At the end of the book, shorn of his frames of reference, aware that he has lost both Ann and Rose, Jacques Revel has nothing left other than the notes we are reading:

> Now that everything has crumbled about me I have nothing left but this pitiful accumulation of futile phrases, like the ruins of an unfinished building, the partial cause of my downfall, incapable of sheltering me against the torrential sulphurous rain, against the surging pitchy waters that lap with a low booming sound, against the perpetual assault of that rumbling, sneering laughter that spreads from house to house and runs round my own wallpaper.
>
> This is the deplorable end of my attempt to struggle; nothing is now left me, comtemptible thing that I am, but to acknowledge my defeat, my undeniable and irremediable defeat, without the slightest hope of revenge, as though I were already dead: my defeat and your incontestable power, horrible amorphous town that I detest, the disproportion of our strengths. [p. 226]

It would thus seem that Revel's undertaking is a disastrous failure. The interrogation of the past and the search for meaning in his experience are fruitless; the glittering avenues of myth and fiction lead only astray. To acknowledge such a loss is to question, indeed, why so much passion and intelligence have been expended in creating false leads. Most painful of all is the failure of Revel's own journal to save him, for it seems to be as ineffective a talisman as *The Murder of Bleston.* Let us recall the hopes placed on the diary itself, the protagonist's desperate wish to wake up (Revel as Réveil) from the opaque forgetfulness of his stay in Bleston. The journal is his effort to see clearly, to reclaim his possessions from the grips of the city, to define and thereby salvage his experience. Consciousness is, however, more than a matter of opening one's eyes; it is a process of incessant scrutiny, of disciplined, pinpointed illumination within the dark immensities of the mind, of firm recall of what one was, of believing in one's continuity. Its exercise resembles the work of the geologist: "and while I wander, seeking for a meaning to my life, through that waste land that I have become, groping over vast banks of deposit, I suddenly stumble at the edge of a cleft at the bottom of which the original soil is laid bare, and thus I can gauge the thickness of the silt which I must plumb and filter in order to recover my bedrock, my foundations" (pp. 110–111).

It would seem that such labors have been in vain because Revel's orientation is false. Revel's vision is defective, for he has systematically misconstrued personal relations, beginning with his blindness concerning Lucien and James, and ending with his *mauvaise foi* regarding his treatment of Ann and his astonishment over the extent of his own attachment for Rose. These misconceptions, camouflaged by the journal and noted only when they explode into his consciousness, constitute a chain of errors, mocking the hungry reader as well as the baffled protagonist. Jacques Revel's stay in Bleston is a personal failure.

Could it be otherwise in a novel so exclusively devoted to charting a city? First and foremost there is Bleston, constituting the medium of his thoughts and the arena of his acts. The most telling sign of its sway is to be seen in its manifold presence throughout the novel. It usurps the whole field of Jacques's vision, reducing all other characters into derivative functions: Horace Buck as pariah, George Burton as subtle, mocking outsider, James Jenkins as believer and defender of its cult, Ann Bailey as dispenser of maps, Rose Bailey as temptation to betrayal. All are phantoms of the city, dependent upon it for their meaning. None has intrinsic personal value—

at least, not in the eyes of Jacques Revel. Jacques inevitably reads them as he reads *The Murder of Bleston*, the maps, the museums and cathedrals and fairs: his guide to Bleston. Thus it is apt that his evenings are increasingly spent with his journal while Lucien and James entertain the Bailey girls. There is little authentic depiction of human relationships in this novel, no sense of intimacy or touch. Jacques represses his feelings, desires but is afraid of Rose, likes but fears Horace Buck, uses but betrays Ann, befriends but does not know James. We cannot visualize these characters as people because Jacques perceives them as functions or shadows. There is perhaps one moment of human tenderness, of recognition, in this novel, and it takes place, strangely enough, in a dental clinic. Jacques discovers Ann "in the great ward with its five buzzing rows of instruments of torture," sees her "sitting openmouthed, terror in [her] eyes," sees the look she gave him "from the depths of that terrified childhood within you which you could no longer control, taken unawares, that look which nobody but me has seen, which was meant for nobody but me, and which made me forever the confidant of that part of you which would never have been revealed had you not been in pain" (p. 225). It is a haunting scene, appropriately modern (dental clinic) and mythic (instruments of torture [*machines saignantes et suppliciantes*], sense of ritual sacrifice, the young man in the spotless coat grinding away, the terror). It is a moment of knowledge, a glimpse of the hidden human truths that *Passing Time* does *not* deal with: childhood, fear, intimacy. Jacques, truly at the heart of the labyrinth this time, thinks he is merely in a dental clinic, eschews the search for Ariadne, and comforts Ann:

For a few moments we went into Willow Park, which was like a lonely wood at that time of year. Dusk was rapidly falling; I took your head between my hands and for a long time I stroked your brows with my thumbs as though to banish your pain, without daring to go further because in a tenuous dream I had begun to hear Rose's voice whispering, speaking such delicious French, the only voice that spoke French to me in those days, Rose's voice had begun whispering to me, leading me away from you. [p. 225]

As the scene ends, the French-speaking, sirenlike Rose-Phae-dra intervenes, supplants intimacy with myth, touch with language, showing us the fragility of human contact within Revel's scheme of things. *Passing Time* is not—despite the wants of its protagonist—a psychological novel, for its optic is resolutely upon the myriad patterns of meaning and the immense, intricate, obsessive stage, not the actors. Within such a framework Jacques Revel's self-serving use of people and places and myths is fatally egocentric and doomed to failure. His "story" does not jell; his myths do not quite fit. He is lost among the profuse objects of his inventory.

There remains only the journal, the statement of his loss. And that is both the substance and the meaning of *Passing Time*. By renouncing and exploding the network of detective story and classical allusion, Butor—and Revel—effect a modern myth of man and his setting, of the invincible need for order and the tenuous but precious record we bequeath. In this context failure may still be redeemed, for a kind of order emerges from the statement of Revel's loss; neither mystery nor biblical nor classical, it is the picture of a city, a picture of Bleston's significance for Jacques Revel. Like the detective story, like his own query for meanings, the final patterns of significance emerge in retrospect, transforming what we know. The greatness of *Passing Time* lies in its remarkable *volte-face*, the virtual resurrection occasioned by viewing the novel as the exploration of Bleston rather than the personal experience of Jacques Revel. Jacques will render Bleston. The city demands an authentic, unstylized, unglamorized, unmythicized, unimagined expression:

I am Bleston, Jacques Revel; I endure, I am tenacious; and if some

of my houses fall down, don't let that persuade you that I myself
am crumbling into ruins, that I'm ready to make way for that
other city of your feeble dreams, those dreams that through my
power have grown so thin, so obscure, so formless and impotent
—maybe you fancied last April that the framework hidden within
these walls foreshadowed that dream-city? But my cells reproduce themselves, my wounds heal; I do not change, I do not die,
I endure, my permanence swallows up all attempted innovation,
this new face of mine is not really new, you can see that, it is not
the first sign of my contamination by that imaginary city which
my enemies contrast with me, although they can never describe
it; no, no, this is the present face of an old, though not an ancient,
city. [p. 208]

In this context the animosity between the Jenkinses and the
author of *The Murder of Bleston* takes on significance. We
are repeatedly told how the detective novel focuses essentially
on the Old Cathedral with its stained glass windows, whereas
the New Cathedral is treated with scorn. Revel must transcend this mythological *parti pris* (in this sense, Bleston does
seek revenge on Burton); he must discover the New Cathedral
with its statues of the arts and sciences, its sculptured men-
agerie; he must embrace the spirit of the real city, the living
arena of his countless walks, the soot, the sulphurous odors, the
new buildings, the fairs, the authentic ugliness, threat, and
vitality of the modern city. Thus the extraordinary nightmare
where the New Cathedral literally begins to breathe and swallow the onlookers is like a warning to Revel: take cognizance
of the real Bleston.

Jacques's diary must be transformed from an unsuccessful
detective story, a fallacious retelling of myth, into an "exploratory description, basis for future deciphering, future illumination." The detective story and the myths are misleading only
if Revel tries to don them as tailor-made apparel. As suggestive, imaginative structures, they will be indispensable in the
"exploratory description"; but they are only part of a much

larger, less self-addressed network that Jacques must establish: "I shall have to acquire the closest possible knowledge of you, in these numbered days, a knowledge of all the articulations of your body" (p. 235).[28] The Jamesian dictum that the artist is the man for whom nothing is lost is realized in the dramatic valorization accorded at the end of *Passing Time*. Bleston must be brought to consciousness. Like any city, it is a reservoir of culture and history, extending through time and space, capable of enriching its inhabitants through an awareness of its plenitude, of the depths and treasures concealed beneath its opacity. The nostalgia for the classical past and the implicit refusal of the modern city stem from Revel's fearful awareness of Bleston darkness, of abdication, of meager and mean lives:

the wind sent . . . the meager unsmiling men and women, with eyes like stagnant water never quite free from the icy film of fear, back to the homes where a precarious peace awaits them, peace painfully acquired at the cost of relentless effort, great stubbornness and patience, long attrition, with so much renounced and rejected, so much buried, besmirched and betrayed, so many humiliations endured, so many needs unfulfilled, such vital secrets lost, so much forgotten. [p.112][29]

---

[28] "All the articulations of your body" is my translation of Butor's "toutes ces articulations de ton corps," because Jean Stewart has omitted the phrase entirely.

[29] Jean Stewart was faced with the impossible task of rendering the impassioned, rhythmical, alliterative, almost incantatory French of Butor's passage. As a result, the English is more neutral in its tone, and the reader is less likely to sense Revel's authentic humanitarian response to the crushed, unfulfilled lives of Bleston's inhabitants:

"... le vent . . . levait des armées complices de poussière, et . . . chassait, pressés comme au coeur de l'hiver, toutes ces femmes sans hanches, tous ces hommes sans épaules et sans sourire, tous ces regards d'eau de mare où le gel jamais blanc n'en finit pas de desserrer les tenailles de sa peur, qui les chassait vers leurs maisons, médiocres fours où cuit pour eux le pain d'une tranquillité précaire, péniblement acquise à grands renoncements,

Here, then, is the real task. Jacques's tireless pilgrimage and his insistent interrogation cannot be enlisted for his private needs, but they will serve in the collective labor of awakening Bleston, of "restoring" it to its people. As ingredients in Jacques's personal drama, the unending inventories of itineraries, restaurants, and cathedrals do not cohere, but as elements of a "future deciphering," they begin to coalesce. We must finally realize that archeology and geology are not metaphors, but are rather the substance of Revel's activity, whereas his personal longings are a foil. His authentic role is to uncover Bleston's riches, to evoke "the whole geological evolution of the region from age to age . . . Bleston, Bellista, Belli Civitas" (p. 219). In this light, the layers and tiers of inquiry and detail in his journal assert their hidden geological significance and can be redeemed. Let us actually reconsider the long passage dismissed as fruitless:

I deposited on the livid green eiderdown the *Evening News*—which in its general layout was just like the copy I have bought this evening from the same paper-seller in front of the chemist's, although every line of the text is different—the red square plan of bus routes, which still lies today, soiled, crumpled and dog-eared, among my other papers on the left corner of my table in this pleasanter room to which I only moved a month later—and that long rectangular booklet the colour of milky tea, the big map, identical with the new clean copy which I have bought since, at the same newsagents, from the same Ann Bailey, and which I am now turning over between the fingers of my left hand to check my statements and make them more precise; and I sat for a long time on the chair, the one chair, with its upright wooden back, staring at them, smoking the last cigarettes out of a packet of Churchman's, waiting for my strength of mind to come back. [p. 40]

enfoncements et abandons, à grands ensevelissements, obscurcissements et trahisons, à grandes humiliations bues, exigences tues, à grands secrets perdus, à grands oublis" (pp. 122–123).

The astonishing repetition of the *Evening News,* the news-agent, the bus itinerary, the two rooms, the map, the paper store, Ann Bailey, is exemplary of the style of *Passing Time.* Somewhere, between the terms of those repetitions, is the story of Jacques Revel, his search for a decent room, his burning of the map, and his deception of Ann Bailey. To grasp the human volume between the repeating but differing terms is to recover the depth of experience and the passing of time. But such repetition is more than a laborious shorthand intended to evoke Revel's life; it is the instrument of a great classification, for Bleston too is caught between its integers. The three Chinese restaurants, the eight carefully evoked parks reserved for the traveling fair, the three copies of *The Murder of Bleston,* with their different images of its author, the recurrent bus trips, the detailed walks, the descriptions of the same places at different times of the year, the repeated interrogation of the tapestries, such lines of force—comprising the real bulk of Butor's novel and stubbornly refusing to be enlisted in a story —transcend the small life of Jacques Revel and constitute the grids of Bleston, the outline for a new kind of map, one that would register the living pulse of the city, take measure of its true dimensions. The prime repetition is, of course, that of the two cathedrals, and the true map which *Passing Time* seeks to render would be one "where the two Cathedrals appear as the two poles of an immense magnet which disturbs the trajectory of all human atoms in its neighbourhood, according to the stuff they are made of and the energy with which they are charged" (p. 163).

Such a chart reflects a new order, a way of organizing and reorganizing the vast details, many of them unseen and forgotten, or ignored, that compose the living patterns of a city. The enterprise is supremely Cartesian in the sense that it entails human mastery over the surroundings, but it is achieved at a cost that would have baffled Renaissance optimism. Revel will bring Bleston to light and life, but he will be extinguished.

His evocation and his coordinates will have symmetry and harmony, but he will be absent: "I know that the story which had been unfolding ever since I first came here has now reached its end, that the pattern is complete, now that this has happened without my knowledge, in despite of me and yet by means of me, making me suffer almost to the point of death and turning me into the ghost that I now am—now that Ann and James have come together . . . just as did Rose and Lucien a month ago" (p. 231). The Jenkinses will be reconciled with the Burtons, and the disparate warring elements of Bleston will fuse through the suffering of Revel. Like the spider and his web, the work of art evolves through the life and experience of the artist; it is not a question of imposing a form but rather of living it. Léon Delmont returns to Paris to write the experience of his recognition; Pierre Vernier sacrifices his life to order the world about him, and that sacrifice is an integral and necessary part of the order effected. Michel Leiris has spoken of Butor's art as a kind of "losing is winning,"[30] and Ludovic Janvier has stressed the suffering required to make reality "spill out."[31]

We are now able to reinterpret the materials of mystery and myth. Burton's definition of the detective's mission, coming in the middle of the novel, characteristically assumes its full significance at the close of the book:

The aim of his whole existence is that tremendous moment in which the power of his explanations, of his disclosure, of the words by which he tears off veils and masks, uttered generally in a tone of grave melancholy as if to soften the terrible, dazzling light they shed, so welcome to those whom it sets free but so cruel, so appalling, so blinding too, the power of his speech actually destroys the criminal, achieves that death that confirms

---

[30] Michel Leiris, "Le réalisme mythologique de Michel Butor," postface to 10/18 ed. of *La Modification* (Paris, 1966), p. 310.
[31] Ludovic Janvier, *Une Parole exigeante* (Paris: Ed. de Minuit, 1964), pp. 147–172.

and crowns his work—that moment when reality is transformed and purified by the sole power of his keen and accurate vision. [p. 135]

Such clarity has a price. The terrible meaning of Burton's prediction emerges only at the close: "A major part of the relations existing between the participant in the drama were maintained only through the errors, ignorances and lies which he abolishes; the actors group themselves in a new pattern from which one member of the former grouping is automatically excluded" (p. 135). Revel will disappear, will become anonymous like his ancestor, the unknown French artist who created the tapestries, like the painting glimpsed at the Jenkinses of a "fugitive monarch, cloaked and crowned, rushing through a dense forest full of wolves with luminous eyes" (p. 48).

In lucidly recording his experience, his delusions and losses, the imagined façades of Bleston and the real spirit of Bleston, Revel performs a strange act of penetration and complicity, of defeat and victory:

And so I thank you, Bleston, for taking such cruel and blatant revenge on me; I shall have gone from you in less than a month, but I shall still be a prince over you since, by acknowledging my defeat, I have managed to survive (as you secretly wished me to) the fate you had in store for me, I have not been engulfed; and now, having endured the ordeal of your fury, I have become invulnerable, like a ghost; I have won from you this offer of a pact, which I accept. [p. 234]

Revel accedes to a kind of mystical insight into the conscience of the city; his suffering enables him to perceive Bleston's lament, Bleston's urge for expression: " 'When shall our strength be set free? When shall we see our velvet spread out, our metals gleaming? When shall we be cleansed and you too, Jacques Revel?' " (p. 237). The completed diary will be the portrait of Bleston, the transformation of Jacques's disorder into Bleston's order. The recording agent, subject and then vehicle of his record, is finally eclipsed by it:

As for the blank sheet of paper on which I am writing, it too is a thick mask of paint, like the blank rectangle on the back of the book in front of me, the book I bought in midwinter in a second-hand bookshop in Chapel Street; but a mirror lies beneath the thick layer of paint that I am scratching with my pen as though with a knife, that I am burning away as though with a blowpipe, and gradually, through the cracks that my words make, my own face is revealed in its coating of thick grime, my own face being gradually cleansed by misfortunes and my stubbornness, and yours behind it, Bleston, your face ravaged with inner conflict; and yours will shine through more and more clearly, until nothing can be seen of me but the glitter of eyes and teeth, while yours is consumed at last in an amplified incandescence. [p. 247]

The purifying vision of the detective, like the "blowpipe," cleanses and discloses Bleston, transforms it into art. The yearned-for light and clarity of the Cretan sky will be rendered to Bleston by Revel's journal, because the rain and clouds and soot and opaque forgetfulness can be penetrated in no other way. The flames of despair present in the filmed destruction of Rome, the violence and misery of Horace Buck, Revel's burning of the map, must be changed from heat to light. The ubiquitous, ambivalent motif of fire in this novel—destruction and purgation—is finally equated with the alchemical effect of Revel's chastened vision: "I see you now, Bleston streets, I see your walls and your inscriptions and your faces; in the depths of your seemingly vacant stares I see the gleam of a precious raw material from which I can make gold; but how deep I must plunge to reach it, what efforts I must make to secure and collect all that dust" (p. 242).

Thus, Butor, after succumbing to the dangers of false reconstruction, finds a redeeming value only in the selfless commitment of the searcher. For Jacques Revel, there is no suitable arrangement of events, no "solvable" Bleston murder.

Butor's protagonist is ritualistically sacrificed to the story he tells. Yet his eclipse is graced with insight, and his story with value. Butor has written a modern *Bildungsroman*, but the setting, rather than the self, must be built; and he has attempted both to point out and to reject the subjective fantasies and preconceived grids which distort experience and impede vision. Measured against our need for patterns and structures is a world that demands, in terms that are appropriate and relevant, to be charted. The self-oriented, psychological mode of traditional fiction is not adequate to such demands. Butor's undertaking lays bare the shortcomings of our egocentric reading. Our conventional expectations of "story," of human relations, and our conventional boredom with the details of setting are painfully exploited and exploded in *Passing Time*. Unaccustomed to viewing art as orientation, we may fail to interrogate maps for meanings, or people for place. If charts (not only maps but also body counts) are to repossess the meaning inherent in them, and people to reveal the conditions that form them, some kind of synthesis must be effected. A new literature must evolve, Butor is saying, epic and didactic, wherein the buried treasures of our setting and the lost time of our experience are brought to light and recomposed into a new order. More, not less, vision is needed, but it must be directed outward rather than inward. The hegemony of the individual—his loves, feelings, sufferings—is rejected, and the appetites of the self must yield to the knowledge of the community. The novel can be a serious instrument of epistemology. Whereas, in an earlier age, Malraux's hero strove to leave a "scar on the map," Butor, more the surveyor than the adventurer, seeks to devise the chart.

Alienated Vision: Proust, Borges,
Claude Simon, and Robbe-Grillet

The body of literature considered in this chapter tends to
subvert the central notion of vision to which most of this book
has been devoted. One may, of course, still talk about the
human optic in Borges, Simon, or Robbe-Grillet, because their
books do contain human characters and the problems of orientation therein are urgent. These novels also contain human
plots, but they are organized and determined largely according to inhuman, mechanical laws. What matters here is not
the authors' attitudes: the erudite gamesmanship of Borges,
the metaphorical associational structure of Simon, the non-
anthropomorphic thrust of Robbe-Grillet. Whatever the authors' intentions, the works depict people as agents, integers,
and ciphers in an enterprise that uses rather than expresses
them. Literature has doubtless always shown the discrepancy
between desired patterns and actual events; *Lord Jim* and
"The Beast in the Jungle" dramatize that conflict. But the
emerging cogency of the work, the meaning that the work
gradually posits—even when human structures are annihilated,
as in tragedy—has been on a human scale.

The focus of this chapter is on the particular quality of
vision that may still obtain in works where the configurations
enacted and the *Kunstwille* informing the writing have little
or no human reference. The novel can produce no equivalent
to abstract art, despite the various claims (structuralist *et al.*)

that literature is solely a language system. The centrality of vision, of human reference, cannot be truly obviated for the crude reason that (1) the medium of literature (that is, language) is unavoidably referential and posits, irrepressibly, human meanings and (2) we, human beings, read it and yoke it willy-nilly into our own sphere.

Implicit in our discussion is the example of Joyce. He was dealt with in the preceding chapter because his work does not actually subvert human pattern but rather tends to democratize the elements of the novel, to transform priorities of plot and character into harmonies of language. But Joyce significantly leaves the issue open, and *Ulysses* contains, within its almost infinite inventory of words and things, fully drawn characters. Bloom, Stephen, and Molly do exist, and they carry out—even if marginally—their own functions as well as those of Joyce. Joyce's world is large; unlike the novelists discussed in this chapter he can accommodate all systems; the human breakdown implicit in his pluralism is never dramatized.

If modern fiction's tendency toward formal rather than human cogency is obviously related to Joyce, its debt to Proust may be somewhat less clear. What was experimental in his work regarding the depiction of character, the disappearance of conventional plot, even the treatment of time, has been so absorbed by his posterity (readers as well as writers) that we are sometimes at a loss to prove why he is important. The comprehensive picture he affords of a dying class and a developing narrator, of the gradual emergence of social and psychological laws and the resultant loss of illusions, makes his work, as Harry Levin has shown, the *summa* of nineteenth-century French realism.[1] Equally clear, equally nineteenth-century, is the romantic-symbolist dimension of his work: the multifaceted theme of the artist, the literary impressionism, the con-

---

[1] Harry Levin, *Gates of Horn*, pp. 372–444.

fessional posture, the subjective optic. Yet, if we take a careful look at some of the essential aspects of his work, such as the function of art and the role of fictions, we can see the germs of a derealizing process, celebrating creativity but menaced by solipsism, that fully flourishes only in the mid-century *nouveau roman.*

Few commentators have failed to remark the importance of metaphor in Proust. Leo Bersani, in particular, has substantially influenced my reading in his study of Proust's complex, creative fiction-making process.[2] Proust fits into my study as a transitional figure, a writer for whom the elusiveness of appearances and the disintegration of personality can still be redeemed. Borges, Claude Simon, and Robbe-Grillet retain the Proustian notion of perception as the imposition of form and fiction, but they radically alter the role of the perceiver, making him spectator or victim or dreamer rather than self-asserting artist. The seeds of such alienation between the vision and the viewer are readily discernible in Proust, but it is precisely that final act of possession, or ordering the multiple, overly rich, knowledge-resisting, contradictory images of the World into a sense of identity which distinguishes Proust from those who follow.

Early in *Swann's Way* the boy, Marcel, discovers that literature affords an entry into the depths of experience that remain closed to physical perception:

A "real" person, profoundly as we may sympathize with him, is in a great measure perceptible only through our senses, that is to say, he remains opaque, offers a dead weight which our sensibilities have not the strength to lift. . . . The novelist's happy discovery was to think of substituting for those opaque sections, impene-

[2] Leo Bersani, *Marcel Proust: The Fictions of Life and of Art* (New York: Oxford University Press, 1965), and *Balzac to Beckett: Center and Circumference in French Fiction* (New York: Oxford University Press, 1970), pp. 192–240.

trable by the human spirit, their equivalent in immaterial sections, things, that is, which the spirit can assimilate to itself.[3]

The whole Proustian drama is laid bare in Marcel's definition: literature is a means of replacing human opaqueness with something we can *know* and *possess*. Gradually this protective, almost digestive, notion of art will change, as Marcel begins to realize that an artist's creation, like the magic lantern, is a means of seeing the world through another's eyes, an invitation to collaborate with genius. The world is not thereby possessed, or divested of its opaqueness; but vision can be shared. Thus, Bergotte intrigues Marcel essentially as a focus, a particular lens through which reality is reflected:

Whenever he spoke of something whose beauty had until then remained hidden from me, of pine-forests or of hailstorms, of *Notre Dame de Paris*, of *Athalie*, or of *Phèdre*, by some piece of imagery he would make their beauty explode and drench me with its essence. And so, dimly realizing that the universe contained innumerable elements which my feeble senses would be powerless to discern, did he not bring them within my reach, I wished that I might have his opinion, some metaphor of his, upon everything in the world. [p. 72]

The world remains *other*, but its variety and impenetrability enable it, in Proust's view, to conjure forth our deepest responses. Those imaginative responses, excessive or futile or "wrong" in life, may find expression in art and thereby constitute our deepest and most authentic signature. Psychologically, such a notion permits one to regard, even to exploit, others as a means of self-discovery, to utilize their opaqueness as a stimulus for self-expression:

I had guessed long ago in the Champs-Elysées, and since established to my own satisfaction, that when we are in love with a

---

[3] Marcel Proust, *Remembrance of Things Past*, tr. C. K. Scott Moncrieff (New York: Random House, 1934), I, 64. Subsequent quotations are from this edition.

woman we simply project into her a state of our own soul, that the important thing is, therefore, not the worth of the woman but the depth of the state; and that the emotions which a young girl of no kind of distinction arouses in us can enable us to bring to the surface of our consciousness some of the most intimate parts of our being, more personal, more remote, more essential than would be reached by the pleasure that we derive from the conversation of a great man or even from the admiring contemplation of his work. [I, 627]

The protective dimension of such a position is obvious as penetration of others is abandoned in favor of self-penetration. But, Proustian self-scrutiny is not idle. The self is realized through the images one projects on the World, through the organization, transformation, and deformation that one's vision effects. Proust's novel depicts the psychological frustration of such activity as well as the aesthetic liberation it affords.

More profoundly than the style of Bergotte, the entire work of Elstir is a metaphorical expression of his identity, his originality. Elstir's inversion of water and land motifs in his seascapes testifies to his ability to use the world as his medium. As a disturbing pendant to the seascapes, however, there is the portrait of Miss Sacripant, with its insistence on the transvestite, the ambiguity and malleability of physical forms. Again, a major theme of Proust's work is sounded, and the concept of the *inverti*, which will haunt the narrator and permeate the novel, is seen aesthetically as a sign of the artist's power, his ability to manipulate forms and cause metamorphoses. As disturbing as it may be morally, the notion of the *inverti* is a recognition of the freedom and opaqueness of others. The excruciating doubts about Odette's or Albertine's lesbian adventures stem from a peculiarly creative form of anguish. More precisely, it is a theory of fictions, a form-giving impulse in response to one's fears (again psychological distress may be equated with aesthetic richness). The French term *inverti* strikingly differs from the English "homosexual" or "lesbian" in its emphasis on the morphological, or the formal notion of reversal rather than a substantive denotation of sexual behavior. Beckett has brilliantly depicted Proust's characters in terms of flora, referring to his "complete indifference to moral values and human justices. Flower and plant have no conscious will. They are shameless, exposing their genitals. And so in a sense are Proust's men and women. . . . Homosexuality is never called a vice; it is as devoid of moral implications as the mode of fecundation of the *Primula veris* or the *Lythrum saliceria*."[4] Beyond shamelessness, however, the floral metaphor suggests metamorphosis itself. The various and manifold avatars of Charlus, Odette, Mme Verdurin, Gilberte, *et al.*, are more overwhelming in their diversity than their particularity: their moral or psychological traits seem to interest Proust considerably less than their astonishing transformations and transmutations.

Proust's world and his style seem larded with explanations, with ever emerging laws to account for appearances, but the reader readily senses that no amount of insight and evidence can adequately stabilize or "explain" the endless flow of changing roles and evolving essences; any character can be anything at any time and probably will be at one time or another. There is only one law in Proust's work, and it is the one that his artists embody, some consciously, others unwittingly: the law of metamorphosis. When the Curé at Combray explains somewhat pedantically to Eulalie that her namesake in Burgundy would be Saint Eloi, that "the lady has become a gentleman" (I, 80), he is merely corroborating etymologically what we see sexually, socially, artistically, and psychologically at work everywhere in the novel. Marcel's grandparents are convinced that Swann can only frequent the progeny of brokers and bankers; Marcel thinks that the two *côtés*, that of Swann and that of Guermantes, are as distinct

---

[4] Samuel Beckett, *Proust* (New York: Grove Press, n.d.), pp. 68–69.

and irreconcilable as east and west; Léonie refuses to believe
that even a stray dog in Combray is unlabeled, unaccounted
for. Proust's novel *inverts* such fixed beliefs and pieties at
every turn, showing the world and its inhabitants to be as
myriad as the church at Combray whose memorial stones
"melt like honey" or surge out "in a milky, frothing wave,"
whose windows are "a mountain of rosy snow" and where the
light, at times, took "on all the iridescence of a peacock's tail,
then shook and wavered in a flaming and fantastic shower,
distilled and dropping from the groin of the dark and rocky
vault down the moist walls, as though [the boy were penetrat-
ing] along the bed of some rainbow grotto of sinuous stalac-
tites" (I, 46–47). One does not penetrate such a world, just
as one possesses precious little in Proust (a lesson that Swann
and Marcel repeatedly learn). A metamorphic world is endless, yielding unsuspected and unlimited riches, but providing
no final knowledge. Elstir's paintings of Odette and the mixed
urban-seascapes show us neither the essential Odette nor nature
as it is; they show us Elstir, his profound knowledge of metamorphosis. Bergotte's metaphors are not truth, but a rich, even
priceless awareness of what pine forests and hail storms and
Phèdre were to the artist.

Revelations in Proust are not truth-giving, because they are
ongoing; they are accretive rather than supplanting. The volume of Proust, the immensities of time and space, whether
they be Combray in a teacup or medieval France in Françoise
or Geneviève de Brabant in the large-nosed, pimpled Duchesse
de Guermantes, are neither undercut nor misleading in the
final analysis. Their richness and their beauty remain, although
life is mean and reality stinting. Not unlike Rosa Coldfield's
"might-have-been" tale of love between Bon and Judith, herself and Sutpen, Marcel's prodigious, erroneous, creative imagination does not need truth for its authority. Contrary to the
Faulknerian overpass to love, however, Proustian transcendence goes beyond the real so that it may return to the self.

Faulknerian evidence is beggared by the urgency of touch and mutuality; Proust's visible anticlimactic surprises (Françoise killing the chicken, Léonie's relief that her husband is indeed dead, Vinteuil putting the music deliberately in view, the all too real features of Oriane, la Berma, his grandmother, Venice, the discovered or suspected homosexuality of every character in the work) do not ultimately deflate Marcel's illusions, but rather add to his gallery of portraits. They will become the impenetrable, but reflective components of his mirror. They will teach him that others are unknowable, but not so the self. The richness of error, seen in the glamour of Guermantes and the interwoven sea-flower-bird mystery of Albertine and the girls on the beach, is not tarnished because Oriane and Albertine are. The metaphorical vision leads, as Proust shows again and again, to disillusionment and frustrates our hunger, but it permits us to possess in our minds and express in our art a fullness and beauty that may be realized in no other way. The self harbors this vision, but it is so remote, so forbiddingly absent from all social intercourse, that the path toward it is one of solipsis and the pleasures it affords are masturbatory in essence. Perhaps it is pleasure itself that so peculiarly marks Proust's work: the pleasure we take in those full-blown metaphorical descriptions sovereignly indifferent to accuracy or inaccuracy, the "inhuman world of pleasure" which each character deviously but maniacally pursues, the final emerging pleasure (equated, in Proust, with maturity) of solipsis itself, of possessing through one's metaphorical evocation of the world, not the world but oneself.

The theme of lost illusions informs the nineteenth-century French novel, articulating the work of Stendhal, Balzac, and Flaubert. It is equally present in Proust, as Marcel becomes disillusioned about the magic of names and places, as the otherness of the world frustrates his hunger, and reality invariably falls short of romantic expectations and imaginative investments. However, unlike Madame Bovary who is destroyed by the discrepancy between dream and reality, Marcel gradually learns that the illusions and fictions he entertains may be infinitely valuable as expressions of the self, as tentative assertions in a kaleidoscopic world. Experience tends to become a testing ground for fictions, redeemable particularly in retrospect, always open and enticing. An event is not "over" in Proust, but rather incorporated into the immense volume of a life capable of being reworked, relived. Nothing can be wasted because everything can be added to the repertory of the self. As Bersani says, the novel *creates* Marcel's continuity: "the metaphorical connections the narrator now establishes among different moments of his life give a psychological unity to what he had felt was the history of discontinuous personalities."[5] Hence, the self emerges through its metaphorical power. It is expression. It is also derealization. The world tends —despite the exquisiteness of its details and the "depth" laws that animate it—to become spectacle, surface, theater, as the portrait of the artist take on unity and continuity.

In the work of Borges, Claude Simon, and Robbe-Grillet, the fictions become autonomous, and the structures and patterns of vision, far from secretly and cumulatively defining the self, reign alone, inhuman and authoritative.

In his Introduction to Borges' *Other Inquisitions*, James Irby shrewdly remarks that "any theme set forth by Borges will be refuted by him somewhere else."[6] Consequently, his work resists cubbyholing, and it can be enlisted to illustrate a particular thesis only by means of discrete nuances or dishonesty. Nonetheless, the bulk of his "metaphysical" tales, his speculative essays and forays into literary criticism deal with

[5] Bersani, *Marcel Proust*, pp. 6–7.
[6] James E. Irby, Introduction to J. L. Borges, *Other Inquisitions 1937–1952*, tr. Ruth L. C. Simms (New York: Simon and Schuster, 1968), p. xiv.

the problems of time, pattern, and identity that have preoccupied us throughout this study. Borges' treatment of these
issues is peculiarly modern. At the outset, Borges dispenses
with the conventions of continuity, character, and cogency
that usually govern fiction. Thus, to compare Borges with
Proust and Joyce and other Moderns is inevitable. But we
must not ignore that his very stories—filled with vivid historical examples, literary allusions from all epochs, Eastern, classical, medieval, Renaissance, and modern philosophical inquiry, all combining to illustrate that notions of reality and
vision always have been of concern to literature—scoff at such
recent comparisons. What is modern about Borges is what he
does with his heresies about time and development; what distinguishes his work from philosophical speculation and makes
it particularly relevant to our study is the problematic effort
to make human meaning out of the multifaceted, multileveled
spectacle that his mind perceives. The order that emerges
comes at a great cost and in the wake of such debris (wrecked
identities, manipulated lives, lapses into the void) that we may
legitimately question just how human it is. The path toward
order leads Borges' personages through eclipses and abstract
form principles, and it is that tension between a desired harmony and a witnessed destruction which characterizes the
vision of his work. What has been abundantly commented on
and celebrated in the art of Borges is the intricate, glittering
formal achievement; his work is conceded to be elegant, so-
phisticated, lucid, cosmopolitan, and esoteric. The claim for
poignancy, for pain, is made less often, and my aim here is to
illuminate the cost, the human dimension (which Borges rarely
overlooks) that underlies and finances his prodigious patterns
and cosmologies.

In one of his essays Borges remarks that an infinite number
of different biographies could be written about any person.
Not the whim of the observers, but the multiplicity of the
subject is responsible for such variety. Any description of

"identity" or "character" would be encyclopedic; moreover, Borges suggests, the separate traits, moments, facets of our lives are wholly discrete, discontinuous, autonomous. Many of his stories evoke people either searching for "themselves" (the portrait of Shakespeare in "Everything and Nothing"), or utterly unaware of the figure their life is creating. Léon Bloy's statement, "No one knows who he is" (which Borges enjoys quoting), is handsomely embodied in "Death and the Compass." The mixture of detective story and esoteric doctrines about the identity of the Name produces the perfect surprise ending, when the detective Lönnrot discovers that he is the object of the game, the Name of the victim. The criminal, Red Scharlach, counted on Lönnrot to pick up the hints, and the detective is ultimately caught because of his fundamental identity (emphasized by the affinity of their names) with the man he is searching for. Borges does not proceed as Sophocles did with Oedipus, and the emphasis is less on riddles or ultimate knowledge than on the compulsive itinerary enacted by the detective, a kind of trancelike ballet in which the dancer thinks he is awake. This story is very obviously a labyrinth parable, for Lönnrot dutifully follows the clues and makes his way to the heart of the maze; there he meets both himself and death. "The House of Asterion" recounts the same myth, but from the inside this time: whereas Theseus-Lönnrot explores the labyrinth in the detective story, the monster itself narrates this one, revealing its longing for Theseus, for deliverance and redemption. Our traditional view of the myth is enlarged, for we realize that the story is not of Theseus and the minotaur, of hero and horror, but—rather than such discrete, isolated elements—of a union, of a desired and wrought harmony. The Conradian strain of secret correspondence between hero and villain (see "The Life of Tadeo Isidoro Cruz" and "The Other Death" as well as "Theme of the Traitor and the Hero") often takes the form of such dramatic reversals as in the minotaur story. "The Shape of the

Sword" is not outfitted with a surprise ending, a confession that the narrator is, in fact, the traitor, merely because Borges is a master of dramatic irony: Vincent Moon as witness-narrator and Vincent Moon as traitor-protagonist *merge*, through the scar, through the atonement of the harsh criticism, through the strategy of the tale. Likewise, the brief note "Borges and I" depicts, in a personal mode, the same enigma of identity. This revealing piece clearly states the schizophrenic division and tension implicit in so many of the tales about "doubles." In some cases the final link is accomplished without strife; thus Edward FitzGerald and Omar ben Ibrahim al-Khayyami, separated by time, country, and temperament, are, according to Borges, fused into a single poet. The work of Kafka, says Borges, not only creates its precursors, but furnishes the unique perspective according to which diverse writers coalesce to form a new whole: before Kafka, they were autonomous; after him, there is a new identity constellation.

In some stories the transition from truncated part to new whole is not achieved without a certain violence. Thus, Borges recounts Runeberg's concept of Judas as the secret mask of God: "God made Himself totally a man but a man to the point of infamy, a man to the point of reprobation and the abyss. To save us, He could have chosen *any* of the destinies which make up the complex web of history; He could have been Alexander or Pythagoras or Rurik or Jesus; He chose the vilest destiny of all: He was Judas."[7] It matters little whether Borges *believes* such a thesis; what counts is the recurrent phenomenon of a *part*, a discordant part (Judas), being welded by the vision of Borges (or those whom he cites) into a larger harmony. In "Deutsches Requiem," Otto Dietrich zur Linde mysteriously embraces his position as subdirector of the con-

[7] Jorge Luis Borges, "Three Versions of Judas," tr. James E. Irby, in *Labyrinths*, eds. Donald A. Yates and James E. Irby (New York: New Directions, 1964), p. 99. Unless otherwise noted, all quotations from the stories are from this edition.

centration camp at Tarnowitz. The reasoning behind this acceptance reveals a submission to the Order principle that directs our lives, the elusive principle that Borges seeks to ferret out in each of his tales: "Thus, every negligence is deliberate, every chance encounter an appointment, every humiliation a penitence, every failure a mysterious victory, every death a suicide. There is no more skillful consolation than the idea that we have chosen our own misfortunes; this individual teleology reveals a secret order and prodigiously confounds us with the divinity" (p. 143).

What would therefore seem to be discord, conflict, antithesis, is ultimately revealed as pattern. The unity that is forged derives from an idealism that radically differs from the relationships observed in earlier writers. In *Père Goriot* and *Great Expectations*, the education of the protagonist consists in discovering *for himself* a deeper order than the visible one countenanced by society. For Borges, the final order need not be "real," nor is it necessary that the actors in the drama perceive its wholeness. He is working from the ancient *topos* of the World as Book, but with the understanding that the ultimately perceived coherence is retrospective, *ex post facto*, a made thing, frequently made of broken fragments and disjointed, ruptured lives. His famous story, "Tlön, Uqbar, Orbis Tertius," perfectly embodies the virtues of an *intelligible* creation: "How could one do other than submit to Tlön, to the minute and vast evidence of an orderly planet? It is useless to answer that reality is also orderly. Perhaps it is, but in accordance with divine laws—I translate: inhuman laws—which we never quite grasp. Tlön is surely a labyrinth, but it is a labyrinth devised by men, a labyrinth destined to be deciphered by men" (p. 12). Many have doubtless considered that statement to be the key to Borges' aesthetic and philosophical beliefs. But "Tlön" is a bloodless creation; its perceptible order does not contain the chopped-up lives and fates encountered in the other stories.

Tlön is a world where pattern and form may be wrought at

will, but often it is not so. Too frequently, the reader may notice only the glittering patterns and elegant systems, but not the muted pain. In "The Garden of Forking Paths" we have the supreme example of labyrinth fiction: we watch the protagonist, Yu Tsun, twist the hands of fate, coerce the living events into a fatal, preordained pattern; we see too how the enactment of the famous Ts'ui Pên labyrinth story turns the paradox of friend-enemy into grisly political truth. And yet, there is more to this story than the synchronization of schema and life; there are also the muffled character relationships, Yu Tsun's own tortured role as spy, his almost pathological fear of the powerful, ubiquitous Richard Madden, his growing veneration for Stephen Albert, a man who is "no less great than Goethe." The gradual revelation of Ts'ui Pên's creation, *The Garden of Forking Paths*, is synonymous with the growing attachment for Albert. As the story climaxes with the murder of the revered man, Borges does not emphasize the completed pattern (either labyrinthine or political): instead he tells us, in words that are strangely reminiscent of Rosa Coldfield, what they cannot have told us: "He [The Chief] knew my problem was to indicate (through the uproar of the war) the city called Albert, and that I had found no other means to do so than to kill a man of that name. He does not know (no one can know) my innumerable contrition and weariness" (p. 29). Still more disturbing beneath its apparent symmetry is the tale of Emma Zunz. Here we see the perfect crime, the substitution of art for life, of imposed pattern on lived experience. Emma is, in a perverse way, an artist figure, one who coerces life into her mold, who deceives the judge and jury with her artifact. In provoking a sordid sexual encounter so that she can seek revenge under the guise of rape, Emma has an ideal alibi: "Actually, the story *was* incredible, but it impressed everyone because substantially it was true. True was Emma Zunz' tone, true was her shame, true was her hate. True also was the outrage she had suffered: only the circumstances were false, the time and one or two proper names" (p. 137). But can we overlook the cost of her achievement? Borges has carefully presented Emma as virginal, shy, almost abnormally afraid of men; to complete her work, she is obliged to violate her life, to twist and deform herself in order to impose her art.

However, even an art which tolerates little human assertion within its limits may be a celebration of human appetites and would-be conquests. Borges enlarges our world, but he does so—honestly and movingly—at our expense. Much has been written about the mirrors and Chinese boxes in his work, strategies for endless reflections and limitless expanse. But the real value of his work does not depend on optical illusions; it is a more vital matter of exploding and transcending the confines in which the impoverished, circumscribed self ordinarily keeps house. It is a true idealism in which spirit can outrun and outperform matter, in which a man awaiting death at the firing squad can find that extra year necessary for completing his play. It is an infinitely open world, extending temporally and spatially in all directions. Everything is ours if our vision is broad and bold enough to claim it: Pierre Menard can rewrite, repossess, and force us to rediscover the *Quixote;* Kafka can reunite his precursors. And yet, as we saw with Joyce, the penalty for such freedom and multiplicity is the loss of our oneness. Borges is willing to pay that penalty, and Tzinacán, the suffering, questing, imprisoned magician who has deciphered the God's script, captures the world but loses himself: "Whoever has seen the universe, whoever has beheld the fiery designs of the universe, cannot think in terms of one man, of that man's trivial fortunes or misfortunes, though he be that very man. That man *has been he* and now matters no more to him" (p. 173).

Lest one think that our universe may be enlarged only through dream, or erudition, or closing one's eyes to the tangible, visible one, Borges also wrote stories about fidelity to the awesome material world we live in. The tale of Funes is that of a man who *sees* the universe, who sees it in its relentless variety and multiplicity. His mind is the repository of all the severed images he has ever perceived: "His own face in the mirror, his own hands, surprised him every time he saw them. . . . He was the solitary and lucid spectator of a multiform, instantaneous and almost intolerably precise world" (p. 65). Unlike the cosmopolitan, blind scholar who transforms the world into abstract, timeless patterns and myths, Funes does not need to leave his chair or to imagine anything at all. He merely sees. He is, Borges reminds us, incapable of thought, because thought is generalizing, and generalizing is forgetting. Therefore, he too pays. He has none of the consoling patterns and short cuts of the mind, and the rich totality of his perceptions is paralyzing and chaotic. Expansion, whether it be visual, imaginative, or erudite, carries its dangers, and Borges does not disguise them.

Identity is desired, but our experience is unconnected. Like the alienated voice of "Borges and I," we live countless, divided lives. The need for harmonies that informs his work can rarely be satisfied within the scope of a single consciousness. Collage, allusion, and cyclical forms make sense of the world, but we are more the ingredients than the beneficiaries of such a process.

The mosaic polish of Borges' art is composed, as all mosaics are, of broken pieces. Unlike the literary fragments shorn up by Eliot in "The Wasteland," the tales of Borges honor the pain of discord, separateness, ignorance, and—even more compellingly—harmony itself. He seeks, like the narrator of "The Library of Babel," that final book which will make intelligible order of everything. He reveres the dream as a realm of transcendence where the realistic limits of time and space are overcome. Aware of man's single ignorance, he celebrates our joint humanity and admires Whitman's desire to be like, and to be, all men. Conscious of time which robs us of our estate and erases our memories, he seeks to refute it, thereby repossessing the richness of our experience. His concept of eternity, illustrated in "The Aleph," is a discovery of all the grids and coordinates of reality, the infinite variety of which beggars our perceptions. Each life, each second contains eternity, and Borges hungers to possess it. If living is a process of erosion and seepage, art can restore our legacy: "Archetypes and eternity—words—promise more certain possessions. What is certain is that sequence is intolerable and niggardly, and that generous appetites desire all the minutes of time and all the variety of space."[8] His characters' truncated lives are, in some sense, salvaged by the vast cosmologies into which Borges inserts them. The private vision is disjointed, but the larger framework is redemptive. His art, as John Barth has pointed out, is comparable to Menelaus wrestling with Proteus or, better, to Theseus finding his way—skillfully and surely— through the intricate labyrinths of his own making.[9] Never forgetting his limited and blind humanity, Borges uses his fantastic knowledge and erudite fantasy to expand the picture, to make an ordered artifact in which human gestures become intimations of harmony and identity.

If metaphor is both creative and expressive in Proust, it is no less liberating in the work of Claude Simon. But whereas Proust ultimately finds identity in the diversity and richness of the mind's images, Simon's novels become progressively impersonal. The distance between *The Wind* (1954) and *Les Corps conducteurs* (1971) typifies the itinerary of the *nouveau roman:* from mimesis to *écriture.* It is no accident that the

[8] Borges, *Histoire de l'éternité* (Paris, 10/18 ed.), p. 162. My translation from the French.
[9] John Barth, "The Literature of Exhaustion," in *The American Novel since World War II,* ed. Marcus Klein (Greenwich, Conn.: Fawcett Publications, 1969), pp. 267–279.

novels chosen for this study, Butor's *Passing Time*, Robbe-Grillet's *In the Labyrinth*, and Simon's *The Flanders Road*, are transitional works of mid-career. Each of these novels is, in some sense, psychological despite itself. *The Flanders Road* is Claude Simon's last truly anthropocentric novel because its style is still—precariously and tragically—in the service of its characters. It is the tenuousness of the novel's psychological reference, the brilliant vital resistance of language and style against the pressures of human cogency that mark *The Flanders Road*. The earlier Faulknerian rhetoric is still there, with its present participles and emphasis on imagination, but in this novel Simon seems to discover that words and thoughts and phrases follow their own impulses and, as it were, dictate their own conduct. In the later novels such stylistic behavior, flitting from one description to another, sovereignly indifferent to the strands of *anecdote* it weaves and entangles, constitutes a clear case of *écriture*, a novel about the possibilities of language. In *The Flanders Road*, the predominance of style over meaning is assessed humanly: Georges's experience is presented in whirling, kaleidoscopic images, merging and shifting and recurring according to the laws of metaphor and analogy, but interrogated in vain for meaning or depth. Such interrogation is anthropomorphic, and is not found in the "liberated" novels that follow.

The fundamental theme of *The Flanders Road*, like that of all Simon novels, is disintegration, decomposition. Only the elements seem real to Simon: the earth, the wind, the grass, the rain. These elemental forces are matched by a kind of disembodied violence and fury that periodically seizes his characters or emerges through them in moments of truth. Against these constant forces is the manifold, complex world of human beings, filled with structures and patterns of culture, morality, and language; each Simon novel dramatizes the onslaught—almost molecular in its elemental indifference—against rational forms. The rotting fruit in *The Grass*, the decaying corpse in

The Palace, the rusty, abandoned farm equipment in *The Battle of Pharsala* assert the futility of human effort; but only in *The Flanders Road* has Simon created a framework truly adequate to his belief in chaos: war, or rather, a man's attempt to make sense of his war experience. Presented through the memories of Georges, the fall of the French front is part of a larger process of decomposition, one that entails the erosion of all forms of cogency. Thus, Georges's evocation of the retreat reflects the interrelatedness of the rain, his fatigue, the collapsing front, and the collapsing, elusive past:

in full retreat or rather rout or rather disaster in the middle of this collapse of everything as if not an army but the world itself the whole world and not only in its physical reality but even in the representation the mind can make of it (but maybe it was the lack of sleep too, the fact that we had had almost no sleep at all in ten days except on horseback) was actually falling apart collapsing breaking up into pieces dissolving into water into nothing.[10]

The phenomenon of matter returning to its original state is recurrent in the novel. Most striking is the decaying horse:

something unexpected, unreal, hybrid, so that what had been a horse (that is, what you knew, what you could recognize as having been a horse) was no longer anything now but a vague heap of limbs, of dead meat, of skin and sticky hair, three-quarters covered with mud . . . already half absorbed apparently by the earth, as though the latter had stealthily begun to take back what had come from it. [pp. 25–26]

We are likewise told that war hastens the decomposition process in all matter, that metals rust far more rapidly, that a general sort of elemental anarchy threatens. As Georges feels a growing numbness in his arm, we detect the same inexorable process: "watching, impotent, the slow transmutation of his

[10] Claude Simon, *The Flanders Road,* tr. Richard Howard (New York: George Braziller, 1961), p. 15. Subsequent quotations are from this edition.

own substance starting with his arm that he could feel dying gradually, growing numb, devoured not by worms but by a slowly mounting tingle that was perhaps the stirring of atoms in the process of permutating in order to organize themselves according to a different structure" (pp. 247–248).

The ultimate awareness of chaos, the Conradian immersion in the elements, is the upshot of *The Flanders Road*, but the apprenticeship is so radical and complete that there is little place for recognition or knowledge. Simon does not believe that chaos teaches. It annihilates, brutally, cleanly, absurdly, as in the case of Wack's death:

the expression dazed, stupefied, as though astonished by the sudden revelation of death that is finally known no longer in the abstract form of that concept with which we have grown accustomed to live but rising up or rather striking in its physical reality, that violence that aggression, a blow of unheard-of unsuspected disproportionate unfair undeserved brutality the stupid and stupefying fury of things that have no need of reasons to strike like when you run headlong into a lamppost you hadn't seen lost in your thoughts as they say then becoming acquainted with the idiotic revolting and fierce wickedness of cast iron. [p. 90]

Moreover, the chaotic principle is not amenable to the constraints of language and the conventions of fiction. Hence the bitter sarcasm reserved for Georges's father, Pierre: "Being the son of illiterate peasants, he's so proud of having been able to learn how to read that he's deeply convinced that there's no problem, and particularly no problem standing in the way of humanity's happiness, that can't be solved by reading good authors" (p. 226). Simon's quarrel is with language itself ("words invented in the hope of making palatable—like those vaguely sugared pellets disguising a bitter medicine for children—the unmentionable reality" [p. 186]), and each novel seems to try to crack the ordered shell of language, to attain some viscous, visceral, authentic realm beyond it.

But the chaos uncovered in this novel neither kills the hero nor reduces him to silence; otherwise there could be no book. Instead it dominates Georges's mind and his acts, giving style to his story and removing meaning from his life. For the memories coursing through Georges's thoughts are not depicted in random fashion; they are articulated as tightly and cohesively as anyone could desire. But the grammar dictating their order is alien to human cogency; it eschews sequence and development in favor of another schema. The extraordinary resemblances among the characters, the predictable roles they assume are the result of a rigid, analogical system, not mimetic observation. Corinne resembles the farm girl resembles the young wife in the painting; Reixach repeats the gestures of his ancestor; the *boiteux* vainly tries to keep his sister-in-law from fornicating, just as Reixach's wife Corinne was sexually promiscuous with Iglésia and others; the old General commits suicide because of the spectacle of his staff in complete disarray, an event that mirrors the two Reixachs' discoveries in the eighteenth and twentieth centuries, possibly even Georges's own war experience. The groupings and recurrent images that structure Georges's narrative evoke an archetypal pattern of betrayal and collapse. The process of mutation and decay permeates the moral dimension of the novel, giving Georges's thoughts a deterministic, obsessional character. In each case we witness the utter collapse of principles or rational structures under the onslaught of chaos, presented in the form of sexual disorder or the kind of "moral diarrhea" brought on by the war. The pattern becomes ritualistic, predictable: the decaying horse, the numb arm, the dissolving rain, the rush of the blood and the frenzy of the body in response to the omnipresent, identical milk-white female flesh with its swelling breasts and dark, beckoning crevices. This is hardly reliable narration, in the sense of *choses vues*, but it is compelling as an index of Georges's mind, as a serial presentation of chaos.

Georges's perception and presentation are articulated by reversals. The discovery of chaos, like any discovery, is not gradual, and Simon wants to convey it with immediacy. Thus we see the same shock value in Wack's "discovery" of death as in the involved fictive versions of the death of Reixach's ancestor. The collapse paradigm is fully illustrated by the story of Reixach's ancestor, seduced by the democratic euphoria of Rousseau, spectator of the defeat of his troops by the Spanish, returning home to find his young wife fornicating with a servant. The trauma is presented with a touch of *guignol*, as Simon hides lover and gun in the closet: "he who had already been dragging for the last four days the heavy, rotten and stinking corpse of his disillusions . . . [walking] to the closet, opening the door, and then receiving in the head that pistol bullet fired at point blank range" (p. 203). Perhaps the most unsettling image of trauma is that of the disguised maid because there the connection between sexual disorder, violence, and deceptive appearances is made explicit: "like the solitary old lady, discovering the boots that stick out beneath the skirt and the thick hair with which the cheeks are covered now, suddenly realizing with horror as the soup is served that the elderly serving-woman she hired that morning is actually a man, realizing then, and irremediably, that she will be murdered in the night" (p. 80). The structure of this complex sentence, with its mounting clauses and suspense, its delayed fatal disclosure, reflects the discovery process itself and renders the shock all the more palpable. These brutal surprises, momentary glimpses of the chaos lurking behind forms, punctuate *The Flanders Road*, rendering both what Georges has seen and what it has done to him.

Georges's posture is one of stunned interrogation; the urgency of his need for meaning transforms those countless evocations of exhausted riding and marching in the rain into a quest. There is hunger for food, knowledge, and, above all, sex; but gratification is thwarted according to the strategy of trauma and reversal we have already noticed. Thus, Georges's glimpse of the girl in the stable occasions a kind of mythic, erotic reverie: "A warm white thing like the milk she had come for at the moment they had arrived, a kind of apparition not lit by the lamp but luminescent, as if her skin were itself the source of the light, as if that interminable night ride had had no other reason, no other purpose than the discovery at its end of this diaphanous flesh modeled in the night's density" (pp. 40–41). The same motif is picked up midway in the book with comparable mythic overtones: "we weren't in the autumn mud we weren't anywhere a thousand years or two thousand years earlier or later in the middle of madness murder the Atrides, riding across time the night streaming with rain over our exhausted horses to reach her discover her find her warm half naked and milky in that stable by the light of that lantern" (p. 121). Finally, near the close of the book, we again encounter the familiar words, but notice that Simon has included the payoff this time: "and I the horseman, the booted conqueror coming from the depths of the night from the depths of time coming to seduce to carry off the lily-white princess of whom I had dreamed for years and just when I thought she was mine, taking her in my arms, embracing her, holding her close, finding myself face to face with one of Goya's horrible old crones" (p. 272).[11]

The hideous old woman is less distressing than the range of possibilities she opens up. It is not a question of staying away from closet doors or not hiring maids with rough complexions (although that might help); what is frightening is the prospect of living among instantaneous, monstrous mutations, the kind that war particularly favors. Consider, for example, the episode where Georges and Iglésia, trying to escape machine-gun fire, are attempting to blend in with the hedges: "and the

[11] The final and controlling version of sexual fiasco and thwarted desire, may well be the frenzied lovemaking with Corinne that literally generates many of the coursing memories of the novel. Corinne is never Goyesque, but the novel itself records, *is* a straining for gratification that is not achieved.

countryside still looked like a well-pruned garden, what do you call those bushes, shrubs or rather conifers grass-plots geometrically shaped gardens *à la française* making careful interlocking curves groves and nooks for marquis and marquises disguised as shepherds and shepherdesses seeking each other in disguise seeking finding love death" (p. 79). The passage constitutes a microcosm of the novel as a whole. The French garden, with its symmetries and harmonies imposed on nature, is the very quintessence of Cartesian optimism, of human assertion; in time of war this haven of rational forms becomes labyrinthine, concealing death and destruction. Likewise, the masquerade motif is operative, and the eighteenth-century *galanterie* thinly disguises the lust and hunger ("seeking each other in disguise seeking finding" is calm compared to the breathless French *se cherchant à l'aveuglette cherchant trouvant*). Finally, just as the sanctity of the garden is obliterated, so too is the final discovery, that of death, not sexual gratification, and Simon's style again conveys the shock by insisting on the insidious similarity (in French) of those words: "*l'amour la mort.*"

Thus, Simon's connective system is in no sense purely mechanical or formal; his mutations and surprises are meaningful, for they ineluctably terminate in death or chaos. The house that Georges incessantly scrutinizes in hopes of spying the mysterious girl behind the shade is described in precisely the same terms as the place where the machine gunner is waiting for them to pass: "The brick house over there!" The most richly suggestive network of related and merging images deals with holes, some gaping, some beckoning. Thus, the horse's wound is described as "the lips of what was more a hole, a crater than a wound" (p. 105); Wack's mouth in death is "wide open like a hole" (p. 157). Implicit in each of these descriptions is the fascination and hunger of sex: "that hairy mouth that thing with an animal's name, a term of natural history—mussel sponge valve vulva—suggesting those deep-sea and blind carnivorous organisms still furnished with lips, with hair: the orifice of that matrix the original crucible that he seemed to see in the entrails of the world" (p. 41). There is a sense of the abyss in this novel, filled as it is with holes, craters, gullies; the fascination and hunger Georges feels in their presence is constant, although the orifices themselves change without warning. Hence we see Georges hiding in a ditch: "watchful, stiff, now completely numb and paralyzed with cramps, and as motionless as the dead nag, his face buried in the thick grass, the hairy earth, his whole body flattened as if he were trying to vanish between the lips of the ditch, to melt, to slip, to sink altogether through this narrow crevice to re-join original matter (matrix)" (p. 249). Several pages later, Georges's sensation of himself making love is described as "there was nothing left of my body but a shrunken wizened fetus lying between the lips of a ditch as if I could melt into it disappear there engulf myself there" (p. 262).

To read *The Flanders Road* is to forge a new grammar, to articulate experience according to the constants of hunger and desire. Ordinarily discrete acts merge into each other, adumbrate a hidden but imperious ordering scheme which is nothing other than the vision of the novel. It is not surprising that Simon, attentive to the moments where chaos surfaces, views the sexual act as particularly explosive. The lovemaking scenes in *The Flanders Road* may well be the most dazzling in modern literature, and the analogical style, blending images and memories of different kinds of hunger, evokes sequences of ecstatic liberation. The following description typifies Simon's version of "tripping":

so I threw myself on the ground dying of hunger thinking The horses eat it why not me I tried to imagine to convince myself I was a horse, I was lying dead at the bottom of the ditch . . . and then it would be the grass that would feed on me . . . in other words up above it would go on growing still indifferent and green just as they say hair goes on growing on dead men's heads the only difference being that I would be eating the dandelions by the root [a weak short cut for Simon's brilliant *"je boufferais les pissenlits par la racine bouffant là où elle pisse"*] our dripping bodies exhaling that sharp pungent odor of roots, of mandragor, I had read that shipwrecked men that hermits eat roots acorns [the French word *gland* is powerfully ambivalent here] and then she took it first between her lips then far back in her mouth like a greedy child it was as if we were drinking each other slaking each other's thirst gorging on each other feasting famished, trying to appease calm my hunger a little I tried to chew it, thinking it's like salad, the harsh green juice putting my teeth on edge a sharp blade cut my tongue like a razor, burning. [pp. 263–264]

As the woman's body and the grass merge back and forth, we are aware of a vertiginous exchange; identity, stability, focus are swept away in the rush of blood. The act of love is wholly impersonal, unleashing forces that bandy about the human participants. Orgasm, like war, reveals the inhuman chaotic principle: "that permanent and inexhaustible stockpile or rather reservoir or rather principle of all violence and all passion that seems to wander imbecile and idle and objectless on the surface of the earth like those winds those gales without any other purpose than a blind and negative fury shaking wildly whatever happens to lie in their path" (p. 293).

In this light the reversal images of shock and trauma are linked with the recurrent motif of bestiality and, as its logical extension, metamorphosis. Making love, Georges describes himself as a dog, "my tongue hanging out galloping panting both of us like dogs" (p. 297), as a goat, "crawling under her exploring in the darkness discovering her enormous and shadowy body as though under a milk-giving goat" (p. 261), as a monkey, "clinging like those baby monkeys beneath the belly of their mother to her belly to her many breasts burying myself in that tawny clamminess" (p. 262). There are innumerable puns dealing with the words *bâton* and *monter*, particularly in regard to Iglésia's affair with Corinne; frequent mention of sodomy between men and goats, in regard to the peasants. Georges recalls the old album in which there is a page devoted to centaurs. The animality at the basis of "human" nature emerges in *The Flanders Road*. Struck brutally on the head in the dark train car filled with prisoners of war, Georges meditates on the adequacy of his humanistic education:

it was probably something like a mule or a horse that was stuffed into this car by mistake, unless we were the ones who were in this car by mistake since its original purpose was to carry animals, unless it's no mistake at all and they filled it with animals the way it was meant to be filled, so that we've become something like animals without realizing it, I think I remember reading somewhere a story like that, men changed with a tap of a wand into pigs or trees or stones all by reciting some Latin verses. . . . And so he's [Georges's father, Pierre] not completely wrong. And so after all words are at least good for something, so that in his summerhouse he can probably convince himself that by putting them together in every possible way you can at least sometimes manage with a little luck to tell the truth. I'll have to tell him that. It'll make him happy. I'll tell him that I've already read in Latin what's happened to me, so that I wasn't too surprised and even to a certain extent reassured to know that it had already been written down, so that all the money he's spent too to make me learn Latin wasn't completely wasted either. [pp. 101–102]

It is always possible to interpret the phenomenon of men turning into animals as moral allegory. But, just as Kafka has chosen to treat its realistically in "The Metamorphosis," Simon, even when he is only using simile, emphasizes the strictly morphological dimension of metamorphosis. To become an animal is more alarming than to act like one; to be sure, there are no real mutations in *The Flanders Road*, but the organization of the novel reflects a world of tumbling forms and emerging forces. Georges's experience defies and mocks him, asserts its hidden links and analogical structure despite his efforts to yoke it into a meaningful pattern.

Simon's novel is the reverse image of *Absalom, Absalom!* (which it strongly resembles); the French work registers a failure of the imagination, an inability to believe in depth, penetration, or the efficacy of affective form. Both books seem circular, but, whereas the thrust necessary for telling the Sutpen story is adumbrated by Rosa and achieved by Quentin and Shreve, nothing is accomplished in *The Flanders Road*; there is no sense of an ending. Things are out of joint, Chaplinesque: "for a second I saw the soldiers of the two armies chasing each other round and round the block of houses like in the Opera or those comic films people dashing in those parodic and burlesque chases the lover the husband brandishing a revolver the hotel chambermaid the adulterous wife the bellboy the little pastrycook the police then again the lover" (p. 212). Because things merge, it makes little difference whether Georges is hiding in a ditch or making love to Corinne five years later; the decaying horse and Reixach brandishing his saber may surge forth at any moment, enigmatic and obsessive. The imaginative effort of Georges and Blum to create a story out of the portraits is a brilliant—but pitiful—parody of the ritual of storytelling enacted by Quentin and Shreve. Perhaps Harvard dormitories are more conducive to fabulation than prison camps; in any event, Simon's characters are whistling in the dark, doomed by tuberculosis and starvation rather than the Southern past, able to conceive only autoerotic pornography rather than a vision of love. Above all, Simon records a failure of depth, a failure of the mind to make sense of one's experience, one's past. *Absalom* testifies to a belief in feeling as knowledge, as a means of penetrating the past and making it render its human truth. Georges fails in this, and the style of his story both records and explains that failure. He can neither control nor order what he sees because his vision is shaped by the forces of hunger and chaos that seize him. His integrity is literally divested from him, as his body merges with the animals and his experiences rush together and apart in ungovernable patterns.

Within such a framework, the human being is an alien measure, and vision can only record the endless outbreaks of chaos. There can be no knowledge or penetration. Georges may pierce Corinne like a ram, but he cannot "know" her. He may long to go through the mirror, to be on the other side of the grass, but death is no answer. The myriad physical world, like the brick house, can be scrutinized indefinitely, but it will yield no more than the eye of the dying horse does: "its long velvety eye pensive gentle and blank in which I had nevertheless been able to see our tiny figures reflected" (p. 293).

The reader of *The Flanders Road* must submit to its despotic style, accept its cogency rather than his own. Because reading profoundly resembles thinking, in that both inevitably seek pattern, Simon's novel is tragic for its protagonist and disturbing for its reader. We cannot dismiss its images of shock and reversal, its motifs of metamorphosis and animality as mere technique because there is a narrator suffering that style, swept along and ultimately broken by it. In that sense alone, there is an ending to *The Flanders Road*; as Georges's reverie closes back on itself, querying whether the whole adventure was just a dream, we sense that we have come, not to the beginning, but to the snapping point of a mind, the point where something fragile and crucial breaks. Georges's trauma is over. Simon has found his strategy, his form of orchestration, and the subsequent novels will be even more radically articulated by analogy and parallel. But the human reference, the obsession with chaos and decomposition that makes sense, human sense, of the presentation will become more and more discrete. The outrage, the fatigue, and the interrogation tend to be discarded, like obsolete appendices that either no longer serve a function or can no longer be tolerated.

Before writing about the work of Alain Robbe-Grillet, one is obliged to take note of the criticism, much of it tendentious, polemical, and written by Robbe-Grillet himself, that surrounds his novels and films. There are two rather distinct and mutually exclusive interpretations of his work: the first assessment, in response to the early novels *The Erasers* and *The Voyeur*, insists on the objective, nonanthropocentric character of his descriptions, the refusal of depth and psychology and plot in favor of a nonreferential depiction of surfaces. In the words of the most influential proponent of this view, Roland Barthes:

interiority is put in parentheses, things and spaces and man's itinerary between them are promoted to the rank of subject. The novel becomes the direct experience of man's environment, but man is shorn of psychology, metaphysics and psychoanalysis in his encounter with the objective milieu he discovers. Here the novel ceases to be chthonic, infernal; it is terrestrial; it teaches us to look at the world no longer with the eyes of the confessor, or the doctor, or God (all significant hypostases of the classical novel) but with the eyes of a man who walks in the city with no horizon other than its view, no power other than that of his eyes.[12]

Speaking of the strange one-dimensionality of Robbe-Grillet's world and characters, Gérard Genette remarks:

whatever they do or think, they are wholly *outside*, with their "memories," their "desires," their "obsessions" spread out around them on the sidewalk like unwrapped merchandise. Those verses of *Plain Chant* come to mind, in which an entire dream personnel is realized and, consequently, destroyed:

[12] Roland Barthes, "Littérature objective," *Essais critiques* (Paris: Ed. du Seuil, 1964), pp. 39–40. My translation.

Ainsi je voudrais voir suivre dehors ta trace
Le bétail de ton rêve, étonné d'être là.[13]

There are no nooks, crannies, shadows, hidden depths, or disguised characters in Robbe-Grillet. There can be no faulty vision because everything is visible. The act of penetration, underlying both the experience of reading and experience in general in all of the novels studied in this book, is futile in a world without secrets.

And yet, as Bruce Morrissette has patiently shown (and Robbe-Grillet's later articles document), a psychological reading of the novels is indeed possible.[14] Not only the frequently erotic and sadistic material, but the one-dimensionality itself, the exteriorization of past, present, future, lies, wishes, the echoes and repetitions are the very image of a deranged psyche and constitute (rather than describe or analyze) a psychological vision. By putting in the tenses and distinctions in voice and mood that Robbe-Grillet has suppressed, we can move from recurrence to sequence to plot and character, and thereby humanize the work.[15] Robbe-Grillet's own insistence

[13] Gérard Genette, "Vertige fixé," postface to *Dans le labyrinthe* (Paris 10/18 ed., 1964), p. 285. My translation.

[14] Bruce Morrissette, *Les Romans de Robbe-Grillet* (Paris: Ed. de Minuit, 1965).

[15] Gérard Genette ("Sur Robbe-Grillet," *Tel Quel*, No. 8 [Winter 1962], 39) has humorously but pointedly exposed the danger of such a reading:

"Une tentative comme celle de M. Morrissette revient à peu près à remettre consciencieusement dans ses plis tout ce que Robbe-Grillet a non moins soigneusement déplié, ce qui suppose qu'on tienne pour nulle la seule réalité indiscutable du roman, sa seule matière: son écriture. On récrit telle page au subjonctif, telle autre à l'optatif, tout un chapitre au futur antérieur. Comme une bonne ménagère, on compte les morceaux de glace, et l'on conclut que telle scène, quoique postérieure, nous ramène en arrière: on oublie simplement qu'en fait, tout est ici et maintenant, et que tout autre lecture que la lecture *au présent* n'est qu'un

on the subjective, and therefore human, origin of the configurations in the novels, reveals, as Genette has shrewdly argued, a need to justify: it is "the conflict between a positivist intelligence and a fundamentally poetic imagination."[16]

To see if one can still speak profitably—and honestly—of vision in such fiction, let us consider his most haunting novel, *In the Labyrinth*. Unlike the clearly defined, therefore possibly blind, narrators and characters of Balzac, James, Faulkner, or even Joyce, Robbe-Grillet's soldier is unspecific, undefined. It is not a matter of reader ignorance, but of character emptiness, or perhaps, openness. The soldier's situation is only marginally particularized: he seeks vainly to deliver a mysterious package to an unknown person at an unknown intersection. But there seems to be no inner reality, no anguish (merely fatigue), no psychology. The soldier is wholly defined in terms of his itinerary, and each conversation, rather than localizing or individualizing the speaker, tends to subvert the possibility of meaning or identity. Thus, the exchange with the doctor parodies the traditional functions of dialogue and recognition:

Immediately the soldier goes into a more detailed explanation; but no sooner has he begun than he is overcome by doubt and de-

---

exercice scolaire, tout juste bon à montrer plus clairement ce que n'est pas le récit de Robbe-Grillet. Revenons à notre camelot, avec son étalage à la sauvette: un gendarme surgit: '*Rangez-moi tout ce matériel, et plus vite que ça!*' le camelot fourre précipitamment ses jeux de cartes, ses gommes et ses montres dans ses poches, et le gendarme, c'est-à-dire le critique attentif note avec soin dans *quelle* poche est rentré *quel* object. Très intéressant. Mais une fois terminée (tant bien que mal) l'opération remballage, où est le délit? On a bien le droit de se promener avec des ficelles dans ses poches, non? Et voilà le critique pris à son piège: plus de délit, plus de procès. 'Reconstruire' un roman de Robbe-Grillet, c'est l'*effacer*."

[16] Genette, "Vertige fixé," p. 305. My translation.

cides to confine himself, out of caution, to a series of incoherent phrases without apparent connection, for the most part incomplete and in any case quite obscure to his interlocutor, in which he himself, moreover, becomes more involved at each word. The other man does not show any sign that his attention is flagging; he listens with polite interest, his eyes squinting slightly, his head tilted to the left, showing no more comprehension than astonishment.

The soldier no longer knows how to stop. He has taken his right hand out of his pocket and moves it forward, clenching his fingers like someone afraid of losing some detail of a memory he thinks he is about to recapture, or like someone who wants to be encouraged, or who does not manage to be convincing, and he continues talking, losing himself in a plethora of increasingly confusing specifications, suddenly conscious of this, stopping at almost each step in order to start again in a different direction, convinced now, but too late, of having blundered from the beginning, and not seeing any means of extricating himself without planting still deeper suspicions in this anonymous pedestrian who merely mentioned the temperature or some banal subject of the sort, or who even asked him nothing at all—and who, moreover, continues to say nothing.

Even while struggling in his own nets, the soldier tries to reconstitute what has just happened: it must have occurred to him (but this now seems incredible) that the man he has been running after since his arrival in the city was perhaps this very man, with his silk-sheathed umbrella, his fur-lined coat, his big ring. He has wanted to allude to what he expected of him, yet without revealing his true mission, permitting the man, all the same, to determine it, if he was actually the man for whom the box wrapped in brown paper was intended, or at least the man who could say what must be done with it.[17]

The situation is melodramatic, filled with visible details ("silk-sheathed umbrella," "fur-lined coat," "big ring," "box wrapped

[17] Alain Robbe-Grillet, *In the Labyrinth*, tr. Richard Howard (New York: Grove Press, 1960), pp. 142–143. Subsequent quotations are from this edition.

in brown paper") and seemingly bristling with significance. But Jamesian conjecture and Faulknerian alternatives are ruthlessly parodied. The desired revelations, the longed-for depths are not forthcoming; the movement toward meaning turns upon itself, and the result is the "erasing" so characteristic of Robbe-Grillet's work.

Not merely is there no humanly defined center of gravity, no "interiority" in the soldier, but his endless journey is composed of meetings and patterns without significance. Robbe-Grillet presents groupings that customarily have value, but he empties them of content and only utilizes them formally. Thus we see the same(?) woman, child, invalid, and photograph, but speculation concerning their relationships is vain. On several occasions the child specifically denies meaning: "He is not my father." Configurations that ordinarily suggest value are only configurations; facial expressions, when interrogated, are just an arrangement of features; characters and buildings reappear, but they may be different. The discussion in the tavern about the defeat at Reichenfels is a case in point: in contrast to the heated assertions that the defeat was occasioned by "rotten officers," the soldier emphasizes the meaninglessness of such distinctions: " 'Anyway,' the soldier says, 'it all comes down to the same thing now. Sooner or later they'll get us' " (p. 166). For the soldier there is no cogent ordering of events, no single sequence that takes precedence; one might say that he has no perceptual grammar, that in the face of defeat or death no arrangement is intrinsically more valid than others. Such a point of view, essentially that of moral nihilism, in the case of the defeat of Reichenfels, informs the narrative impetus of the work, endowing it with total freedom in content and total rigor in form. The vital center of the work is in its verbal propriety (*signifiant*); meaning (*signifié*) is malleable, and, as it were, an afterthought. Already implicit in Joyce's work, the priority of formal pattern over human cogency is militantly at the core of Robbe-Grillet. As Genette has noted,

Robbe-Grillet's novels are organized according to three related principles: natural analogies (streets, houses, châteaux, corridors, buildings, doves, eight-shaped objects, bayonet-shaped objects, look alike and may fuse into one another); artificial reproductions (photographs, engravings, paintings, novels within the novel creating a "fictive" world that resembles and often blends in with the "real" world of the works); repetitions and variants of the story (hypotheses and fantasies becoming real, memories and hallucinations existing on the same plane as the events, incidents recurring over and over in similar but slightly differentiated versions). These principles of composition are not discretely embodied in the texture of the story: they brutally articulate the writer's material, asserting their independence from any and all sources. Analogy replaces sequence and becomes a morphological principle. In *In the Labyrinth*, as Genette has written,

a subtle and continuous process of variations, multiplications, fusions, reversals, substitutions, metamorphoses and anamorphoses is operative in the characters, places, things, situations, acts and words. The soldier, the child and the young woman are successively split and merged; houses and streets are telescoped; a painting comes alive; real scenes are frozen into a painting; conversations are begun, repeated, distorted, dissolved; gestures are developed and sublimated; objects have changed ownership, place, time, form, matter; the world of the real and that of the possible have exchanged qualities; an entire city and a moment of history have glided toward and away from each other in an imperceptible displacement.[18]

In the face of such mobility, can one still speak of vision? Is *In the Labyrinth* an elaborate configuration of formal motifs, or is it a story of human beings? Is the structural principle alone real and the characters merely grist for its mill? Or is there a plausible psychological explanation (fatigue, sickness,

---

[18] Genette, "Vertige fixé," pp. 303–304. My translation.

hallucination) that would account for the shifting scenes and plateaux of the novel? Both and neither. On the one hand, if we acknowledge the autonomy of *écriture*, if we suppress the human reference, the book becomes an adventure in spatial form, a wholly exteriorized spectacle articulated by surface analogy. Time and depth would be no more present than they are in the recurrent motifs of tapestries and wallpaper. Such a work celebrates the freedom of the author, his commitment, not to "reality," but to his medium (words) and his imagination. On the other hand, there is a psychological dimension to Robbe-Grillet's work. Instead of psychoanalyzing the soldier or narrator or the narrative focus and thereby determining what particular psychosis might engender such "distortion," let us look at the protagonist without preconceptions. His thoughts, scant though they are, are perfectly innocuous; even his great fatigue and later wounds do not authorize the kind of subjective reversal that we encounter with James's governess or Faulkner's Jason, wherein what the character sees might be construed as a mirror. Robbe-Grillet's soldier simply lacks the subjective complications or equipment that would justify such a reversal. The fusion of scenes does not result from his fatigue; rather—and this is quintessential—we must conclude that his fatigue comes from walking the treadmill Robbe-Grillet has placed him upon. Likewise, his wound is not the origin of any distortions, but the result of the author-narrator's decision. In short, the soldier—much like the reader—is assaulted by the entire arsenal of Robbe-Grillet's tricks. For him, as for the reader, objects fuse into each other, reappear, disappear, change, jump, and dance according to the analogical principles already mentioned. Finally, he, like the reader, is attempting to make sense of the steps he is being put through and the changing scenes in which he merges. His effort to understand is never explicit; there is no questioning, no pathos. Yet, his very perseverance in delivering the box testifies to a human compulsion of a different order from the world he inhabits. It is that discrepancy which accounts for the book's haunting power. To interpret the substance of Robbe-Grillet's fictional world, with its pirouetting forms and merging structures, as the psychosis of either narrator or character is to "derealize" what is primary and to displace the authentic psychological dimension of his work. The style does not record a *fait accompli*, a deranged optic; it *causes*, as we watch, the disorder and suffering.

For there is psychology, and consequently, there is vision. It is the vision of a person wholly subjected to a rigorous, deterministic form principle, one that replaces his human exigencies with the author's sense of *écriture*. The soldier is sacrificed to style, to literature. One is entitled to speak morally, in terms of sacrifice, because the soldier—despite his function as pawn, as mere formal motif—obviously conceives of his mission humanly. Like many of Robbe-Grillet's characters, he seeks human meanings, depth, in a world of surfaces and figures. The scene is ordered and harmonious, filled with faces and objects that cohere formally. The soldier is the messenger of disorder, vainly attempting to coerce the gliding forms, to deliver his package. Human meanings can tolerate very little mobility, and the free-wheeling structure of *In the Labyrinth* easily undermines the soldier's task, mocks his sense of purpose. The failure is not tragic because the quest is devalorized by the world of the book; the soldier doesn't become insane (he hasn't sufficient "interiority"), but simply dies, leaving the scene untroubled in its superficiality.[19]

There remains the narrator. Almost invisible, he is nonethe-

---

[19] In the later Robbe-Grillet, we are treated to a more harmonious world, one without intrusive desires for human significance. The failure of the soldier, of A in "Marienbad," or N (the French visitor-narrator) in "L'Immortelle" to adjust to the dizzying formal machinery of the work, is wholly absent from the untroubled, programmed marionettes who embroider the surface décor in *La Maison de rendez-vous* and *Project for a Revolution in New York*.

less all-powerful, since he creates the story of the soldier by contemplating the objects in his room: a box wrapped in brown paper, a painting on the wall. Presumably, these elements are the *real* genesis of the story, and the patently fictional, tentative developments that follow illustrate the creative but specious work of the writer. A still more suggestive origin of the fictive story, the abortive effort to impose human meanings, is the fissure in the wall opposite the writer's bed:

To the right of the large, luminous circle whose circumference it regularly follows, there is, at the corner of the ceiling, a slender black line about an inch long and scarcely noticeable: a crack in the plaster, or a spider web covered with dust, or some trace of a bump or scratch. This imperfection in the white surface, moreover, is not equally visible from every point in the room. It is particularly apparent to an observer near the base of the wall to the right, at the other end of the room, looking up along what is virtually the diagonal of this wall, as is normal for someone lying on the bed, his head resting on the bolster. [p. 117]

The crack in the plaster is the crevice through which the human element emerges, constituting by its very presence the flaw in an ordered scheme. The story is vitiated in its genesis, and its claim to cogency is precarious. In this light we may interpret the frequent scenes of potential violence or destruction as an index of the story's fragility: the bottle of wine leaning dangerously on the waitress's tray, the ever threatening suspicion or even terror on people's faces when they encounter the soldier ("bringing terrified faces to half-open doors, necks craning, eyes anxious, mouths already opening to shout" [p. 56]), the soldier's dream that he is carrying a grenade about to explode, a grenade most certainly representing the box he carries with him. That pitiful, derisory box is what two centuries have done to the poignant glove box given to Rastignac by Madame de Beauséant. At the close of the story the grenade goes off in the form of a machine gun, and the box, the ultimate parodistic symbol of depth and mystery and human affirmation, is at last opened. Finally we have real content: names and sequences come pouring out, giving us a third-rate, patch-work, "realistic" rendition of the events. The hastily put together *anecdote* is too threadbare to be convincing, less real than the potential chaos surrounding the story, less vital than the analogical forces articulating the story.

Yet, if the fissure is more authentic than the story issuing from it, the psychological component would appear to collapse. At this point we need to consider the figure lying on that bed, regarding the fissure, imagining the story. It is possible to relegate this aspect of the novel—the narrator visibly fabricating a story from nothing—to the well-stocked category of plays within plays, Chinese box stratagems, and so on. To do so, however, would be to overlook the particular quality of storytelling we have here, and the implicit, inescapable ethical dimension of such storytelling. For there is a dialectic here. The narrator's freedom of creation (and, by extension, Robbe-Grillet's freedom)[20] can be exercised only at the expense of the soldier. There is, doubtless, in all fiction the kind of authorial manipulation that Gide has dramatized and that Sartre has deplored; in Robbe-Grillet, however, it is exalted, travestied under the name of liberty and passed off as non-anthropocentric honesty. All of Robbe-Grillet's work is characterized by exploitative self-assertion—sometimes epistemological, sometimes aesthetic, sometimes erotic. *Last Year at Marienbad* gives fullest expression to this kind of rape, whereby the man's efforts to create meaning, to create the woman's past, to coerce those elusive Baroque statues and

[20] At the risk of being perverse, I would like to call attention to the cover of the 1962 10/18 edition of *Dans le labyrinthe*. We see a circular maze with the face of Robbe-Grillet at its heart, like a bemused but patient minotaur. How strange that all roads lead to Robbe-Grillet himself. *Le hasard objectif!*

corridors into the sanctuary of their love, reflect a fusion of all the different varieties of persuasion. Thus, the eroticism in Robbe-Grillet, from *The Voyeur* to *Project for a Revolution in New York* and including all the films, is part of the same self-assertion, or more precisely, tyranny that we see elsewhere. In *The Voyeur*, Mathias's sexual exploitation is related to the larger pattern of aesthetic tyranny which forces him to view the world in terms of figure eights and other deterministic analogical patterns. In *In the Labyrinth* the despotic principle is fully dramatized in the person of the narrator. Those opening lines are chilling:

> I am alone here now, under cover. Outside it is raining, outside you walk through the rain with your head down, shielding your eyes with one hand while you stare ahead nevertheless, a few yards ahead, at a few yards of wet asphalt; outside it is cold, the wind blows between the bare black branches; the wind blows through the leaves, rocking whole boughs, rocking them, rocking, their shadows swaying across the white roughcast walls. Outside the sun is shining, there is no tree, no bush to cast a shadow, and you walk under the sun shielding your eyes with one hand while you stare ahead, only a few yards in front of you, at a few yards of dusty asphalt where the wind makes patterns of parallel lines, forks and spirals.
>
> The sun does not get in here, nor the wind, nor the rain, nor the dust. [pp. 7–8]

We may admire the hypnotic cadences, the exercise of authorial freedom, the independence of the *signifiant*, the assertion of *écriture* over pedestrian reality, but our aesthetic euphoria should not blind us to the calculated, inevitable cruelty that makes the feat possible. *Our* vision is atrophied if we do not perceive the dialectic between the exposure (and, like trained circus animals, exploitation) of the soldier and the protected comfort of the narrator, the exhausted and absurd pilgrimage of the soldier and the supine figure gazing at a fissure in the wall. Let us not forget that a labyrinth is a hu-

man-made, rational structure, an expression of human creativity; it is terrifying only to those who do not understand its
design, those trapped in it. There is a scene where the soldier,
put through a number of tricks, perseveres in finding an exit;
it is a remarkable scene because the tentativeness of it reflects
both the narrator's aesthetic quandary (where does the soldier
go next?) and the desperation, even the implicit threat of a
character who wants out:

He notices at this moment that the door is ajar: door, hallway,
door, vestibule, door, then finally a lighted room, and a table with
an empty glass with a circle of dark-red liquid still at the bottom,
and a lame man leaning on his crutch, bending forward in a precarious balance. No. Door ajar. Hallway. Staircase. Woman running from floor to floor up the spiral staircase, her gray apron
billowing about her. Door. And finally a lighted room: bed, chest,
fireplace, table with a lamp on its left corner, and the lampshade
casting a white circle on the ceiling. No. Above the chest is a
print framed in black wood. . . . No. No. No. [pp. 88–89]

At what point do we change those periods into exclamation
points? One doesn't need to be a sleuth to see that the soldier
has found his way into the narrator's room, is looking at the
picture that is his origin. The "No. No. No." betokens more
than the suicide of the story; it is a refusal, possibly even a
fearful refusal, of "confrontation" between narrator and protagonist.

To deny that such narrative strategy has ethical implications, or to say that moral strictures are out of place in assess-
ing Robbe-Grillet, is actually to transform the soldier into a
pawn, to regard his itinerary as part of a figural composition,
not as a human quest. It is to deprive the book of its suffering
and poignancy, the real pathos it has—not because we insist on
putting in depth where it does not belong, but because the
soldier's *geste* is ineluctably a human action, an image of help-
lessness and struggle that is *there* on the page, not merely in
our minds—unless we agree to abstract it into mere pattern.

Moreover, Robbe-Grillet is counting on us to respond humanly. He could have applied his analogical technique to things. In using people as his motifs, Robbe-Grillet can claim neutrality only if we are willing to grant it. Robbe-Grillet has insisted that his art is an invitation to freedom, that what the reader "is being asked to do is no longer to accept a ready-made, completed world, a solid world, shut in on itself, but on the contrary, to participate in an act of creation, in the invention of the work—and the world—and in this way to learn to invent his own life."[21] It sounds good. But the formal tyranny of his work, bequeathing an image of man wholly alienated, wholly programmed by mechanical principles, seems to bear out his belief that "the present age is . . . that of the regimental number."[22] Robbe-Grillet is playing a shrewd game with his readers: to read him "his" way as an exercise in forms, to discount the anthropomorphic problem of his vision, is to divest his work of the real interest it has, for Robbe-Grillet ultimately has precisely as much depth as we do. And therein lies the challenge of his work.

[21] Robbe-Grillet, *Towards a New Novel*, p. 110.
[22] *Ibid.*, p. 61.

Conclusion

To interpret fully the evolution charted in this book is not easy. However, my study of the modalities of vision and response in the novel from Balzac to the *nouveau roman* should afford some insight into the decline of humanism. I do not mean "humanism" as a repository of particular, Western values, but rather humanism as a focus, a means of relating the appearance of the planet and the activities of the species to human concerns. It is not a question of man occupying the center of the universe, but of the struggle to impose meaning on reality, a struggle that literature has always reflected, that reading has always embodied. Literature need not revel in orgies of significance and depth. Philosophically, it has been respectable since Kant and the romantics to assert the primacy (and, implicitly, the alienation) of the mental image, the subjective awareness against the "real" contours of a world that we can never apprehend. Borges himself has neatly traced the growing autonomy of perception through Berkeley and Hume. Existentialism and phenomenology also provide an intellectual background for these developments in fiction, exposing the quest for meaning as increasingly problematic and precarious. But the novel has essentially either assumed a world of meanings, or has been in search of those meanings (which amounts to almost the same thing, regardless of the outcome of the search).

At a certain point, however, the modern novel seems to reject the humanistic burden of achieving knowledge, while maintaining the forms of interrogation. The mystery form generates a search for answers: Balzac provides them with flourish, James conjectures them through refinement, Faulkner creates them through feeling, Butor situates them by sacrificing the agent to the scene, and Robbe-Grillet rejects the question, making the need for depth and meaning seem an intrusion in his immaculate world. The waning belief in depth, the inability or refusal of the novel to educate its characters and readers, the apparent and ambivalent shift of authority from writer to reader, the conception of literature as a nonreferential verbal structure—these developments in fiction stem from and reflect problems and crises that go far beyond the confines of literary history. Such an evolution sheds light on the "knowability" of the world; it also traces the diminishing powers of the self. In his book, *Loss of the Self in Modern Literature and Art*, Wylie Sypher has convincingly charted the decline of anthropocentric humanism from the romantics to the present; he is looking for what can still be redeemed:

Is it possible, while the individual is vanishing behind the functionary throughout the technological world, to have any sort of humanism that does not depend upon the older notions of the self, the independent self that is outdated or at least victimized by the operations of power on its present scale? Any such humanism must come to terms with our sense of the anonymity of the self, must therefore get beyond any romantic notion of selfhood. The importance of recent painting and literature is here, for both suggest that we must no longer confuse humanism with romantic individuality or with an anthropomorphic view that put the self at the center of things.[1]

Sypher argues that the diminished egos and collapsed selves of

[1] Wylie Sypher, *Loss of the Self in Modern Literature and Art* (New York: Vintage Books, 1962), p. 14.

twentieth-century anti-painting, anti-theater, and anti-novel must be seen as a reaction against the romantic individualist legacy. The case for painting is the most intriguing, and the *art brut* of Jean Dubuffet does, in fact, suggest a kind of libidinous realism, an art that "loves the world and loses the self in the world without either renouncing the world or seeking to master the world. In fact, this sort of painting could be the most complete surrender to the world that has occurred in Western art."[2]

Whereas the eclipse of the self is the precondition for the globality of Dubuffet's work, Sypher's thesis concerning the "new" humanism in literature is less convincing. We have seen, in Butor's *Passing Time*, a paradigm of the transition from romantic self to impersonal art, but Butor is using language not color, human plots not pigments and textures; the result is little joy and celebration, much suffering and anguish. The writers whom Sypher discusses are Beckett, Sarraute, Ionesco, and Robbe-Grillet. Sarraute's tropisms reduce the self to a random collection of impersonal urges, a seesaw of fears and appetites in which notions such as personality or identity are hopelessly anachronistic. Robbe-Grillet is wisely dealt with in summary fashion because, as we have seen, the self interests him primarily as marionette. Beckett is clearly among the most arresting literary figures of our time from this point of view; he has shown us in infinite, agonizing detail that the extinction of the self is no easy matter. The self seems to have its own logic, even when ours wears out, and the path of decay and dissolution seems endless, sustaining new forms and new soliloquies in each Beckett work. Beckett shows us over and over that there is something irreducible at the core of the human enterprise, that we can never be totally dispossessed. The ills and leakages of our existence may instill a yearning for the void, but the self, nonetheless, perseveres: "With Beckett the

[2] *Ibid.*, p. 125.

affirmation is gone; but the paradox remains, for after the self has shriveled, the human remains—in some unlocalized area of perception or response. To repeat: we have an existence, however unwillingly, after we have lost an identity; and we do not seem to be able to diminish this existence below a certain point."[3] Beckett was not dealt with in my study, but the residual humanism of his work, more impressive in its endurance than in its decay, may serve us as a *critical posture*. The self is not extinguishable; even where it functions minimally as character, or is beset by systems and forces, the reader of fiction cannot discount it from the picture.

Wisdom (and the rationale for reading fiction) may well lie in such a recognition, an ultimate awareness that the human is an indestructible locus, the physical and mental set which we are, which mocks and painfully contains our guerilla wars of disbelief, of erosion and illusion, of changeability and discontinuity, of impersonal systems and inhuman laws. Free or not, we are. We may be the creatures of societal forces, sexual forces, economic forces, physiological forces, genetic forces, linguistic forces, and still other, yet-to-be-discovered, eagerly awaited forces; yet we are the arena in which these forces have their play. Even Borges, master of abstractions and transformations, acknowledges the primacy of that residual self: "Time is a river which sweeps me along, but I am the river; it is a tiger which destroys me, but I am the tiger; it is a fire which consumes me, but I am the fire. The world, unfortunately, is real; I, unfortunately, am Borges."[4] We may be philosophically erasable and culturally encroached upon; we may be inauthentic, insincere, and incomplete; but the most casual empiricism testifies to our ongoing presence. The educated mind tends to make short shrift of such evidence, not to see, but to see merely beyond, to seek the graph, the system,

[3] *Ibid.*, p. 154.
[4] Borges, *Labyrinths*, p. 234.

the generality, the meaning instead of the increasingly vulnerable but ineradicable self. This waning belief in the individual, in character, must eventually wring the neck of fiction, but the fictions studied in this book staunchly register both the limitations and the possibilities of the self. The novel, with its symbiotic relationships between character, plot, and form, can be defined as the arena in which the self lives and dies. Unlike other literary genres, fiction—because of its lifesaving "impurities"—cannot avoid showing us human beings in their ecological setting. Because the novel reveals, willy-nilly, how the self perceives and adjusts to its environment, a study of vision and response records not only how men make sense of the world, but how much space they take up, what balance they achieve, how they use (or are used by) their fictional universes.

In the work of every writer discussed we see the widening awareness of relation, threatening the self with violation, yet hinting of greater fullness, of undreamed-of syntheses. In the earlier novels the paradigms of fiction are adequate to such transitions and translations: Rastignac experiences Goriot, Mme de Beauséant, and Vautrin as parent figures, chooses masquerade over fullness in a society where the links are broken and the cash nexus alone prevails; but he, and we, have been educated, have been enriched didactically even if impoverished ethically; likewise, Pip must broaden his codes, learn to assimilate Magwitch and Orlick in his scheme of things, to assign human rather than fairy-tale values to Estella and Miss Havisham, in short, to see that the self is implicated in a vast network of forces, a network that, in Dickens, is synonymous with plot. The fictive frameworks accommodate the expanding self in Conrad, Ford, and James as well. Conrad is nothing if not unsuspected affinities and doubles, an arduous itinerary of commitment and betrayal, of ever wider patterns of recognition and responsibility; the aptness of the reversals in Ford, the manner in which the tragic, muted tale of destruction replaces the shrill, ironic comedy of errors, everything in *The Good Soldier* suggests an emerging picture, a drama of fine and not-so-fine motive where the innocent and the naive (not merely Dowell, but also Nancy and Leonora) play out roles and form patterns far beyond their own ken. My reading of *The Turn of the Screw* emphasizes precisely how the governess functions far more powerfully and fatally as *character* than she knows. In James the world of relation refuses to be the plaything of our mind, the product of our motive; it emerges inexorably as fact (as it does in "The Beast in the Jungle"), not as ghost story but as murder story. James's tale of the supernatural is utterly real; there is nothing virtual (or "might-have-been") about the governess's vision; she is embarked on a course where her imagination and her gestures are increasingly at one, until they finally merge in the death scene, where everything is finally expressed, where all the educations—Miles's, the governess's, our own—are completed. In Bernanos and Faulkner the expansion of the self explodes the fictional norms. The large areas of uncertainty in *Monsieur Ouine*, the ambiguous relations between characters, the bouts of drunkenness and stupor, the pervasive, cancerous role of Ouine himself, give rise to a murky, fluid universe where the contours of story and character are eroded, where the central acts are unseen, where the self is fitfully imprisoned: Philippe must flee his gilded cage, Arsène must transcend his flesh, and the clinical perspective of the doctor and the professor must yield to a more generous recognition of spirit and sensation. Faulkner's work is an unending inventory of the riches and reaches of the self: Caddy informs all of *The Sound and the Fury*, although she is not present; the fullness of the past in Benjy's and Quentin's sections, the reality of its ghosts, and the immediacy of its hold are volatile forces buried inside the main characters. Faulkner taps these sources, and they overflow into the narrative of the present, despotically sweeping everything along with them. Not merely the history, but the internal chemistry of the Compson family has been evoked. In *Absalom* the fictions are endless, too many and too rich to be encompassed in a story but surely true as indexes of the self. The self spills out in Faulkner's art, as it cannot in life and does not in history, overwhelming us with "what they cannot have told" us, showing us inner kingdoms that need no evidence, culminating in an ecstatic liberation from its "earthly tenement," an epiphany of brotherhood that illuminates both the destruction of the family and the cause of the War.

These are works of the engaged, exploring self; the scale of the exploration is gradually enlarged, as the confines of the Maison Vauquer open up into a murkier realm in *Great Expectations*, become still more puzzling in Conrad and Ford until, in James, the area to be investigated, the territory to be charted, and the data to be interpreted are so filmy and ethereal that the motive of the searcher alone remains visible. Yet Rastignac's dramatic confrontation with two real worlds, rendered in real dialogues, is not unlike Dowell's meditations on motive, the governess's ghostly intercourse, or Quentin and Shreve's fabrications; in each case the fictional universe draws out the self, reveals it embroiled in nets and relationships beyond what it had dreamed of. Control and will and lucidity may be lacking, but the self is committed and extended into every nook and cranny of the work. In such art the education of both characters and reader lies in seeing that that fullness, all those plots and stories and seemingly discrete events and characters, must revert back to and nourish the self. Sometimes the education fails: Rastignac cannot absorb the fullness of both Goriot and Vautrin; he will bury Goriot. Dowell is broken by the contraries of his story, just as Nancy and Edward were. But Pip's vision is chastened and broadened, his sense of self more resonant and committed to the world as he assumes his bonds with Magwitch and recognizes Orlick and the others as human; Rosa Coldfield's fairy tale, her celebration of love are not a discrete, virtual subplot, recounted in italics in the fifth section of *Absalom*: that experience must be absorbed into the selves of the two boys in the dormitory before they can enact and create their own love story. And where the dissonances cannot be absorbed into a growing self, where the self either cracks or resists, then the only controlling view, the only overview left to be expanded and educated is that of the reader. All these fictions serve in a process of aggrandizement and enrichment.

It is worth insisting on this orientation because it underlies the notion of humanism that runs throughout this book, and it provides the line of demarcation between the first three chapters and the last two. The materials of Kafka, Joyce, Butor, Proust, Borges, Simon, and Robbe-Grillet are, as the world is, there; they defy or subvert enlistment into the absorptive enterprises of the self, whether that self be character or reader. In some books the self tries to master, or at least discover its relation to, the universe in which it is placed; in others the sense-making syndrome is either absent or atrophied, and the self serenely functions, coequal with the writer's other objects, in the achieved artifact. Of the two kinds of fictions, the first are obviously painful, but the second, when read as human documents (should we—can we—read them otherwise?), are truly intolerable. Kafka's characters seem to be refining endlessly away at the world they inhabit, but the myopic ratiocination does not begin to illuminate the stage or educate the player. In Joyce the human elements have integrity, but they are unrelated. We are forced to go to extraordinary lengths to connect the world of the work, its verbal pyrotechnics and allusive interplay, to the needs of its characters. It is absurd to say that certain chapters are written the way they are because they reflect Bloom's point of view, or anyone else's—the voices are Joyce's. The work indeed makes its innumerable statements, but among them is the lesson that the allegiance of the artist is to his language, his own resourcefulness and prowess, whether or not his characters are displaced in the undertaking. In Butor we see an explicit treatment of the displacement between self and setting, but the eclipse is graced with value; Revel is turned into a phantom, but Bleston's immensities are adumbrated in his journal, and the city's inhabitants are to be —somehow—enriched by his loss. Proust's self is both the richest and most ghostlike of all; the world it haunts and the people it encounters are mercilessly beyond its reach, inciting prodigious appetites and expensive-expansive errors. Yet the absorption process is very much in effect, so much so that the world finally becomes fodder for the infinite metaphorical creations of the self. The excesses and investments of the imagination are no less real and priceless, simply because life vulgarly undermines them; thus the self in Proust, like the genie in the bottle, is physically contained but capable of infinite expansion, of sustained implosions, of repossessing its own estate, of controlling the world by internalizing it. Borges' mosaic world is composed of fragments shored up against his ruins, and his art consists in putting them together in strange and wondrous ways, in making concord out of discord, in healing disunities; but one does not work in human materials with impunity, and his man-made, *ex post facto* harmonies are achieved in pain. Wholeness soothes the mind, whatever form it may take, but the personal frame of reference in Borges is too diminished for absorption or enrichment to take place. There is along with the dizzying sense of expansion an awareness, even if muted, of incompletion and disconnectedness. Simon and Robbe-Grillet are the most contemporary of the writers discussed in this book, and in their works the creation of any identity, given the encroaching, allpowerful systems in which the self is immersed, is problematic. Trauma and hunger articulate the dreamscapes of Simon's hero, and the result is the collapse of all forms; but the accelerated decay is matched and even surpassed by couplings and fusions, by a metaphorical, associative logic that has become real, yoking together, recalling, and merging events that the protagonist undergoes rather than coerces. Finally, we have the fully autonomous vision in Robbe-Grillet, the rendition of character as mere component, as element in an exercise in forms. Never before has a world of victimization and automatism been so acutely depicted as in the work of Robbe-Grillet; here the absorption is wholly reversed, and character is transformed into surface design. We have come full circle. The work has devoured its people, rather than the other way around.

Yet, even in Chapters 4 and 5 character remains; the self is not and cannot be lost. It is true that the fullness of the fictional universe is no longer transformed into the paradigms of relation for the protagonist. The character may find his experience indigestible; he may find himself shunted off into a corner of a book that has other concerns; he may be snuffed out altogether. Yet, as a locus at the very least, the self continues to exist, inferentially if not observably. This minimal existence must not be minimized because it accounts for both the anguish and the interest of much modern fiction. Proust's Marcel encounters only discontinuity, within himself and in others; such discoveries are inevitably painful, for we live with the illusion of stability. He gradually learns to value the imaginative richness of his illusions, regardless of their viability in life, but we, as readers, must not discount the real pain, the real fiascoes that attend Marcel's life experience. The aesthetic richness and the human cost are not separable. Likewise Bloom's wisdom consists in embracing a conception of life in which individual assertion is virtually nil; he is able to countenance his own cuckoldry by turning to notions of relativity and serial repetitions that the individualist Odysseus never contemplated:

If he had smiled why would he have smiled?
To reflect that each one who enters imagines himself to be the first to enter whereas he is always the last term of a succeeding

one, each imagining himself to be first, last, only and alone, whereas he is neither first nor last nor only nor alone in a series originating in and repeated to infinity. [p. 715]

Such acceptance is kin to resignation, and that smile is nonetheless of a man who does not enjoy being cuckolded; this is not enviable adjustment. With Butor and Simon we see characters in the process of being dispossessed. Their needs and their psychology irreversibly recede into the background as their visions take on authority; Revel is expelled from Bleston as phantom; Georges is powerless before the kaleidoscopic but rigorous onslaught of his past experience. Yet these books are immensely moving, moving in ways that other novels of Butor and Simon are not; they affect us because the self, even if displaced and presiding over its dissolution, still has squatter's rights, still constitutes an inviolable locus. Both Revel and Georges bear witness to their own loss.[5] The modern novelist need not disguise our alienation, nor should he artificially eliminate the self altogether: dual recognition of man's impoverishment and his response is not necessarily a dead end; it may be, in the words of Wallace Stevens, a point of departure:

> From this the poem springs: that we live in a place
> That is not our own, and much more, nor ourselves
> And hard it is, in spite of blazoned days.[6]

[5] The depiction of the *processes* alone (whether it be the organizational principles of Bleston or the fusion of lovemaking, hiding in a ditch and eating grass) would be structurally dazzling but without human reverberation. Such is, in fact, the case for works such as Butor's *Mobile* and *Description de San Marco*, Simon's *Bataille de Pharsale* and *Les Corps conducteurs*, Robbe-Grillet's *Projet pour une révolution à New York*, and the later work of Nathalie Sarraute as well. Things and scenes and words merge into one another at will as the artist asserts his shaping and connecting power, but the effort to assess the mechanisms, to relate the spectacle to the needs of its characters is absent. These later works have much more "freedom" and mobility than those chosen for discussion here, but such aesthetic autonomy is achieved at a high cost.

[6] Wallace Stevens, "Notes Toward a Supreme Fiction," *The Palm at the End of the Mind* (New York: Vintage Books, 1972).

It is that enduring ability to recognize and celebrate our estate, even when it is "hard," that it makes it possible and even necessary to speak of the human reference in even the most non-anthropocentric art. It is in this light that Robbe-Grillet's work must be read; the character may, through the laws of analogy run wild, merge with the wallpaper, but that too can be assessed humanly.

We have seen that the nature and function of character, of the self, evolve in the course of the novel from Balzac to Robbe-Grillet. If the character's sense of things is an index of vision, then it is clear that response takes us into the realm of plot. It is worth mentioning Frank Kermode's *Sense of an Ending* in this respect, for he has written with brilliance and authority about the rationale for fictions, the uses—literary and otherwise—of plotting. Our fictions, according to Kermode, have always oscillated between the consolations of form (of beginnings and endings and order) and the respect for contingency (the inhuman, amorphous real). Thus, our stories perform something precious for us because

they find out about the changing world on our behalf; they arrange our complementarities. They do this, for some of us, perhaps better than history, perhaps better than theology, largely because they are consciously false; but the way to understand their development is to see how they are related to those other fictional systems. It is not that we are connoisseurs of chaos, but that we are surrounded by it, and equipped for coexistence with it only by our fictive powers.[7]

If we view fictions as human instruments of mediation, their referential value becomes primary, and they will flourish or wane in terms of their explanatory power, in terms of their *vraisemblance*. But the novels studied in Chapters 4 and 5 sug-

[7] Frank Kermode, *The Sense of an Ending: Studies in the Theory of Fiction* (New York: Oxford University Press paperback, 1966), p. 64.

gest a notion of plotting radically different from such mediating concerns. These plots are often only ostensibly exploratory, but actually the occasion for verbal high jinks, metaphorical embroidery, or abstract design. The referential power of language itself is recognized as arbitrary, and the plot is often a simple-minded smokescreen (meant to be taken seriously only by the equally simple-minded) for the more arcane experiments actually taking place: game theories being illustrated, associative language patterns unfurling, secret or unconscious psychodramas being enacted. In an age or literary climate where meaningful order is either unavailable or incredible, the writer may take refuge in the propriety of his medium, his *écriture*.[8]

Along these lines the developments in linguistics and anthropology in our century have doubtless played their part. We now know that language is not merely a transparent vehicle for human expression, that it is a system of signs, that a writer's use of it implicates both himself and his culture in ways that have little to do with the "content" of his statement. The

[8] John Barth, in *Lost in the Funhouse* (New York: Bantam Books, 1969), has explored the proposition that the so-called crisis of literature is essentially a technical problem, that the conventions of narrative may be ailing and exhausted, but that reality is doing just fine: "The fact is, the narrator has narrated himself into a corner, a state of affairs more tsk-tsk than boo-hoo, and because his position is absurd he calls the world absurd. That some writers lack lead in their pencils does not make writing obsolete" (p. 108). In point of fact, *Lost in the Funhouse* is very much a transitional work in the same manner *Passing Time, The Flanders Road*, and *In the Labyrinth* are; it records the breakdown and exhaustion of the mimetic, naturalistic tradition and announces the possibilities of a mythological solution. Moreover, it has the painful wholeness of the novels studied in this book; that is, it accepts the realist premise even while exploding it. Thus, the novel gives us the very experience of exhaustion, explores the *cul-de-sac* of the "consciousness-syndrome" in writing, and ends up in a mythological framework that is credible and moving precisely because of what precedes it.

authority of form over meaning, of code over content, already implicit in Joyce, has a certain scientific basis, and one of the reasons that fiction tends to be about its own *modus operandi* is because the writer's medium—words—has lost its innocence.

From a socioeconomic point of view, Lucien Goldmann has accounted for the work of Robbe-Grillet in terms of reification, of the reduction of people and values to a state of things, a phenomenon inherent, according to Marxist ideology, in a capitalist ethic of exchange.[9] Complementing Goldmann's thesis and corresponding more closely to the emerging fiction of autonomous structures would be an explanation related to some of McLuhan's analyses of mass media. Not just the images of the media and the immediacy of the world at large brought within our ken, but the overwhelming visual, material complexity of the modern world, the pressures of pluralism and heterogeneity, the proliferation of objects which we use but neither create nor understand, make for a scene of such competitive variety that our minds are glutted with images, fragments, pieces of the world we live in. They crowd each other, overlap, merge, and, ultimately, neutralize one another. Once we begin to perceive reality as a manifold panoramic surface it is a short step to initiate the articulation process, to provide grids and analogies, parallels, and polarities. Finding pattern—any pattern—is a way of staying sane. But, to preserve a sense of the human is an incessant exercise in depth, in empathy, in discriminations. To respond humanly is to penetrate beyond the surface vision, to eschew formal similarities in favor of depth and insight. Penetration (even if it is illusory) alone enables us to hallow the uniqueness of each experience, or, as it were, to make it unique and therefore significant. Jerzy Kosinski's recent novel, *Being There*, illustrates the human sterility that results from a saturation of images (television in

[9] Lucien Goldmann, *Pour une sociologie du roman* (Paris: Gallimard Collection Idées, 1964), pp. 281–333.

this case); the protagonist passively perceives the world as a series of images, wholly without depth, serenely undifferentiated in value or nature. The formalist approach to reality is reductive if pushed too far, because it asserts the unifying formal characteristics of "different" phenomena while ignoring or de-emphasizing the particularities. To make sense of the world and to order the world are not identical enterprises; they may well be contradictory. Thus, Robbe-Grillet can allot the same meticulous care (and, hence, lack of importance) to his lost soldier and to the design of wallpaper.

But it should be evident by now that even the writer who claims to be interested solely in words or abstract designs is obliged to play our game as much as we are to play his. It is true that he establishes the givens, but then we have the last word. And it is appropriate that we should, because we bring the book to life, yoke (by our very presence) whatever the writer has created into a human reference, our own. We are not merely consumers or even the makers of reputations, but more importantly, we are the reasons why books are written, the necessary climax to the author's courtship. We consent and even desire to be wooed by artists because they have something precious to contribute to our lives. Our need, as Kermode has said, is elemental: "Men, like poets, rush 'into the middest,' *in medias res*, when they are born; they also die *in mediis rebus*, and to make sense of their span they need fictive concords with origins and ends, such as give meaning to lives and to poems."[10] Being "in the middest," we seek orientation, and, hence, books which themselves depict a search for patterns, for origins and ends, must have a special appeal for us. From Balzac's Rastignac to Robbe-Grillet's soldier, the books dealt with in this study are about finding one's way, and we read them doubly, reflexively, seeking both to order their lives and our own. In Balzac and Dickens the authentic codes and

---

[10] Kermode, *Sense of an Ending*, p. 7.

patterns become visible even if they are not honored; and we are lessoned. The conjectural realism of Conrad, Ford, and James explodes simplistic notions of motive and effect, dramatizes the abyss between our self-enclosed vision and the immense network of relationships in which we are immersed. There is aptness and propriety in their art. In Faulkner and Bernanos the affective, the irrational, and even the supernatural reign, brutally expanding our sense of self and plot, immersing us sensuously before enlightening us cognitively. But enlightenment does come.

There is no such gratification for us or for the characters in the novels dealt within the last two chapters. Our yearning for order and stability is thwarted as we are confronted with the mobility of modern fiction. We can tolerate very little mobility in life; sanity requires constants, as many of them as possible. That is probably why we cling so tenaciously to fixed images of the self, of our past, of others; it is why we embrace routines and conventions and clichés. Yet, surely since Heraclitus, life has been identified with flux. We need no recourse to literature or philosophy to prove such a claim: a cursory glance at our selves, our growing hair and nails, our intake of food and output of excrement, our changing moods and decaying flesh, our defective memory and precarious commitments, our incessant role-playing and ethic of sincerity, our fragile, fitful, arbitrary sense of identity; these, the facts of our lives, make for little stability. So, as Kermode says, forms that are too fixed are unacceptable, are sensed to be obviously specious in an ironic age. But it is uncertain that we are ready for the metamorphoses and kaleidoscopic activity of modern fiction. Let us begin with Kafka, for he has the courage to be literal: the depiction of Gregor Samsa, of the child's wound in "A Country Doctor," of the omnipresent reversals and dilemmas in the longer works, belongs quite simply to a world that we cannot (afford to) recognize as our own. Metamorphosis is equally the law of Proust's work, the key to all sexual, artistic, and social behavior; we have seen that recognition of such a law is the prime ingredient of the artistic vision, but we might also consider that its attendant mobility (not to say, chaos) makes much of life intolerable for Marcel, constitutes, in fact, a good reason for retreat within the self. My reading of Joyce emphasized the parity of his work, his strangely one-dimensional, egalitarian vision in which anything can be, or become, all things if the powers of language, allusion, or associative logic will support it. Likewise, in Borges, the shape of people's lives is divested of its discreteness, is meshed—sometimes smoothly, sometimes forcibly—into the Book the author is devising. *The Flanders Road* presents such transformation somewhat less explicitly than Kafka's work, but with infinitely more pathos; Simon exploits it for all the shock and trauma it contains, and his character is unhinged by it. The case for Robbe-Grillet has been stated several times, and there is no need to belabor the obvious.

By now, it is clear that the merry-go-round, topsy-turvy, transformational worlds of modern fiction are, if taken seriously, sinister, that they are murderously unstable, and that the most minimal conditions for sanity could not be met in such confines. What is less clear is why the readership of these novels does not respond. The criticisms and the praises leveled at "modernism" are essentially technical in nature, emphasizing that such an idiom and such a strategy are, rightly or wrongly, those of our age, that such formal prowess or experimentation is either reprehensible or desirable, according to one's aesthetic criteria. And then the specialists take over, and the charts appear. I contend that these novels are significantly, disturbingly, of our age and that they impose human burdens on the reader. If we do respond to them with fullness, if we try to ascertain the ethical dimension of their formal achievement, if we seek orientation in them, then we must find them tragic and revealing documents of our age: tragic because human assertion is either subordinated or annihilated, and revealing because that is our age. That is why one returns to Faulkner, with nostalgia but also with the kind of need Kermode has described. Like the other modern writers, Faulkner has no illusions about permanency, and one is tempted to compare the shock and trauma of his work with that of Simon: Sutpen's Hundred, Sutpen himself, Charles Bon, and even Charles Etienne de Saint Velery Bon appear without warning, "abrupt" onto the scene, like the "oldentime *Be Light*." The townspeople never do go beyond stunned incomprehension. Not merely trauma, but metamorphosis itself is present: Ellen Coldfield's incomprehension of the role she is to play is repeatedly depicted by the images of butterfly and cocoon, of "substanceless shell," of mutation. Yet the lesson we must draw from *Absalom*—and it is a comforting lesson for readers "in the middest"—is that there are no transformations or men without a past. Not exactly causality, but certainly causes do emerge from *Absalom;* and primal among them is the image of the child in front of the white mansion, standing before a closed door, injured and preparing, already, his design. That scene of nonrecognition—so vastly unlike the nonrecognition that articulates *Ulysses*—both announces (in historical time) and confirms (in the reader's time) the pattern of blindness at the moral heart of the work. Origins and ends *and their importance* are made clear. Sutpen's design and his accomplishment are the work of the self-made man, the man without a past, blind to the humanity of others. And he is destroyed. He fails because, in Faulkner, the self is not safe behind closed doors and creeds. *Absalom* is about the reader himself, about our response to art and to others. We are asked to reread and reimmerse ourselves endlessly in this novel, until our involvement is like Quentin's: "*But you were not listening, because you knew it all already, had learned, absorbed it already without the medium of speech, somehow from having been born and living beside it, with it, as children will and do: so that what your father was saying did not tell you anything so much as it struck, word by word, the resonant strings of re-membering"* (pp. 212–213).

We must open ourselves to Faulkner's story, identify with it, just as Quentin and Shreve must labor both together and with the ghosts of Charles and Henry if the story is to be born at all. The fluidity and transcendence requested of Quentin and Shreve, requested of us, is finally identified with the very essence of continuum, the flowing blood: "not two of them there and then either but four of them riding the two horses through the iron darkness, and that not mattering either: what faces and what names they called themselves and were called by so long as the blood coursed—the blood, the immortal brief recent intransient blood which could hold honor above slothy unregret and love above fat and easy shame" (p. 295). It is, if you like, mobility and metamorphosis: Quentin and Shreve are transformed into Charles and Henry, and we are perhaps all four of them. But it is metamorphosis of infinite value, because from it is born a moment of order, expansion, and liberation. Nonetheless it is only a moment. The world cannot be stopped or transformed; the Sutpens cannot be saved. Quentin and Shreve cannot sustain the vision; not only will they separate, but Quentin (as we know from another volume) will die. The Faulknerian moment of illumination and overpass is followed by a ruthless reentry into the real, and that sequence may well epitomize the precious briefness of art. If we open ourselves to literature, it is so that we may return, renewed, to living, with a fuller sense of the human. But return we must, as the book (or the museum or the concert) closes. It is because, indeed, we are single, isolated selves, diminished and even dispossessed, that the transcendence and shared vision of art hold out such beauty.

We too can view the world solely as a sequence of images and patterns. Buildings, trees, faces, and bodies may be depicted as graphs, blueprints, and body counts; or they may be an invitation to private ecstasies and opaque truths. Beyond and despite logic and systems, we make our lives and we help make our truths. As Shreve said, in *Absalom*, "there are some things that just have to be whether they are or not, have to be a damn sight more than some other things that maybe are and it don't matter a damn whether they are or not" (p. 322). To be sure, the modern critic will speak of romantic delusions and affective fallacies. Our affective fallacies, however, constitute the facts of our lives, and they may be worth more, in that realm, than our scientific evidence. It is possible that response has always been sluggish and inert, and that modern man is no more anesthetized than his predecessors. But the emphasis on systems, the appeal of abstract, clinical, reductive approaches to people and problems, the often dehumanizing rage for order, have, it seems, never met with such grace and approval as they receive today.

Mystery may be based on a specious sense of depth, but it can be humanizing. The growing involvement of Rastignac in the misfortunes of Goriot, the empathy of Quentin and Shreve toward the story of Sutpen, provide a paradigm of vision and response. In this light we may define reading a novel as an invitation to response, a priceless entry, as Proust said, into the field of vision of another. More profoundly, reading is an act of vitalization because we are called upon to invest the sequence of white pages and black print with human meanings. Like Pip, Dowell, Jacques Revel, we are compelled to scrutinize, to revise, to extend depth, resonance, nuance—and ourselves—to the people and puzzles and patterns and language we have confronted. Reading is a humanistic adventure, not because the world of depth is philosophically true, but because our need for meaning is real and our ability to respond is good.

Index

VISION AND RESPONSE
IN MODERN FICTION

Designed by R. E. Rosenbaum.
Composed by York Composition Co., Inc.
in 11 point linotype Janson, 2 points leaded,
with display lines in Deepdene.
Printed letterpress from type by York Composition Co.
on Warren's No. 66 text, 50 pound basis,
with the Cornell University Press watermark.
Bound by Vail-Ballou Press.